SHARED GROUND
AMONG JEWS AND CHRISTIANS

A SERIES OF EXPLORATIONS

VOLUME III

Overcoming Fear Between Jews and Christians

Editor
James H. Charlesworth

with
Frank X. Blisard
and Jerry L. Gorham

THE AMERICAN INTERFAITH INSTITUTE
CROSSROAD • NEW YORK

1992
The Crossroad Publishing Company
370 Lexington Avenue, New York, NY 10017

Printed in the United States of America

Library of Congress Cataloging-in-Publication Data

Overcoming fear between Jews and Christians ; editor, James H.
    Charlesworth ; with Frank X. Blisard and Jerry L. Gorham
        p.   cm.— (Shared ground among Jews and Christians ; v. 3)
    Papers presented at a conference.
    Includes index.
    ISBN 0-8245-1265-0
    1. Judaism—Relations—Christianity—Congresses.   2. Christianity
and other religions—Judaism—Congresses.   3. Christianity and
antisemitism—Congresses.   4. Fear—Religious aspects—Judaism—
Congresses.   5. Fear—Religious aspects—Christianity—Congresses.
I. Charlesworth, James H.   II. Blisard, Frank X.   III. Series.
BM535.083   1993
261.2'6—dc20   92-31262
                                                              CIP

Participants and Contributors

Irvin J. Borowsky
Founding Chairman
American Interfaith Institute
Philadelphia, Pennsylvania

Hugh Anderson
Professor of New Testament
Emeritus
Faculty of Divinity
University of Edinburgh
Edinburgh, Scotland

Peder Borgen
Professor of New Testament
Department of Religious Studies
University of Trondheim
Trondheim, Norway

James H. Charlesworth
George L. Collord Professor of New
Testament Language and
Literature
Princeton Theological Seminary
Princeton, New Jersey

R. Alan Culpepper
James Buchanan Harrison Professor
of New Testament Interpretation
The Southern Baptist Theological
Seminary

Richard K. Fenn
Maxwell M. Upson Professor of
Christianity and Society

Department of Church History
Princeton Theological Seminary
Princeton, New Jersey

Eugene J. Fisher
Secretariat for Catholic-Jewish
Relations
National Conference of Catholic
Bishops
Washington, D.C.

Paul D. Hanson
Bussey Professor of Divinity
The Divinity School
Harvard University
Cambridge, Massachusetts

Martin Hengel
Professor of New Testament and
Early Judaism
University of Tübingen
Tübingen, Germany

Christopher M. Leighton
Executive Director
Institute for Christian-Jewish
Studies
Baltimore, Maryland

Doron Mendels
Faculty of Humanities
The Hebrew University
Jerusalem, Israel

Roland E. Murphy, O. Carm.
George Washington Ivey Professor
  Emeritus of Biblical Studies
The Divinity School
Duke University
Durham, North Carolina

John T. Pawlikowski, O.S.M.
Professor of Social Ethics
Department of Historical and
  Doctrinal Studies
Catholic Theological Union
Chicago, Illinois

Alan F. Segal
Professor of Religion

Barnard College
Columbia University
New York, New York

W. Barnes Tatum
Professor of Religion and
  Philosophy
Greensboro College
Greensboro, North Carolina

Elie Wiesel
Andrew Mellon Professor of the
  Humanities
University Professor
Boston University
Boston, Massachusetts

Contents

Illustrations

(between pages 92–93)

Foreword

Irvin J. Borowsky

Every Jew can vividly recall the very moment when he or she was first introduced to fear of historical and contemporary anti-Semitism, the reality of hate, and the scope of violence against the Jewish people. The information woven throughout family histories, photographs, and the media was irrefutable and shocking. For those of us who had been raised in an environment of ecumenical culture and education, protected by the umbrella of the great "American Dream," the other reality which was presented, the reality of debasement against our people, of hideous violence, of a "Final Solution" that surrounded and destroyed whole families, whole communities, and almost completely decimated a whole people, was too surreal to fully grasp at once.

But as the oral stories emerged from our families (for no family was left untouched), as the impeccable facts and supporting documents by scholars burst upon our world, claims of ignorance and denial shrunk. Initially, the core residue of this "enlightenment" was anxiety and fear.

But in recent years, a new response to the horrors of anti-Semitism have arisen within the Jewish community worldwide . . . a response that demands that fear be part of the memory, but not part of the answer to Jewish-Christian dialogue.

The role of Christianity in making Auschwitz a reality cannot be denied. Human beings nurtured in the traditions of the church actively participated in the Holocaust because they were taught to see themselves within the essence of light and goodness and to see others as darkness and evil. The Jewish people, even today, are presented in the New Testament as the essence of 'the other' and, therefore, to be feared and hated.

It is time to lift the veil of self-deceit. It is time to address the fact that Christian teachings were, in large measure, responsible for the ability of the Holocaust to occur.

Just 50 years ago, within this century, the hideous scope of the "Final Solution" reduced the Jewish people to less than fourteen million survivors. In the past 1000 years, one out of every two Jews born into the world has been murdered as have two out of five Jews in this century alone. One out of three living Jews was murdered just 50 years ago, including a million-and-a-half children. All were murdered in Europe by anti-Christians claiming they were protecting Christianity.

The strength of future Christian and Jewish relationships must be built on historical truth that recognizes fear as well as intellectual honesty. Dialogues that are merely polite and passionless are limiting at best.

As a Jew, I feel safe in a world that practices Christianity. My fears focus on the small number of words in the New Testament that need to be more accurately translated from the Greek if we are to eliminate anti-Semitism. These words are a barrier to peace. They are powerful weapons that bigots use against my grandchildren.

New Testament passages that foster hatred of Jews must be modified. Proper reconstruction of the New Testament that includes the social and political environment of the first century and the clarification of Jesus' crucifixion by Roman soldiers is essential.

Words are, indeed, major tools for teaching trust or injecting poison. There are words in the New Testament that have provided references for bigots to create prejudice and distrust; to accuse and abuse.

As a result of those words, "Jews" are blamed for the death of Jesus. Jews from ancient times to this very day are damned in prose that defames all Jews. These New Testament references have been used by Hitler and others to set the stage for hostility and the murder of those whose roots were from the same stock that nurtured Jesus.

In this enlightened time, there are millions of Christians who are also fearful whenever anti-Semitism raises its ugly head.

They work diligently in interfaith programs and publish statements explaining that Christianity does not blame contemporary Jews for crimes against Jesus and Paul. Yet, throughout the world, new converts to Christianity as well as those who are re-discovering their Christian faith, are inspired by the Bible. Until the scriptures are translated more factually, misinformation and hate will be handed down to future generations of Christians, and the tides of violence will rise again and again and again.

In light of all the studies and statements and explorations, it's especially shocking that the gospel passages which have been used by fanatics throughout history to vilify the Jews as "Christ-killers" have been retained in all new editions of the Bible for future Hitlers to use and quote. If Mark, John, and Paul had the benefit of knowing that their writings helped define tragic realities for their own people, they would surely have modified the hate-filled references that are still published in the New Testament today. There is no doubt that their intentions were to capture the spirit which Jesus exemplified while on earth . . . his spiritual leadership of courage, of commitment and of love.

From the time Jesus was a child he was exposed to the barbaric treatment of his fellow Jews by the Roman invaders and their collaborators. Historians have estimated the number of Judean collaborators who assisted the Roman conquerors at a small number: Roman-appointed priests, tax collectors, moneychangers, and temple guards. These were the authorities whom Jesus challenged, not the other 99% of his coreligionists.

Jesus stood up to oppression. He spoke out against cruelty. He had a faith that inspired the writers of the New Testament and, if permitted to be an example, it is this faith that will inspire the modification and removal of inaccurate references to the Jewish people from the New Testament and from Christianity.

Let us join together to extend our research and resources to Bible publishers. Let us help them understand that the use of the word "Jew" in the exclusive sense as the enemy of Jesus represents a misguided, incorrect and, ultimately, harmful reflection of an entire people.

Clearly, the success of this magnificent objective will be a major step in overcoming fear between Jews and Christians.

IRVIN J. BOROWSKY,
Founder and Chairman
American Interfaith Institute

Acknowledgments

We appreciate the courtesy of Professor Elie Wiesel for allowing us to republish his "Why I Am Afraid." This was originally published in E. Wiesel's *A Jew Today*, translated from the French by M. Wiesel (New York: Random House, 1978).

Abbreviations

Modern Publications

AB	Analecta Biblica
ABRL	Anchor Bible Reference Library
ANF	A. Roberts and J. Donaldson, eds. *The Ante-Nicene Fathers: Translations of the Writings of the Fathers down to A.D. 325*, 10 vols. (Edinburgh, 1868–72; rev. and repr., Grand Rapids, Mich., 1950–52)
ATR	*Anglican Theological Review*
BibTr	*Bible Translator*
BZAW	Beitrage zur Zeitschrift für die alttestamentliche Wissenschaft
CCARJ	*Central Conference of American Rabbis Journal*
CF	*Classical Folia*
CH	*Church History*
ChrCent	*Christian Century*
CTSR	*Chicago Theological Seminary Register*
DownsRev	*Downside Review*
EcumTr	*Ecumenical Trends*
ES	The Encounter Series
EvT	*Evangelische Theologie*
ExpT	*Expository Times*

GCS	Die griechischen christlichen Schriftsteller der ersten drei Jahrhunderte
GOTR	*Greek Orthodox Theological Review*
HRT	*Harvard Theological Review*
HUCA	*Hebrew Union College Annual*
IBS	*Irish Biblical Studies*
ITQ	*Irish Theological Quarterly*
JBL	*Journal of Biblical Literature*
JE	Singer, I., et al., eds., *The Jewish Encyclopedia*, 12 vols. (New York and London, 1901–06)
JES	*Journal of Ecumenical Studies*
JRH	*Journal of Religious History*
JSS	*Jewish Social Studies*
LCC	Library of Classical Christianity
LCL	Loeb Classical Library
NEH	National Endowment for the Humanities
NovT	*Novum Testamentum*
NovTSup	*Novum Testamentum*, Supplements
NTS	*New Testament Studies*
OTP	Charlesworth, J. H., ed., *Old Testament Pseudepigrapha*, 2 vols. (Garden City, N.Y., 1983–85)
PatrSorb	Patristica Sorbonensia
RelStRev	*Religious Studies Review*
RevExp	*Review and Expositor*
RIL	*Religion and Intellectual Life*
SAC	Studies in Antiquity and Christianity
SBLDS	Society of Biblical Literature Dissertation Series
SBLMS	Society of Biblical Literature Monograph Series

SBLTT   Society of Biblical Literature Texts and Transla-
             tions

SGAJC   Shared Ground Among Jews and Christians: A
             Series of Explorations

SIDIC   *Service International de Documentation Judeo-
             Chretienne*

SJLA   Studies in Judaism in Late Antiquity

StPatr   Studia Patrologiae

TD   Textes et Documents

TW   Theologie und Wirklichkeit

TWAS   Twayne's World Author Series

VTestSup   *Vetus Testamentum,* Supplements

Church Fathers

AdvJud   Tertullian, *Adversus Judaeuos*

AdvMarc   Tertullian, *Adversus Marcionem*

l Apol   Justin Martyr, *Apoligia* No. 1

DialTrypho Justin Martyr, *Dialogue with Trypha*

HE   Eusebius, *Ecclesiastical History*

Paed   Clement of Alexandria, *Paedagogus*

Prot   Clement of Alexandria, *Protrepticus*

Strom   Clement of Alexandria, *Stromata*

CHAPTER ONE

Fear: A Perennially Present Anguish

James H. Charlesworth

> *"Of all the bad passions fear is most accursed."*
> William Shakespeare

The American Interfaith Institute convened a symposium of Jewish and Christian experts in Philadelphia in 1987. In the past participants were asked to prepare papers as authorities on texts or social phenomena. This symposium was different: the specialists were urged to look back over their life and to reflect on the fear that has accompanied them over the years, and to assess it in light of guiding traditions. Two concerns brought random perspectives into a common focus: the fear Jews and Christians have of each other, and the fears shared by them when facing shared enemies.

Some events of the past few years bring common fears to a zenith. In light of the horrors of the last two hundred years, it is incomprehensible to hear that anti-Semitism is popping to the surface throughout the western world. Note the title of an AP news release from "East Berlin," and dated March 18, 1990: "Fearing rebirth of anti-Semitism."

The SCUD missile attacks rained down terror. They also tore open old volcanoes once quietly sealed in memories designed to be distant. On occasion I was linked by phone with colleagues in Israel.

One conversation with a member of the symposium on fear was riveting. From my comfortable office in Princeton I could sense terror in the voice of a dear friend. He explained how "no one dares venture out at night. . . . We gather together in sealed rooms. We are forced to relate intensely and intimately with loved ones with whom we had tended to drift apart from." He went on, describing an elderly woman who let some magma pour out of a deep crevice: "Have we escaped the gas chambers only to be gassed here?" To hear such words galvanizes you to another.[1] Fear leaves no place to hide.

More recently our fears have escalated again.[2] Early in the morning we are told that the hard-line communists have successfully pulled off a *coup d'état* in the Soviet Union. As we watched television pictures of armored vehicles and massive tanks roll into red square we are told that Gorbachev is ill. Our fears mount as we immediately recognize that lies are again the order of the day. We gasp little prayers of hope but know that the world has changed instantaneously and we are afraid of the consequences. As our blood pressure rises the stock market falls over 100 points in the opening session. Both are barometers that fear has gripped our world.

No one can function in times of terror. No representative work is possible. Fright may evoke flight. But, what if you are "home"? Can one flee to a safer spot?

Fear may also create the impossibility of flight (as William James pointed out).[3] Charles Darwin observed that fear and terror cause the human to lose control of the body and the mind.

Some fears cannot be conquered. We lose; or they abate. Other

---

1. I agree with M. H. Ellis who states, "grappling with the horrific signals the desire to be faithful to the experience of the Jewish people. . . . Awaiting clarity, we travel a path of ignorance toward a destination unknown, a destination that, more often than not, becomes recognizable in the form of nightmare." Ellis, *Toward a Jewish Theology of Liberation: The Uprising and the Future* (Maryknoll, N.Y.: Orbis, 1987) p. 24.

2. I am not convinced it is helpful in light of so much that has happened during this century to distinguish too neatly between fear and anxiety, as did S. Freud and P. Tillich. See Freud, *The Problem of Anxiety* (New York: Columbia University Press, 1936). I find it impossible to agree with Tillich that "fear can be conquered by action." See Tillich, *Systematic Theology* (Chicago: The University of Chicago Press, 1951); the quotation is in vol. 1, p. 191. Fear can make action impossible; it can become a black hole into which actions disappear. Fear can activate the flow of adrenalin, which increases lactic acid formation and decreases the normal benefits from the use of glucose and oxygen.

3. For much of what is presented in the next sentences I am indebted to R. Plutchik's "Fear," in *International Encyclopedia of Psychiatry, Psychology, Psychoanalysis, & Neurology*, ed. B. B. Wolman (New York: Aesculapius Publishers, Inc., 1977) pp. 17–18.

fears are within our controls.[4] Not to wrestle with dispensing them is to bypass the way back to paradisiacal bliss.

Back then, the story (or myth) goes, the human and the animal conversed; and both lived in harmony with the Creator. There was nothing to fear. There was no cold, heat, or inclement weather from which to seek shelter. Food was abundant and delicious. The creator and the created could stroll together in the cool of the evening. The story reappears in the ancient world as a world-wide belief in a distant place, usually called "the Island of the Blessed Ones." It is pervasive in Greek traditions.[5] The Greeks suggest they may have developed these ideas from Iran and India.[6] Indeed, the belief that there is a better world somewhere beyond our reach is an ancient, pre-Zoroastrian, idea in Persia.[7] The story was inherited by the Romans and appears in many of their most influential writings.[8] The belief in a far off "Island of the Blessed Ones" was known in Syria and Egypt.[9]

Most importantly for our western culture, the expectation of a better world, or descriptions of a paradisiacal place appear in the writings of Isaiah, the Dead Sea Scrolls, the *Books of Enoch*, the *Testaments of the Twelve Patriarchs*, *4 Ezra*, and *2 Baruch*, the sayings of Jesus, Paul, and most impressively in the little-known *History of the Rechabites*. Note how the following excerpt reveals that the Abode of the Blessed Ones is free from hatred and fear:

> And again we announce to you, O brothers, that among us there is no sickness, pain, fatigue to our bodies, mutilation, weariness, or temptations; not even Satan's power can touch us, for there is not among us rage, jealousy, evil desire, or hateful

---

4. Senator Bill Bradley, for example, in the Senate argued that "the Republican use of the Willie Horton commercials in the 1988 presidential campaign and the labeling of the 1991 civil rights measure as a 'quota bill' were both meant to divide white and black voters and 'appeal to fear.'" (*The Times* [July 11, 1991).

5. See especially the following: Homer [*Odyssey 6*, 44–45], Hesiod [*Works and Days* esp. lines 159–71], Pindar [*Olympian Odes* II, 68–72], Herodotus [*Hist. Bk.* III], Plato (*Phaedo* cf. 109–112], Strabo [*Geography* 1 and 3].

6. See Philostratus, *Life of Apollonius*, Bk. 3, ch. 15,

7. It shapes descriptions of Yima's golden reign, Mithra's abode, and Yima's subterranean hideaway.

8. See notably the following: Virgil [*Fourth Eclogue* lines 15–25], Lucian [*A True Story*].

9. For Syrian literature see Iamblichus's *On the Life of Pythagoras;* for Egyptian writings see *The Shipwrecked Sailor* and Chaeremon (*apud* Porphyry's *De Abstinentia*). Also, see Philo of Alexandria's *De vita contemplativa* and *De vita*.

thoughts. But (we experience only) quietness and gladness; and (exhibit) love and affection toward God and each other.[10]

These thoughts shared by Jews and Christians reveal both the ways they were able to live with present fears and the manner in which they thought about a better world.

We cannot reopen paradise; but we can bring a bit of paradise a little closer. Why should Jews fear Christians? Why should Christians fear Jews? What can and should be done to remove the dreaded fear that separates us?

This volume is the third in the Series of Explorations. Here are presented the papers given during the symposium in Philadelphia. We must confront our fears; otherwise we are not true to ourselves and forget the errors of the past. Note these words by Erich Fromm:

> The influence of men like Hitler or Stalin lies precisely in their unlimited capacity and willingness to kill. For this they were loved by the necrophiles. Of the rest, many were afraid of them, and preferred to admire, rather than to be aware of their fear. . . .[11]

In the present volume fear is explored from a variety of historical, sociological, and personal perspectives.

One paper was so deeply personal, explaining the fear of being a young Jewish boy in Nazi Germany, that Shemaryahu Talmon felt he could not publish it. His reflections and searing memories, shared with us who heard him, will remain a silent witness to what is incomprehensible, branded far too loosely by a category, "the Holocaust."[12] Surely, such a burnt offering can in no way be acceptable and pleasing to God, no matter how the ineffable One may be conceived or isolated as supra-categorical.[13]

---

10. *HistRech* 14:1; see Charlesworth in *The Old Testament Pseudepigrapha* (Garden City, N.Y.: Doubleday, 1985) vol. 2, p. 458.
11. Fromm, *The Heart of Man: Its Genius for Good and Evil* (New York: Harper & Row, 1964) pp. 40–41.
12. Since that time I walked with him and his wife Panina through Auschwitz and Birkenau. Inexpressible horrors became too real; I was sick for the next five days.
13. One of the tasks of Christian theologians today is to insure that the label "Christian" cannot be used by any who wishes to perpetuate in any form the evil of the Nazi persecutors; that label must be reserved only for those who inherit from the many who died or jeopardized families in the effort to provide refuge from the reign of fear and are willing to die for others. That is the meaning of following Jesus, to take up the cross and follow.

Alan Culpepper, Paul Hanson, Barnes Tatum (whose paper was added to those of the symposium), and Roland Murphy analyze for us certain aspects of biblical and post-biblical literature that provide keys to unlock better and mutual understanding.[14] Such is invaluable for the new generation of Jews and Christians, who may be positioned on a potential turning point in human history.

Richard Fenn, Hugh Anderson, Doron Mendels, Alan Segal, Peder Borgen, Eugene Fisher (whose paper was added to those of the symposium), and John Pawlikowski report on several trends. These may prove to impact the course of relations among Jews and Christians.

Elie Wiesel allows us to republished his "Why I Am Afraid." He now shares with a wider audience his personal reasons why he has been afraid. Martin Hengel reflects on his experiences in Germany before 1945. Christopher Leighton (whose paper was added to the collection) share with us his confrontation with fear in the Soviet Union.

In many of these reflections we can hear the echo of Abraham's fear as he raised the knife over the neck of his son. Others bring to memory the fears of the Israelites as they wandered out into hostile territory, leaving behind the house of bondage, which did have ample food and water. Still other aspects of the following chapters reawake the fears David must have held as he fled King Saul to hide in the watery expanse of the En-gedi oasis, or of Jeremiah when he was taken from his beloved Jerusalem by the Babylonians, or Judas Maccabeus when he saw the Temple desecrated and his brother Eleazar crushed by an elephant. To those who know the Dead Sea Scrolls (or Qumran Scrolls), some aspects of the papers might provide a better understanding of the fear experienced by the founder of the Qumran Covenanters, who were exiled from the Temple and forced to live in the parched desert of Judea. Some papers may awake memories of others, perhaps the priests about to be butchered by Pompey's troops.

---

14. Preparing these chapters for publication I was reminded of Martin Buber's statement: "All religious reality begins with what Biblical religion calls the 'fear of God.' It comes when our existence between birth and death becomes incomprehensible and uncanny, when all security is shattered through the mystery." Buber, *Eclipse of God* (New York: Harper & Row, 1952) p. 36.

Such memories unite Jews and Christians; they are part of our common heritage. In fear of common enemies, in recognition of how fear shreds our shared traditions—and in fear of the Lord in the proper way—we may find ways to remove the fears that abolish our common dream.

CHAPTER TWO

Why I Am Afraid

Elie Wiesel

Perhaps it would be best not to admit it publicly: I feel threat-ened. I am afraid. For the first time in many years I fear the nightmare may be starting all over again. Perhaps it never ended. We may have lived, since the Liberation, a period be-tween parentheses. And now they are closed again.

Is another Holocaust possible? I often asked my students that question. Most answered yes; I said no. By its dimensions, its scope, the Holocaust was a unique event; it will remain so. I explained to them that the world has learned a lesson, that hate and murder transcend those who take part in them di-rectly: one begins by killing others only to massacre one's own in the end. Without Auschwitz, there might have been no Hi-roshima. The annihilation of a people leads inevitably to the annihilation of mankind.

Oh yes, so naive was I that I thought—especially during the early postwar years—that Jews would never again be slan-dered, isolated, handed over to the enemy. Anti-Semitism, I thought, had died under a sky of ashes somewhere in Poland; we had nothing more to fear; the world would never again be insensitive to our anguish. I was convinced that, paradoxically, men of today and men of tomorrow would be protected by the terrifying mystery of the concentration-camp phenomenon.

I was wrong. What happened could happen again. I may be exaggerating. I may be too sensitive. After all, I do belong to a traumatized generation. We have learned to believe threats more than promises. The disquieting signs are proliferating. The sickening spectacle of an enthralled international assembly celebrating a spokesman for terror. The speeches, the votes against Israel. The dramatic loneliness of this universal people. An Arab king presents his guests with deluxe editions of the infamous Protocols of Zion. The desecrated cemeteries in France and in Germany. The campaigns in the Soviet press. The recent *Retro* wave—a trend among writers, movie-makers and others toward retrospective "evaluation" of events surrounding World War II—that vulgarizes the experience. The anti-Zionist, anti-Jewish pamphlets that distort our hopes. One must be blind not to recognize it: hate of the Jew has once more become fashionable.

Nothing surprising, then, that in so many places Jewish existence is in jeopardy again. In October 1973, while the Israeli army was experiencing grave, almost fatal reverses, Western Europe, with only rare exceptions, refused its help and, much worse, attempted to sabotage America's aid. Europe gave free hand to the aggressors, accepting in advance Israel's certain defeat, that is to say, its probable liquidation. And now? Will this people, so young and yet so old, survive the next attack, and at what cost? How many times will Israel be called upon to sacrifice the best among its children? How long can a community of men live in a state of siege, inside a hostile environment? Is a posthumous victory for Hitler conceivable?

For those of us who have lived the human and Jewish condition to its ultimate depths, there can be no doubt: at this point in history the Jewish people and the Jewish state are irrevocably linked; one could not survive without the other. We have rarely been as united. And as alone.

And so the notion of a new collective catastrophe no longer seems preposterous. We already know that as far as we are concerned, the impossible is possible. When it comes to Jewish history, there is nothing unthinkable.

I say this reluctantly and for the first time. I have always placed the Holocaust on a mystical level, beyond human understanding. I have quarreled with friends for making certain easy analogies and comparisons in that domain. The concentration-camp phenomenon eludes the philosophers as much as it does the novelists, and it may not be dealt with lightly. I speak of it now, in connection with the present, only because Jewish destiny has once again become subject to discussion.

That is why I am afraid. Images from the past rise up and cloud current events. Blackmail in some quarters, abdication in others. Overt threats, hidden complicities. Friends who suddenly declare their neutrality. Neutrals whose hostility becomes apparent. The enemy who becomes ever more powerful and ever more attractive. If allowed to have his way—and he is—he will become the god of our cursed age, demanding—and obtaining—the future of a people as a sacrifice.

Not that I foresee a situation where Jews would be massacred in the cities of America or the forests of Europe. Not that another universe of barbed wire will be built or new death factories erected, but a pattern is emerging. One does not speak of genocide; one envisages the end of Israel. That is enough to justify my fear. I feel what my father must have felt when he was my age. Thus, for us nothing has changed. The world is indifferent to our death as, in fact, it is to its own. It has forgotten too soon.

I look at my students, and I tremble for their future. I see myself at their age on a continent in ruins. And I do not know what to tell them.

I should like to be able to convince them that in spite of the official slogans, in spite of appearances, our people has friends and allies. I should like to be able to tell them that in spite of the accumulated disappointments and betrayals, they must maintain their faith in man, that in spite of everything, there are reasons for hope. But I have never lied to them, and I shall not start now. And yet . . .

Despair is not a solution, I know that well. But then, what is the solution? Hitler proposed one. He wanted it to be final, and he was well on his way toward accomplishing his goal while, near and far, God and mankind turned away their gaze.

I remember. And I am afraid.

CHAPTER THREE

The Fear of the Other: An Introduction to the Problem of Social Dread

Richard K. Fenn

Recently a group of young Jewish Americans visited Germany. Staying with German families, they visited concentration camps and discussed the Holocaust with their hosts. One account of the visit notes a combination of fear and fascination in these students. Although filled with anxiety, they felt that they "had to see for themselves."[1] Despite their dread, the students insisted on experiencing a pain that was not initially their own. How can we account for this drive to return to the past and to imagine scenes of horror? Such a drive underlies their dread: their horrible fascination with others' lives that are marked with death. One student in fact tore his hands on the barbed wire at Dachau after seeing the gas chambers. I would like to suggest that the drive stems from the same part of the self that wishes to see in others a double: a mirror image, that anchors and guarantees one's own existence and, sad to say, one's own illusions about oneself. Some of those illusions, unfortunately, are part of the perennial dream of immortality and omnipotence that returns to haunt the human race and can take on demonic proportions.

The desire to double oneself, to have a mirror-image, appeared in a more positive way on the visit just described. The

---

1. *New York Times*, September 27, 1987, p. 14.

Americans wanted to see their experiences and feelings reflected in their German hosts. One student actually said:

> For American Jews, German history ended in 1945. . . . But in the German classroom it was exciting to share a present. I saw a wonderfully warm, concerned German community, *and I hope they saw it in us.*[2] (Emphasis added.)

The desire to see in others a mirror image of oneself ("wonderfully warm, concerned") no doubt is part of the social cement that binds individuals together. Indeed, that desire appears to have inspired these students eventually to dance together and, hugging one another, to say goodbye. The dream inevitably turns to dread, as all mirror-images eventually fade and crack. It is this resulting dread that I wish to discuss here.

The Dread of Community

The individual's search for a "double" is part of the social cement that ties individuals together in communities and societies. Sociologists and others interested in analyzing the ingredients of that cement have noted various attachments, such as primordial ties to blood-kin, to the soil where one was born and will die, and to the accidents of fate. Fate subjects a people to common forces and unites them in a common destiny. They become a people in answering the question of "who are we, together?"[3] As societies become more complicated, however, the ties that bind people together become more complex, and in recent years the state itself and the division of labor have been nominated as primary factors that hold entire societies together. The state particularly has inherited a diffuse aura of sanctity from the previous struggles of a nation and retains a borrowed glory.[4] The state has to pay interest on this borrowed credit, however, in the form of special benefits to an increasingly wide range of interests. The awe with which the sacred was once approached therefore no longer serves as the cement which ties a people together; the bonds of holy fear have been broken in

---

2. Ibid.
3. B. Anderson, *Imagined Communities: Reflections on the Origin and Spread of Nationalism* (London, 1983).
4. E. Shils, *Center and Periphery* (Chicago, 1975).

most modern societies. What is left, I will argue, is a less holy form of dread.

Let us assume that a dominant majority sees itself pleasantly reflected in the mirror of the larger society. Why, then, should there be something fearful and driven about the majority? Despite its apparent security, the majority flees from the notion that it could also see its likeness reflected in the mirror held up by Hispanics or Jews or Blacks. Regardless of a minority's cultural achievements, the small group is frequently considered suspect and is colored in the darker hues associated with uncertainty, decay, and even death. Otto Rank speaks of such profound fear as stemming from "the pathological fear of one's self, often leading to paranoid insanity and appearing personified in the pursuing shadow, mirror-image, or double."[5] I am suggesting that this unholy fear of one's darker side and of death itself remains in a secular society as the social cement that ties together both the Jew and the Gentile: the majority with those who are cast in the darker hues of the imagination.

As societies become more secular, I would argue, it becomes more difficult to detect this fear. Nonetheless, dread—I contend——underlies social interaction, undergirds major institutions like the family, and provides a residue of obedience to the state. When fear was transformed into a holy awe in the presence of the transcendent, the emperor and the temple could compete for loyalty and obedience; people could choose between the sacrifices demanded by one or the other. The more unblemished the sacrifice, the greater the benefit to both the self and the larger society. Those with blemishes (i.e., the impure, the defective, the swarthy, and the sacrilegious) could easily be put beyond the pale. As religious and political claims to a divine authority yielded to the process of secularization, the sacred became the object of a lesser awe. It was such a form of the sacred that Durkheim attributed to the collective representations of entire societies; emblems and institutions, even beliefs and values, could still elicit enough to bind the members of a modern society into a moral community. Of course, the more complex the division of labor and the more relationships were based on contract rather than sacrifice, the more difficult it became to discern the

---

5. O. Rank, *The Double: A Psychoanalytic Study.* (Chapel Hill, 1971) pp. 85–86.

sacred dimension behind special interests. To disclose this dimension was the task of the sociologist, who would point behind the veil of the secular to the sacred source of all covenants.

Durkheim was also aware that there are currents of an unholy fear in modern societies, destructive currents that lead to suicide and other forms of violence when the sacred no longer commands awe and receives appropriate sacrifice. The more diffuse the sacred becomes, the more likely it is that fear will seek a wide range of objects. When that fear was mobilized by the state and directed outward at those who were systematically deprived of their rights, the Nazi state became systematic in its destruction. Occasional sacrifice became continuous and rational rather than caught up in sporadic ecstasies. The Nazi state, pagan and irrational as its enthusiasts were, was an example of the capacity of a secular society to administer fear in continuous and lethal dosage rather than in the spasmodic destruction of a crusade or vendetta.[6] Unholy dread of the darker self took the place of sacred awe and holy fear. Sacrifice became continuous and unlimited.

Dread is therefore the term that I wish to use, rather than awe or fear, to describe the cement that holds people together in the uneasy alliances characteristic of a complex, modern society.[7] That dread is diffuse, often underground, seldom dramatized, and yet relatively pervasive. Profoundly individual as a state of mind, it is so widely shared that it constitutes a common tendency or predisposition. When societies collectively dramatized this dread in collective rites, dread could be mobilized and heightened in displays of political grandeur and military power that issued in calls for commitment and sacrifice. No wonder that Freud spoke of the "dread of the community."

The relatively contrived grandeur of celebrations of the Statue of Liberty or of the Constitution now take on the hype of the Olympics and show-business. Even the waving red flags in European city squares and the burning of torches is an ersatz demonstration of a society's sacred power when compared with the dread inspired by the emblems of Empire and the statue of the emperor that once threatened to destroy the sanctity of the Tem-

---

6. R. Rubenstein, *The Cunning of History* (New York, 1987).
7. S. Freud, "On Narcissism: An Introduction," in E. Jones, ed., *Collected Papers*, vol. 4, The International Psychoanalytical Library, No. 10 (New York, 1959) p. 59.

ple's precincts in Jerusalem. No longer reflecting a sacred cos-
mos, the regalia of the state are more clearly manufactured and
their celebrations more obviously contrived. The fantasies that
once united a society in delusions of grandeur and holy fear
have been replaced by a more diffuse mythology: an implicit,
underground network of unstated hopes and fears that surface
in more fragmented and idiosyncratic demonstrations. A police-
man is shot, a gang of white children pursues a young black to
his death on city streets, swastikas are painted on the facade of
a country club. These are the bizarre and occasional omens of
dread rather than solemn and collective celebrations of holy fear.

In a secular society, terror becomes increasingly random rather
than concentrated in dramatic celebrations. Sacrifices are sporadic rather than scheduled. They may occur at any time rather
than at times determined by the state or required by the sacred
calendar of the religious community. The more secular a society
becomes, the more difficult it is to locate and expunge the
sources of dread in collective actions that bind some together at
the expense of others. It becomes difficult to know who is the
most expendable, and minorities understandably become more
anxious than ever that they will be chosen for sacrifice in a process that seems increasingly difficult to identify, define, locate,
and therefore control in particular times and spaces.

Dread therefore inspires paranoia in majorities as well as in
minorities. Even among those who have political or economic
reasons for feeling secure, there are several reasons for such
paranoia and the reasons are all implicit in Freud's notion of the
"dread of the community." Here I can only mention them briefly
and illustrate them in anecdotes. My intention is to suggest that
until this dread is brought into the full play of public consciousness, it remains as a perennial source of discomfort and danger
and, under conditions such as war or economic collapse, such
dread remains a dangerous source of political unrest and repres-
sion. It then becomes the pernicious cement that ties together a
mass society whose positive linkages have been stretched and
become inelastic or beyond repair.

The Double

The paranoid symptoms of dread can be illustrated in the
well-known case of the "double." Rank, Freud, and others were

fascinated by the appearance of the double both in literary and clinical sources. The double is simply an image of the self toward which the individual forms a fatal attraction. Rank finds in the celebrated portrait of Dorian Gray one of the most obvious examples: a portrait that at first provides a flattering mirror-image slowly becomes an image of impending death.[8] It exercises a fatal attraction over Dorian Gray himself, who can neither face nor disregard the truth it betrays of his own mortality. The portrait inspires the very dread which any image can stimulate in a viewer who, turning toward it in the hope of seeing a reflection of his or her own vitality, finds just the opposite. The residues of self-love keep one riveted on the double, even when the double brings the inevitable, and dreaded, message of death.

Freud, himself very taken with Rank's argument on the perennial appearance of the double in culture and social institutions, argues that there is something uncanny and therefore dreaded about all such representations of the double.[9] The part of the self which observes oneself makes us fascinated with our own reflection, but it also makes us find in the scrutiny of our own conscience the dread gaze of a father who may have had reason to be vengeful. In one's failed ideal-self, moreover, one finds one's own mortality. Dread is thus built into social life as surely as the infant becomes capable of self-scrutiny, of identifying with others, and of desiring the love of forbidden attractions. The ramifications of this notion are clearly too complicated to explore here, but we should come to appreciate why the sources of dread in any society present a clear and sometimes present danger to both Jew and Gentile, black and white.

Consider that one may find one's double in the family, in one's ethnic community, or even in the nation. These are the flowers that spring from what Freud called "the soil of unbounded self-love"; each begins as "an assurance of immortality," but inevitably becomes "the ghastly harbinger of death."[10] Take, for the simplest example, the symbols of American society: the eternal eye over the pyramid on the dollar; or the new Israel which, unlike the old, may yet fulfill in its own life the promises of God in history; or the city set on a hill whose presence resembles that

---

8. Rank, *The Double*, pp. 76ff.
9. S. Freud, "The 'Uncanny,'" in *Collected Papers*, vol. 4, pp. 387ff.
10. Ibid., p. 387.

of the new Jerusalem. Compare such imagery with the plague of national failure, corruption, and indebtedness associated with the names Vietnam, Watergate, Iran-Gate, with the trade deficit and the national debt. Add the statistics documenting the perennial decline of the public's trust not only in politicians and officials but in the basic institutions of American society (the church, the media, the courts, and the military). Images of national vitality and eventual glory have faded, despite the claim that "the pride is back." On the contrary, the decline of public confidence in our fundamental institutions affects all those seeking various nominations to high office. The scrutiny of public figures keeps pace with official surveillance of private citizens. Big brother watches and is watched with increasing vigilance as the ties binding citizens with the nation become more tenuous. *The point is that the portrait of the self that was painted on a national canvas becomes cracked and disfigured, like the portrait of Dorian Gray, until one can scarcely either countenance it or take one's eyes off it.* This is partly what Freud means by "dread of the community." The community, like the figure in fairy-stories and myths which keeps an eye on us and threatens us with disfigurement, becomes uncanny and the object of dread.

Such dread is compounded by a guilty conscience. Freud notes that self-love lies at the source of our attraction to our ethnic community or to the nation, and it is therefore natural that self-love should return to its source (oneself) when the ethnic community or nation disappoint us. To withdraw narcissistic affection from the nation, like withdrawing it from a parent on whom one still depends, is a way of avoiding a wound to our self-love; but withdrawal can inspire considerable guilt. The parent may no longer love the child whose infatuation with the parent has ended; the nation may not love and protect the ethnic group whose affair with the nation is over; so ruminates the guilty conscience. How else can we explain the public demonstrations of patriotism by subordinate minorities except as an appeal for continued love from the nation and, perhaps, as a cover for the minority's love of itself? Such a cover is not unwarranted. Once the Jerusalem Temple ceased to honor prayers for the Roman emperor, in fact, the Roman legions appeared on the horizon. In South Africa, Jehovah's Witnesses remain in jail for their failure to make sacrifices of prayer and of military service to the state. There is some reality in the paranoia inspired by a minority's refusal to flatter itself by honoring the King.

Dread of the community or of the nation increases wherever a certain stigma is associated with one's ethnicity or nationality. A stigma, of course, is quite simply a wound; stigma comes from the inevitable discovery that one's community or nation is no guarantee of life and immortality; it too suffers decline and defeat. The reflection of the self in the ethnic or national mirror discloses the signs of aging and death. No wonder that affection is partly withdrawn, even as the nation or community remain objects of narcissistic curiosity and attraction. But the hunger of a primitive self-love dies very hard indeed. That hunger can nourish an American "Zionism" that seeks vindication and demands an eye-for-an-eye in the way of penalties on its enemies, issues warnings to the disaffected, and harbors no aliens. America the ugly seeks to renew the myth of an America that is pure and beautiful, from which the burden of stigma has been lifted once and for all. Defeat in war or cycles of depression can lead to a cultural despair. That despair may be heightened when the apparatus of the state is controlled by a bureaucracy that will subvert attempts to take it over. Such despair may be varied by independent sources of criticism in the academic world, the churches, the media. Interest groups become adept in self-defense and in appeals to public opinion. As cultural despair mounts, an apparently insecure majority can engage in behavior that, in the clinic, would be described as masochistic, depressed, or even paranoid. Academics may produce a literature which, in the case of nineteenth and early twentieth century Germany, has indeed been called "the politics of cultural despair."[11] Stern's apt phrase for the climate of pre–World War I Germany begins to fit the products of an American elite that despairs of the survival of civic virtues in an individualistic culture. Indeed, many individuals never learn the rudiments of national history or constitutional law, so preoccupied are they with their personal appearance and advancement. Lasch's "culture of narcissism" is filled with descriptions of a paranoid society in which there is no privacy but a war-of-all-against-all.[12] What worries me is that

---

11. F. Stern, *The Politics of Cultural Despair: A Study in the Rise of the Germanic Ideology* (Garden City, N.Y., 1965).
12. C. Lasch, *The Culture of Narcissism* (New York, 1978).

the prophecy of such a society may be self-fulfilling as academics continue to enjoy the stigma of wounded nationalism. Cultural despair is not therapeutic, especially when engaged in by a majority and its academic elites; the hatred of English intellectuals for England itself between the two world wars is a case in point.

The licking of national or communal wounds is a masochistic, pleasurable form of social dread. As Freud has pointed out, the object of dread is really a magnified representation of the earliest self: that self which is itself primitive and therefore engaged in the most primitive—i.e., animistic—thinking. That is why majorities find in minorities an uncanny resemblance of themselves: uncanny because it taps these unconscious, very early mental images in which thoughts are virtually omnipotent. In the face of the minority the majority finds a distorted representation of its own self: a representation particularly of those grandiose impulses and wishes that accompany the earliest stages of narcissism. That is why minorities are so often caricatured as being greedy, power-hungry, untrustworthy, and filled with insatiable sexual desires. That is also why majorities are likely to fear that the minority still has access to hidden, occult powers, to a secret magic that can work its will. No wonder, then, that minorities find themselves the object of a curious fascination that accompanies the sense of dread. Somehow the majority cannot forget the minority and keeps returning to its own preoccupation—and fear—of the minority in question. The minority may thus remind the majority of a beauty or power that was once its own and now is lost.

It is precisely this compulsive drive to go back, again and again, to the minority question that signals the presence of unconscious, indeed neurotic processes. It is as if the majority is driven to return to its dread of the minority, no matter what progress it makes, no matter what turns it takes. In fact, Freud describes his own experience of walking through streets that meandered in many directions, only to find himself back again in the same quarter, where "painted women" were doing business; indeed, they noticed his periodic returns with some interest.[13] The "uncanny" nature of the experience comes from its origins in the desire to return to a period in which thoughts

---

13. Freud, "The Uncanny,'" in *Collected Papers*, vol. 4, pp. 389–90.

seem magically to become deeds and wishes "come true": a magical world, but sufficiently unconscious as to make one anxious when, as so often happens, one's thoughts do appear to become acts and one's wishes happen to come true. Hence the obsessional quality of the majority's preoccupation with the minority. The minority seems to have access to these magical powers in their secret rites, and the majority's envy of the minority leads to a variety of envious thoughts and malicious wishes.

The obsessional nature of this preoccupation also explains why both sides may vow "never again." The obsessed do wish for relief from their circular preoccupations, from the unending cycle of envy and self-blame that stems from unconscious motives and from "omnipotent" thoughts. Both the minority and the majority may be driven to seek a final solution that makes it impossible for these repressed wishes and fears to ever return.

The desperation of the group driven by such recurrent dread of the other accounts for its suicidal tendencies. Constantly to be in the presence of the other can inspire such fatal dread when the other seems demonic. Indeed, as Freud argues, the other group is a "double," an image of one's own group itself, especially in its unconscious, grandiose aspects. That is why the double becomes "a vision of terror, just as after the fall of their religion the gods took on demonic shapes."[14] The Romans indeed took on a demonic shape to the zealots, who feared that emblems and representations of the Roman Empire were magical and evil in their potency; the Romans may well have had an equally superstitious dread of the Jews. Certainly Jews and Gentiles, blacks and whites, perennially overestimate each other's potency and failings. There is a sense, then, in which a majority can be captivated by its own, dreaded image of the minority, in which it unwittingly sees a reflection of its own unconscious strivings for power and of its latent magical thinking. No doubt Blacks and Jews can similarly overestimate the demonic powers of the majority and become captivated in their political imagination. Furthermore both the majority and minority may intentionally "spook" the other by donning extraordinary garments and by marching to the beat of the most intimidating drum. The recent attempt by the Ku Klux Klan to

---

14. Ibid., p. 389.

use white sheets, crosses, and military attire to intimidate blacks is simply another instance of the return to the infantile world of omnipotent fantasies. In adults, however, these fantasies can take on the substance as well as the trappings of political power when ritual fails to give these spirits free play within the most limited of contexts.

What haunts the public preoccupation with the holocaust is precisely the possibility that politics will again pre-empt the play of hope and fear, joy and anguish, that are acted out in ritual. At the end of the visit by American Jews to Germany, there was a party, in which the young Germans danced with their visitors; the *New York Times* reports that the professor who organized the visit

> watched the dancing and hugging with some incredulity. "I never believed it would work like this," he said. "I feel that I should warn them that this is not the whole of Germany, that there are darker sides. So many of them came with fear, and now look at this."[15]

Those who have seen the repressed wishes and fears of childhood acted out in political spheres know that dreams of omnipotent domination can be carried a long way before they yield to suicidal consequences for an entire nation. The professor wishes to keep fear alive because he knows that dread of the other can drive a nation to genocide and collective self-destruction. He was not the only member of the group who was aware of such ghosts: the *Times* account noted that a young Californian reportedly was "haunted" by the memory that Bonn had once had five flourishing synagogues, where only one small synagogue now remains. Dread returns with the memory of a time when the majority nearly succeeded in carrying out its fantasies of omnipotence and of a final solution. It is therefore understandable that a young German should promise: "I can only say that what happened forty years ago won't happen while I live." What fantasies of omniscience and omnipotence underlie such a bold claim? Similar fantasies supported collective dreams of national glory under Nazi leadership not long ago.

---

15. *New York Times*, September 27, 1987, p. 14.

CHAPTER FOUR

The Gospel of John as a Threat to Jewish-Christian Relations

R. Alan Culpepper

The Gospel of John contains some of the most hostile anti-Jewish statements in the Christian scriptures. So sharp is the contrast in that gospel between Jesus' exhortations to his followers to love one another and the hostile references to "the Jews" that Kaufmann Kohler commented that John is "a gospel of Christian love and Jew hatred."[1] Among the most devastating references to "the Jews" one finds the following:

5:16, 18   And this was why the Jews persecuted Jesus, because he did this on the sabbath. . . . This was why the Jews sought all the more to kill him, because he not only broke the sabbath but also called God his Father, making himself equal with God.

7:1   . . . he would not go about in Judea because the Jews sought to kill him.

8:31   Jesus then said to the Jews who had believed in him, . . .

8:37–38   you seek to kill me, because my word finds no place in you.

8:44   You are of your father, the Devil, and your will is to do your father's desires. He was a murderer from the beginning. . . .

An earlier draft of this paper was published as "The Gospel of John and the Jews," *RevExp* 84 (Spring 1987) 273–88.
1. K. Kohler, "New Testament," *JE* 9 (1905) 251.

8:47   He who is of God hears the words of God; the reason why you do not hear them is that you are not of God.

9:22   His parents said this because they feared the Jews, for the Jews had already agreed that if any one should confess him to be the Christ, he was to be put out of the synagogue.

16:2–3   They [the Jews] will put you out of the synagogues; indeed the hour is coming when whoever kills you will think he is offering service to God. And they will do this because they have not known the Father, nor me.

18:36   . . . if my kingship were of this world, my servants would fight, that I might not be handed over to the Jews. . . .

19:38   After this, Joseph of Arimathea, who was a disciple of Jesus, but secretly, for fear of the Jews, asked Pilate that he might take away the body of Jesus.

20:19   On the evening of that day, the first day of the week, the doors being shut where the disciples were, for fear of the Jews. . . .

The effect of these excerpts is chilling.[2] This corpus of hostile references to "the Jews" begins with the report that "the Jews" sought to kill Jesus for healing on the sabbath, builds to the charge that "the Jews" are from the Devil whereas Jesus is from God, intimates that Jesus was killed by "the Jews," and predicts that "the Jews" will persecute and kill the followers of Jesus. Understandably, Jews feel threatened by the inclusion of such references in the Christian scriptures, and indeed atrocities against the Jews may be blamed in part on abuse and exploitation of such passages in the Fourth Gospel.

The purpose of this paper is to draw together and review the issues that are basic for any dialogue on the subject of the Gospel of John and the Jews. The substantial body of literature on the subject has established standard positions and identified questions that remain unanswered. The general observation that the vilification of "the Jews" in John has contributed to the bloody

---

2. For a more complete list see M. J. Cook, "The Gospel of John and the Jews," *RevExp* 84 (1987) 260–61.

record of Gentile persecution of Jews can hardly be contested. Nevertheless, probing beyond this general observation leads one into areas where meanings are ambiguous and biases influence interpretations and conclusions. Five major issues must be addressed, however cursorily:

1. What does *hoi Ioudaioi* mean in the Gospel of John?
2. How does the group characterized as *hoi Ioudaioi* function in John?
3. How did John function in its historical context?
4. Is John anti-Semitic?
5. What is the task of interpretation and dialogue in the present context?

The sequence of these questions is important. Each assumes discussion of the previous issues, and discussion of the latter issues must be informed by sensitivity to the previous questions.

Referents of *hoi Ioudaioi*

The term *Ioudaios* or *hoi Ioudaioi* (usually translated Jew/the Jews) occurs seventy times in the Gospel of John. Studies devoted specifically to identifying the referents of the plural, *hoi Ioudaioi*, in John have typically proposed four or five categories which have either neutral or hostile overtones.[3] First, *hoi Ioudaioi* is used to designate Jews or Judeans in contrast to Samaritans or Gentiles. Such phrases as *he orte ton Ioudaion* ("feast of the Jews"; 5:1; 6:4; 7:1), *pascha ton Ioudaion* ("Passover of the Jews"; 2:13, 11:55), and *basileus ton Ioudaion* ("king of the Jews"; 18:33, 39; 19:3, 19, 21[twice]) may be placed in this category.

This category has sometimes been divided into more specific usages: the Jews simply as people, the Jews in contrast to Gentiles, the Jews in contrast to Samaritans, the Jews as Jesus' contemporaries, and references to customs of the Jews. Little seems to be gained by such distinctions. Most notable (and problematic) among the neutral references is John 4:22—"Salvation is from the Jews."

---

3. See E. Grässer, "Die antijüdische Polemik im Johannesevangelium," *NTS* 11 (1964–65) 74–90; R. G. Bratcher, "'The Jews' in the Gospel of John," *BibTrans* 26 (1975) 401–09; R. Fuller, "The 'Jews' in the Fourth Gospel," *Dialog* 16 (1977) 31–37; U. C. von Wahlde, "The Johannine 'Jews': A Critical Survey," *NTS* 28 (1982) 33–60.

Of more particular concern is the hostile or "typically Johannine" use of *hoi Ioudaioi* to refer to those who rejected Jesus and eventually demanded his death. The use of *hoi Ioudaioi* to characterize the willful rejection of Jesus received its classic expression from Rudolf Bultmann:

> The term *hoi Ioudaioi*, characteristic of the Evangelist, gives an overall portrayal of the Jews, viewed from the standpoint of Christian faith, as the representatives of unbelief (and thereby, as will appear, of the unbelieving "world" in general).[4]

In his definitive study of the use of *hoi Ioudaioi*, Urban C. von Wahlde found that ten previous studies agreed unanimously in identifying the following thirty-one passages as instances of this hostile sense: 1:19; 2:18, 20; 5:10, 15, 16, 18; 6:41, 52; 7:1, 11, 13, 15; 8:22, 48, 52, 57; 9:18, 22a, 22b; 10:24, 31, 33; 13:33; 18:14, 31, 36; 19:7, 31, 38; 20:19.[5] On the basis of substantial support, von Wahlde adds seven instances: 7:35; 8:31; 11:8; 18:12; 18:38; 19:12, 14. Two or more of the ten studies agree in adding seven other verses to the list: 3:25; 8:31; 10:19; 11:54; 18:20; 19:20, 21a.[6] After examining these seven verses, von Wahlde concludes that five represent the neutral use; the other two (8:31; 10:19) present a mixture which he ascribes to the work of a redactor.[7] Beyond identifying the passages that reflect the hostile sense, von Wahlde was concerned to show that, with the exception of 6:41 and 6:52, all the other instances of the hostile sense refer to the authorities. While there is widespread agreement as to the instances that refer to the authorities, there is no such agreement as to which instances refer to the common people. Only four verses (7:15, 35; 10:31, 33) are interpreted by two or more of the

---

4. R. Bultmann, *The Gospel of John*, trans. G. R. Beasley-Murray, R. W. N. Hoare, and J. K. Riches (Philadelphia, 1971) p. 86.
5. von Wahlde, "The Johannine 'Jews,'" p. 41. The ten previous studies reviewed by von Wahlde are: E. Grässer, "Die antijüdische Polemik im Johannesevangelium"; R. Schnackenburg, *The Gospel According to John*, trans., K. Smyth (New York, 1968) pp. 286–87; R. Fortna, "Theological Use of Locale in the Fourth Gospel," *ATR* Suppl. Ser. 3 (1974) pp. 58–94; Bratcher, "'The Jews' in the Gospel of John"; Fuller, "The 'Jews' in the Fourth Gospel"; G. J. Cuming, "The Jews in the Fourth Gospel" *ExpT* 60 (1948–49) 290–92; G. Baum, *Is the New Testament Anti-Semitic?* (Glen Rock, N.J., 1965); R. E. Brown, *The Gospel According to John*, AB 29 (Garden City, N.Y., 1966) pp. lxx–lxxiii; M. C. White, *The Identity and Function of Jews and Related Terms in the Fourth Gospel* (Ann Arbor, 1972); R. Leistner, *Antijüdaismus im Johannesevangelium*, 3 (Bern, 1974).
6. von Wahlde, "The Johannine 'Jews'", pp. 41, 49–53.
7. *Ibid.*, pp. 53–54.

ten studies as referring to the people rather than the authorities. Von Wahlde examines the arguments in each case and finds them unconvincing.[8] Questions might also be raised about 19:7, 12, and 14, but these are judged to refer to the hostile authorities mentioned elsewhere in the Johannine passion narrative.

The effect of von Wahlde's work is to narrow the scope of John's vilification from the people and the authorities to the authorities only.[9] Even granting von Wahlde's conclusions, however, one must still contend with the fact that John uses a general term that elsewhere in his narrative has a broader referent and is not limited to the authorities.

Another significant thesis has been advanced by Malcolm Lowe. Gathering data from ancient Jewish, Christian, and pagan writings, Lowe argues that while among "Gentiles and Diaspora Jews the word had already a secondary religious meaning, . . . the primary meaning of *Ioudaioi* was geographical."[10] The term *Ioudaioi* designated "Judeans" as opposed to people living in other areas, and *Judea* itself could designate (1) Judea in the strict sense, (2) the procurate of Pontius Pilate (including Idumea and Samaria), or (3) the whole kingdom of Herod the Great.[11] The Gospel of John, Lowe concludes, speaks of Judea "only in the strict sense."[12]

Only the key points of Lowe's case for translating every reference to *Ioudaioi* in John as "Judeans" can be noted. The references to the feasts *ton Ioudaion* all occur "in references to feasts requiring a pilgrimage to Judea."[13] Wherever it is clear that Jesus (or the subject) was in Jerusalem, "the words *he orte, pascha* (and other feast names) occur *without* any appendage."[14] The only exception is John 6:4. While others recognize that *Ioudaioi* refers to Judeans in 11:19, 31, 33, 36, 45, 54; 12:9, 11; 19:20, and possibly also 3:25 and 11:8,[15] Lowe concludes that all the references to *Ioudaioi* in John denote Judeans, with the exception of the

8. *Ibid.,,* pp. 44–45.
9. F. Mussner, *Tractate on the Jews: The Significance of Judaism for Christian Faith,* trans. by L. Swidler (Philadelphia, 1984) p. 184, reaches a similar conclusion.
10. M. Lowe, "Who were the *Ioudaioi*?" *NovT* 18 (1976) 106–07.
11. *Ibid.,* p. 103.
12. *Ibid.,* p. 112.
13. *Ibid.,* p. 116.
14. *Ibid.*
15. Bratcher, "'The Jews' in the Gospel of John," p. 409; von Wahlde, "The Johannine 'Jews'," p. 46.

instances in Samaria (in John 4), where "Jews" has "the correct denotation, but lacks the connotation of Judea."[16] The only possible exception Lowe allows is John 18:20.[17] The phrase *basileus ton Ioudaion* means "King of the Judeans."[18] In the hostile instances, therefore, the *Ioudaioi* are Judeans, "either in references to the Judean population in general or (less frequently except after Jesus' arrest) to the Judean authorities."[19]

In the most recent study on the subject, John Ashton responds to Lowe's work by first distinguishing three related questions: (1) who are the *Ioudaioi*; (2) what role or function do they fulfill in John; and (3) why did the evangelist regard them with such hostility?[20] Ashton reviews Lowe's thesis sympathetically, defending its plausibility but withholding final judgment until more historical evidence is adduced.[21] Groups of people were commonly identified by their place of origin or their principal deity.[22] The religious and geographical meanings may, therefore, not have been sharply distinguished. Granting the difficulty of the references in John 6, Ashton accepts that

> wherever *Ioudaioi* is used . . . these are natives or inhabitants of Judea. But to say this is to say very little: the nature and significance of the role they play is left undefined, and the reasons for assigning it to them unexplored.[23]

Ashton perceptively lodges the complaint that neither Lowe nor von Wahlde distinguished between "referent" and "sense." The "referent" of *Ioudaioi* would be "natives or inhabitants of Judea." By "sense" Ashton means the role the *Ioudaioi* play in the gospel narrative.[24] The distinction is essential.[25] In the gospel, historical persons become characters in a narrative in which they

16. Lowe, "Who were the *Ioudaioi*?" p. 126.
17. *Ibid.*, p. 126, n. 79.
18. *Ibid.*, p. 119.
19. *Ibid.*, p. 128.
20. J. Ashton, "The Identity and Function of the *Ioudaioi* in the Fourth Gospel," *NovT* 27 (1985) 40.
21. *Ibid.*, p. 69.
22. *Ibid.*, p. 45; W. A. Meeks, "'Am I a Jew?' Johannine Christianity and Judaism," in Jacob Neusner, ed., *Christianity, Judaism and Other Greco-Roman Cults*, SJLA vol. 12, part 1 (Leiden, 1975) p. 182.
23. Ashton, "The Identity and Function of the *Ioudaioi* in the Fourth Gospel," p. 55.
24. *Ibid.*, p. 57.
25. See R. A. Culpepper, *Anatomy of the Fourth Gospel: A Study in Literary Design* (Philadelphia, 1938) pp. 125–26.

take on varying degrees of symbolic significance and characterize different responses to Jesus.[26] Most previous studies on the identity of the *Ioudaioi* in John suffer from lack of precision because they do not sharply distinguish between semantic and syntactic aspects of meaning, or (using Ashton's terms) between referent and sense.

Distinguishing hostile from neutral instances and limiting the referent to Judeans or authorities, or even Judean authorities, does not address the issue of John's characterization of the *Ioudaioi*, their function in this gospel, or the effect of using the same term to refer both to the hostile authorities and to the (neutral) Jews or Judeans. Rather than describe Jesus' opponents as Pharisees, rulers, scribes, or chief priests (as the Synoptics do), John characterizes the opponents with the more general term *Ioudaioi*, thereby coloring all occurrences of the term in this gospel (at least in retrospect) with the hostile sense. Parenthetically, it is important to observe that John's characterization of the *Ioudaioi* is no less shaped by theology and historical circumstances than is its characterization of Jesus, which has long been recognized as the product of Johannine theology.

At this point the discussion of "the Jews" in the Gospel of John must move from the issue of historical referent to that of narrative function. Historical investigation and interpretation are related but quite separate endeavors.[27] Nevertheless, our review of efforts to define the meaning (referent) of *Ioudaioi* in John confirms four conclusions and focuses four issues for further study:

1. Strictly defined, *Ioudaioi* probably designated a religious group dwelling in Judea. The term was also used more loosely for others related to this group regardless of where they lived. What was the nature of the ambiguity or relationship between "Judeans" and "Jews" in the first-century range of meanings associated with *Ioudaioi*?

2. References to the *Ioudaioi* in the Gospel of John can often be classified in terms of their tone and referent (e.g., neutral/hostile, Judeans/Jews, people/authorities). What is the signifi-

---

26. See E. Krafft, "Die Personen des Johannesevangeliums," *EvT* 16 (1956) 18–32; R. F. Collins, "The Representative Figures of the Fourth Gospel," *DownsRev* 94 (1976) 26–46; 95 (1976) 118–32; Culpepper, *Anatomy of the Fourth Gospel*, pp. 101–48.
27. See R. A. Culpepper, "Story and History in the Gospels," *RevExp* 81 (1984) 473.

cance of such distinctions for plot development or reader response?

3. Only certain Jewish leaders generated hostility toward Jesus. Why does John use the generalizing designation *hoi Ioudaioi*—which carries the burden of the world's rejection of Jesus—to characterize those who were hostile to Jesus?

4. We must be careful to distinguish between referent and symbol (i.e., historical persons and literary characters) when discussing the Jews in the Gospel of John. What is the relationship between these two aspects of meaning in this gospel, and how does it change or develop?

The Function of *hoi Ioudaioi* in John's Gospel

Merely distinguishing and classifying neutral and hostile references to the *Ioudaioi* in the Gospel of John, however, is not adequate. We must ask how the neutral and hostile references are related to one another. A full analysis of the characterization, role, and function of the *Ioudaioi* in John cannot be attempted here. Principal issues will be defined, and the parameters of the narrative role of the *Ioudaioi* will be sketched. Concerns more strictly literary than the four issues just defined also require attention:

1. How does the gospel narrative develop the relationship between the *Ioudaioi*, the crowds, the Pharisees, the authorities, and the world?

2. Is there progressive development and escalation of hostility throughout the gospel or within episodes, or is von Wahlde correct in maintaining that "from the time that they appear on the scene, the 'Jews' demonstrate this attitude which neither increases nor diminishes as the gospel progresses"?[28]

3. How does John explain (or make plausible to the reader) the hostility of the *Ioudaioi*?

In *Anatomy of the Fourth Gospel*, I argued that *hoi Ioudaioi* are one character—not three, four, or five—and that the level of hostility escalates within each episode and from one episode to

---

28. von Wahlde, "The Johannine 'Jews'", p. 35.

another.[29] Further precision may be given to this analysis of the role of "the Jews" by tracing the development of the hostility from one episode to the next. (*Episode* is used here to designate a distinct segment or section of the narrative that contains one or more scenes. The beginning of an episode is usually marked by the phrase "after this" or "after these things," a change of location, and reference to a festival.)

Episode 1 (John 1:19–2:11)

John the Baptizer bears witness to Jesus, and Jesus calls his first followers, among them Nathanael, "an Israelite in whom there is no guile" (1:47). Jesus' first sign allows the disciples to see his glory, and they respond with belief in him (2:11).

The only reference to "the Jews" in this first episode reports that "the Jews from Jerusalem" (later identified with the Pharisees, 1:19, 24) sent messengers to question John. Opposition or hostility may be foreshadowed, but it is not explicit here. The replacement theme is introduced by the reference to the six water pots which were for "the cleansing of the Jews" (2:6), and from which Jesus provides the new wine.

Episode 2 (John 2:12–3:21)

The beginning of a new episode here is signaled by three indicators: (1) the phrase "after this" (*meta touto,* 2:12); (2) a change of location (to Caphernaum, 2:12; then to Jerusalem, 2:13); and (3) reference to a festival, "the Passover of the Jews" (2:13). Jesus drives out the merchants, then interprets his actions to "the Jews" when they question him. The pattern of Johannine dialogue is established: the Jews ask questions, and Jesus gives metaphorical answers full of double meaning which "the Jews" do not grasp (see 2:18–20). The narrator must explain Jesus' response to the reader (2:21–22). Nicodemus, "a ruler of the Jews" (3:1) and "teacher of Israel," comes to Jesus at night but cannot understand Jesus because Jesus is from above while Nicodemus is "earthly" (*epigeia,* 3:12; cf. 3:31). John begins to explore

---

29. Culpepper, *Anatomy of the Fourth Gospel,* pp. 125–32.

the nature and source of unbelief through the characterization of "the Jews" (see 3:18–20).

Episode 3 (John 3:22–36)—An Interlude in Judea

"After these things" (*meta tauta*, 3:22), Jesus and his disciples remain in Judea, where John's disciples debate with "the Jews" about cleansing (3:25).

Episode 4 (John 4:1–54)

This episode begins with only the indication of a change in location due to Jesus' knowledge that the Pharisees had heard of his baptizing (4:1). The Samaritan woman identifies Jesus as a Jew, and the narrator explains that "Jews have no dealings with Samaritans" (4:9, RSV). Later, Jesus declares that "salvation is from the Jews" (4:22), but the hour is coming when the distinction between Jew and Samaritan will be observed no longer: "all true worshipers will worship in spirit and in truth" (4:23). Verse 43 marks a scene change, and the episode concludes in Cana of Galilee.

Among the references to "the Jews" in John 1–4, there is little indication of hostility. At most, the inability of "the Jews" to understand Jesus is portrayed. The seeds of conflict are sown, but they have scarcely begun to grow.[30]

Episode 5 (John 5:1–47)

The beginning of a new episode, and a major division in the gospel, is marked by the three common indicators: (1) "after these things" (*meta tauta*), (2) a festival of "the Jews," and (3) travel to Jerusalem (5:1). Hostility against Jesus arises for the first time when Jesus heals on the Sabbath and declares that God is his Father. "The Jews" question the healed man, and the narrator explains that "the Jews" were seeking to kill Jesus because he violated the Sabbath and committed blasphemy (5:16, 18).[31] The script unfolds slowly, however, and the hostility develops step by step. Jesus responds that "the Jews" have not accepted the witnesses on his behalf: John the Baptizer, the

---

30. *Ibid.*, pp. 91, 126.
31. *Ibid.*, p. 127; see also A. E. Harvey, *Jesus on Trial: A Study in the Fourth Gospel* (Atlanta, 1977) pp. 67–81.

signs, the Father, the Scriptures, even Moses himself (5:31–47). "The Jews" do not believe because they do not seek "the glory of the only God" (5:44). Indeed, they are not faithful to their own heritage: if they believed Moses, they would believe Jesus (5:46).

Episode 6 (John 6:1–71)

"After these things" (meta tauta), Jesus crossed the Sea of Galilee (6:1). The Passover, "the festival of the Jews," was at hand (6:4).

While "the Jews" celebrate the Passover in Jerusalem, Jesus feeds a multitude in the hills of Galilee and then crosses the Sea. When Jesus will not feed the crowd (6:2, 5, 22, 24) again the next day, "the Jews" begin to "murmur" (6:41) and then to fight with one another (6:52) over Jesus' explanation that he himself is "the bread of life" (6:48, 51). Jesus' disciples murmur also (6:61), and many then turn away from him (6:66).

Episode 7 (John 7:1–8:59)

"After these things" (meta tauta), Jesus went to Galilee (7:1), where his brothers challenge him to go to Jerusalem for the festival of booths (7:2).

From the beginning of this episode the reader is warned again that "the Jews" were seeking to kill Jesus (7:1). The warning raises the level of suspense, while the hostility of the exchanges between Jesus and "the Jews" builds to a climax in this episode. The crowd "murmurs" (7:12), but they fear "the Jews" (7:13). The reasons for unbelief are developed fully in this chapter.[32] The authorities seek to arrest Jesus, but he eludes them. Some of the people believe (7:31), whereas the Pharisees "murmur" again (7:32), and "the Jews" question Jesus' enigmatic responses (7:35; 8:22). Because some of the people believe, there is a division (schisma) among them (7:43). Again, Jesus says that "the Jews" are "from below" while he is "from above" (8:23).

John 8:31 is a notorious difficulty. Jesus addresses "the Jews who had believed in him," but they no longer believe (see 8:31b). The hostile exchange that follows raises challenges to both the legitimacy of Jesus' birth and the relationship of "the Jews" to

---

32. Culpepper, *Anatomy of the Fourth Gospel*, pp. 129–30.

Abraham.[33] Jesus claims that their father is the Devil (8:44), so they are not "from God" (8:47). "The Jews" respond that Jesus is a Samaritan and has a demon (8:48, 52). This episode ends with "the Jews" taking up stones to throw at Jesus (8:59). A new peak of hostility has been reached.

Episode 8 (John 9:1–10:42)

The conventional markings of the beginning of a new episode fail us here, but the shift from the intensity of chapter 8 to the new structure of seven scenes in John 9, with their escalating conflict, justify the beginning of a new episode at John 9:1.

Jesus' work brings division *(schisma)* even among the Pharisees (9:16). "The Jews" do not believe that the man Jesus healed had actually been blind (9:18). His parents are afraid of "the Jews," however, because "the Jews" had agreed to cast out of the synagogue any who confessed that Jesus was the Christ (9:22). "The Jews" then question the man himself and finally cast him out (9:34). John 9, therefore, extends the conflict between Jesus and "the Jews" into the affairs of those who were associated with Jesus. Exclusion from the synagogue represents a fresh escalation in the conflict.

The point at which this episode ends is also open to debate. John 10:19 reports a division *(schisma)* among "the Jews," with some claiming that Jesus is a demoniac and others defending him. A new festival, Hanukkah, is introduced in John 10:22, so a new episode could begin at that point, but the action in the following verses brings the hostility to a "flash point" again as "the Jews" take up stones once more (10:31, 33) before Jesus withdraws from Jerusalem (10:40).

Episode 9 (John 11:1–54)

The beginning of this episode is marked by the introduction of new characters (Lazarus, Mary and Martha) and their request that Jesus return to Judea, to Bethany.

Suspense is created by the reminder that "the Jews" had recently attempted to stone Jesus (11:8). "Many of the Jews" had come to comfort the sisters, however, and they are portrayed in a positive light (11:19, 31, 33). They even comment, "see how he

---

33. See R. A. Culpepper, "The Pivot of John's Prologue," *NTS* 27 (1980) 27–28.

loved him" (11:36). Following the raising of Lazarus, "many of the Jews" who were present believed in Jesus (11:45); others reported him to the Pharisees, who conspire against him. The division between receptive and hostile "Jews" that was noted earlier is now complete. Jesus can therefore no longer move about openly among "the Jews" (11:54), so he withdraws to Ephraim.

Episode 10 (John 11:55–12:50)

This episode is closely related to the previous one, but the new episode is introduced by the reference to "the Passover of the Jews" (11:55) and Jesus' return to Bethany (12:1). Surprising as this may be, the first part of the gospel ends with the Pharisees seeking to arrest Jesus (11:57) while a great crowd of "the Jews" cheers his arrival at Jerusalem (12:9, 11).

The only reference to "the Jews" in the farewell discourse recalls Jesus' words about his departure (13:33; cf. 7:33). Although Jesus warns his disciples of the world's hostility and says they will be put out of the synagogue and killed (16:2), "the Jews" are not named explicitly.

"The Jews" return to the narrative at the arrest of Jesus (compare 18:3 [Pharisees] with 18:12 [Jews]). Caiaphas had counseled "the Jews" that Jesus had to die for the sake of the people (18:14; cf. 11:51). Jesus protests that he had taught openly, in the temple, where "the Jews" gathered (18:20). Pilate questions: "Are you the king of the Jews?" (18:33), and later retorts, "Am I a Jew?" (18:35). Jesus maintains that his kingdom is not of this world. If it were, his followers would fight to keep him from being handed over to "the Jews" (18:36). Pilate then reports to "the Jews" that he finds Jesus innocent of any wrongdoing. "The Jews" then appeal to the Law (19:7). The Gospel of John renders its final verdict on "the Jews," however, when they force Pilate to condemn Jesus (19:12) and then respond to his taunts saying, "we have no king but Caesar" (19:14–15). In bitter irony, Jesus is crucified under the inscription, "Jesus the Nazorean, the King of the Jews" (19:19–22).

Fear of "the Jews" followed Jesus' crucifixion. Joseph of Arimathea was a secret believer "for fear of the Jews" (19:38), and the disciples remain behind closed doors "for fear of the Jews"

(20:19). The only other references to "the Jews" following the crucifixion are incidental (19:40, 42).

Conclusions

From this analysis of the role of "the Jews" in John's gospel narrative, the following conclusions may be proposed:

1. References to "the Jews" must be studied in their narrative context. Extracting the references from their place in the structure of the narrative and attempting to distinguish various referents (Judeans, authorities, common people) does not explain John's characterization of "the Jews" or the development of their role in this gospel.

2. Similarly, Bultmann's description of the symbolic role of "the Jews" as Jesus' opponents does not do justice to the division among "the Jews" that is described in John 6–12. "The Jews" are neither a static nor a homogeneous character.

3. "The Jews'" hostility toward Jesus is not constant (*contra* von Wahlde). Instead, we find escalation of conflict within the ten episodes in the first part of the Gospel and progressive development in the plot from one episode to the next.

4. The division between the "Jews" who accept Jesus and those who finally reject him is the most distinctive feature of John's treatment of "the Jews"—not their uniform hostility toward him. The significance of this division in relation to the social context of this gospel now requires further attention.

How Did John Function in Its Historical Context?

Both the social factors that influenced the formation of the Fourth Gospel and the functions of that gospel in that context are important. Specifically: (1) What influenced John's use of the generalization, "the Jews"? (2) Why does this gospel describe division among "the Jews"? (3) How might these aspects of this gospel have been understood by its first readers?

Wolfgang Iser and other reader-response critics have recently helped us to appreciate the importance of a narrative's reflection of values and social codes and norms. By means of commentary, characterization, irony, stereotype, caricature, and conflict, a narrative has the ability to call into question a reader's perceptions and commitments and undermine or defend rival value systems.

Familiar values may be "defamiliarized" in the narrative world by portraying them in a new context. Consequently, new configurations of distance and intimacy between the reader, the characters, and the represented values are created. The Gospel of John in particular handles these dynamics in a masterful way.[34] For example, a change in the reader's attitude toward the Law may be confirmed by the last reference to *nomos* in this gospel, where the *Ioudaioi* answer Pilate: "We have a law, and by that law he ought to die . . ." (19:7).

The complementary proposals of J. Louis Martyn and Raymond E. Brown (though they differ at points) have been widely accepted as the most useful analyses of the specific historical context of the composition of the Fourth Gospel.[35] Relying heavily upon their work, we would sketch the general contours of that gospel's historical setting as follows.

The Johannine community originated in a group of Jews who found the fulfillment of their messianic expectations in Jesus. The teachings of the Beloved Disciple were shaped into homilies for fellow Jews, so the Johannine tradition is deeply rooted in the Hebrew Scriptures and their interpretation (especially in the Wisdom tradition).

For reasons that are not entirely clear, the synagogue began to identify and expel the Jesus-believing Jews from its fellowship. The process was probably similar to the use of the *Birkath ha-Minim* (Twelfth Benediction) but prior to its adoption at Jamnia. This traumatic event is reflected in John 9:22; 12:42; and 16:2.

While the majority of the believers began to form a new community, "secret believers" remained within the synagogue and some of the Johannine Christians may have considered returning to the synagogue. Relying on written sources composed under the influence of the Beloved Disciple, the gospel was composed and edited over a period of years. Eventually, the Johannine community itself split, and the Johannine Epistles were written to encourage and defend the remnant community from the Christological innovations of those who left the community. The Fourth Gospel, therefore, was written to show that Jesus

---

34. See Culpepper, *Anatomy of the Fourth Gospel*, pp. 164, 209–10.

35. J. L. Martyn, *History and Theology in the Fourth Gospel*, rev. ed. (Nashville, 1979); idem, *The Gospel of John in Christian History* (New York, 1978); R. E. Brown, *The Community of the Beloved Disciple* (New York, 1979).

was the fulfillment of Jewish expectations and that those who received him were faithful to the Law while those who rejected Jesus turned away from their own heritage.[36] Martyn has convincingly shown how the Gospel of John develops two levels of meaning.[37] It recalls (1) Jesus' conflict with the authorities, but it also clarifies (2) the issues in the conflict between the Johannine community and the synagogue. Within this context, the Johannine Gospel functioned primarily to encourage the Johannine community, to interpret why the synagogue had rejected them and their messianic beliefs, and to provide the community with a clearer identity as true "children of God."[38] The Gospel of John confirmed that the community was being faithful to Jesus' revelation as it was mediated to them by the Paraclete or Spirit of Truth and interpreted by the Beloved Disciple. Secondarily, this gospel probably also served to encourage the "secret believers" (who were caught between the Johannine community and the synagogue) to declare their faith publicly, to sever ties to the synagogue, and to join the community. By the time of the final editing of John's gospel, other (intra-church) functions are evident also, but these are not relevant for discussion of the Gospel of John and the Jews.

On the basis of this understanding of the setting of the Fourth Gospel, several observations are possible.

1. Both the pervasive Jewishness of the Gospel of John and its sharp polemic against "the Jews" can be explained on the basis of the setting described above.[39]

2. The division among "the Jews" in chapters 6–12, which is peculiar to John, developing as it does from "murmuring" to the belief of some of "the Jews" and the efforts of others to seize Jesus, reflects the division that had occurred within the synagogue.

3. The Johannine Christians believed that they were faithful to the Law while their opponents had shown that they themselves did not understand Moses or the Scriptures (5:39, 46).

4. The Fourth Gospel stereotypes Jesus' opponents as "the

---

36. S. Pancaro, *The Law in the Fourth Gospel, NovTSup* 42 (1975).

37. Martyn, *History and Theology in the Fourth Gospel*, p. 30.

38. See Culpepper, "The Pivot of John's Prologue," pp. 25–31.

39. N. A. Beck, *Mature Christianity: The Recognition and Repudiation of the Anti-Jewish Polemic of the New Testament* (Selinsgrove, Pa., 1985) pp. 249–50.

Jews" because the decisive break between Judaism and Christianity had already occurred, at least in the Johannine setting, and the Jews of the synagogue were persecuting the Christian community. "The Jews," therefore, becomes a term by which the Gospel of John characterizes both Jesus' opponents and the community's opponents. Through this characterization, this gospel offers various explanations for why Jesus was rejected by his own people.[40]

Is the Gospel of John Anti-Semitic?

Sometimes shading distinctions is merely an academic exercise in obscuring an issue or hedging on a response. When answering the question of whether John is anti-Semitic, however, clarity of definition is essential.

J. N. Sevenster, in *The Roots of Pagan Anti-Semitism in the Ancient World* (1975), established several points that are relevant to our discussion. He traced the earliest evidence of pagan anti-Semitism back as far as the Elephantine papyri (fifth century B.C.E.). Ancient anti-Semitism, however, predated modern theories of racial distinctions. Sevenster found not a single indication "that anti-Semitism in the ancient world used the theory of race as a weapon of attack."[41] Instead, the basis for pagan anti-Semitism was the contempt of Jews for pagan religious practices, the autonomy and separation of Jewish communities, and the peculiarities of their religious practices (sabbath observance, circumcision, and food laws).[42]

Although some (e.g., Edward Flannery)[43] regard pagan anti-Semitism as the source of Christian anti-Semitism, Sevenster does not link the two. Douglas Hare's observation is persuasive: "Since gentile converts to Christianity were drawn primarily from those attracted by Judaism, it is not at all likely that Chris-

---

40. Culpepper, *Anatomy of the Fourth Gospel*, pp. 129–30; J. Painter, *John: Witness and Theologian*, 2nd ed. (London, 1979) pp. 71–76.

41. J. N. Sevenster, *The Roots of Pagan Anti-Semitism in the Ancient World* (*NovTSup* 41 [1975] 56); cited by R. A. Hare, "Review of Three Recent Works on Anti-Semitism," *RelStRev* 21 (1976) 16.

42. Sevenster, *The Roots of Pagan Anti-Semitism*, pp. 89–144; Hare, "Review," p. 16.

43. E. H. Flannery, *The Anguish of the Jews* (New York, 1965) pp. 60–61; cited by J. E. Leibig, "John and 'the Jews': Theological Anti-Semitism in the Fourth Gospel," *JES* 20 (1983) 211, n. 8.

tian anti-Semitism is to be explained on the basis of pagan hostility toward the Jews."[44] Little is gained by attempting to trace the roots of Christian opposition to Judaism to pagan anti-Semitism. The two phenomena were generally independent of each other and motivated by different concerns.

A second interpretation relieves the Christian Scriptures in general, and the Gospel of John in particular, of the onus of anti-Semitism by arguing that the Christian Scriptures express a prophetic critique voiced from within Judaism, prior to the separation of Christianity from its Jewish origins.[45] Although, ultimately, such a solution does not succeed, it has the merit of taking seriously the differences in context between modern readings of the Christian Scriptures and the original social context in which they were written. While it is true that Christianity and Judaism were not clearly distinct from each other until at least very late in the first century, the Gospel of John—as we have seen—was written at the point of separation (in one locality) and probably contributed to the ultimate separation between the two. It is far more difficult to interpret John as prophetic critique from within Judaism than it is to view Paul in this way. John serves to widen a breach that had already occurred.

A third line of argument builds on both the symbolic use of "the Jews" as representing the world's rejection of Jesus (Bultmann) and the view that the hostile references to "the Jews" designate the authorities, not the common people (von Wahlde). The following statements are representative and show that leading Johannine scholars have advanced this view:

> R. E. Brown: "John is not anti-Semitic; the evangelist is condemning not race or people but opposition to Jesus."[46]

> Robert T. Fortna: "Whatever animus John may have felt and expressed against the synagogue, it is not in any racial sense antisemitic. He does not set Jew and Gentile against each other. Rather he sees two views of revelation—we would say two religions—in contradiction. . . ."[47]

---

44. Hare, "Review," p. 16.
45. B. Vawter, "Are the Gospels Anti-Semitic?" *JES* 5 (1968) 473, 483; W. D. Davies, "Paul and the People of Israel," *NTS* 24 (1977) 19, 21, 37.
46. Brown, *John*, vol. 1, pp. lxxi–lxxii.
47. Fortna, "Theological Locale," p. 94.

U. C. von Wahlde: ". . . the context of intra-Jewish debate remains a possibility. . . . If the term ["the Jews"] refers only to authorities, it hardly provides evidence that the gospel is an attack on the attitudes of all Jews."[48]

Other scholars have now begun to distinguish anti-Judaism from anti-Semitism and to recognize varieties of one or the other in John. *Anti-Judaism* has been defined as

that attitude which produces a clean break with Judaism theologically, either by thoroughly discrediting the Jewish tradition, as in Marcion's case, or by usurping the Jewish Bible and turning it against the Jews, as in the *Epistle of Barnabas*.[49]

Edward H. Flannery accepts the distinction between *Anti-Semitism* "which must include a note of hatred or contempt of the *Jewish people as such*"[50] and *anti-Judaism,* which "is purely a theological reality; it rejects Judaism as a way of salvation but not Jews as a people."[51] By anti-Judaism, Flannery designates "those oppositions intellectual in nature, whether theological or apologetical, which are bereft of hatred or stereotyping of Jews as persons or as a people."[52]

In response to efforts to exonerate the Gospel of John of the charge of being anti-Semitic, Eldon J. Epp and Janis Leibig, while recognizing the legitimacy of the distinction between anti-Semitism and anti-Judaism, have both concluded that the milder term does not adequately describe John. Epp concludes, "It is difficult to apply to the Fourth Gospel's anti-Jewish attitudes and to their impact upon the reader any term other than *anti-Semitic.*"[53] Leibig nuances her position by using the terms "the antisemitic potential of the Fourth Gospel"[54] and "theological anti-Semitism." The latter, which she derives from Rosemary Ruether,[55]

---

48. von Wahlde, "The Johannine 'Jews,'" p. 33; see also S. Wilson, "Anti-Judaism in the Fourth Gospel? Some Considerations," *IBS* 1 (1979) 46.

49. Hare, "Review," p. 16.

50. E. H. Flannery, "Anti-Judaism and Anti-Semitism: A Necessary Distinction," *JES* 10 (1973) 583.

51. *Ibid.,* p. 582, quoting from his *The Anguish of the Jews,* p. 60.

52. Flannery, "Anti-Judaism and Anti-Semitism," p. 583.

53. E. J. Epp, "Anti-Semitism and the Popularity of the Fourth Gospel in Christianity," *CCARJ* 22 (1975) 49.

54. Leibig, "John and 'the Jews,'" pp. 224–34 passim.

55. R. Ruether, "Theological Anti-Semitism in the New Testament," *ChrCent* 85 (1968) 191–96.

distinguishes John "both from the later racial Antisemitism and from the milder 'anti-Judaic' attitude."[56]

The range of judgments on the issue of anti-Semitism in John makes clear definition and precise judgments important. The basis for the anti-Jewish tone and language in the Fourth Gospel is both theological (or more precisely, Christological) and social. Confession of Jesus as the Messiah led to a relativizing of the authority of Torah that the Jewish community found unacceptable. Expulsion of the Johannine Christians from the synagogue sharpened the conflict and probably contributed to the dualistic thinking of the Johannine community. The dualism evident in Johannine thought—that distinguished sharply between those who belonged to the light, the truth, and the life from above and those who did not—resulted in a severe condemnation of all who did not accept Jesus as the Christ, the ultimate revelation of God.[57]

The conflict, however, sprang from within Judaism, from hostility between Jews and Christian Jews.[58] It involved theological, not racial, differences. While the term *theological anti-Semitism* retains a certain "shock value" applauded by Leibig,[59] it also retains overtones of racial anti-Semitism. Still, the "prophetic critique" or "intra-Jewish debate" positions do not recognize the extent of the breach with Judaism that is already reflected in John. During the process of the development of the Johannine tradition and the composition of that gospel, the bearers of that tradition found themselves displaced from participation in Jewish life.

In defense and explanation of these events, the Fourth Gospel stereotypes the rejection of Jesus as the response of "the Jews."[60] Even if *hoi Ioudaioi* once denoted "the Judeans" or the Jewish authorities, the Gospel of John generalized and stereotyped

---

56. Leibig, "John and 'the Jews,'" p. 226. See also S. Sandmel, *Anti-Semitism in the New Testament?* (Philadelphia, 1978) pp. xix–xx.

57. J. H. Charlesworth, "A Critical Comparison of the Dualism in 1QS 3:13–4:26 and the 'Dualism' Contained in the Gospel of John," in J. H. Charlesworth, ed., *John and Qumran* (London, 1972) pp. 76, 96.

58. J. L. Martyn, "Glimpses into the History of the Johannine Community," in *The Gospel of John in Christian History* (New York, 1978) pp. 102, 107, 119-21.

59. Leibig, "John and 'the Jews,'" p. 227.

60. See R. Lowry, "The Rejected-Suitor Syndrome: Human Sources of New Testament 'Antisemitism'," *JES* 14 (1977) 229–30.

those who rejected Jesus by its use of this term. Fuller succinctly attributed to the evangelist three critical developments:

1. He altered the designation of Jesus' opponents in many places to "the *Ioudaioi*" and introduced this new designation into his own composition.
2. He reinterpreted the issues between Jesus and his opponents in explicitly christological terms.
3. He gave the hostility between Jesus and his opponents a previously unparalleled bitterness.[61]

Perhaps even more importantly, the Gospel of John is the first document to draw a connection between "the Jews" who condemned Jesus and Jews known to the Christian community at a later time. By means of this transfer of hostility, effected by the two levels of meaning Martyn has found in this gospel, the gospel creates a dangerous potential for anti-Semitism.

Norman Beck identified three types of anti-Jewish polemic in the New Testament: *christological,* which identifies Jesus with God; *supersessionistic,* which contends for the superiority of Christianity over Judaism; and *defamatory,* which, as Beck maintains, is not essential to the Christian message but is damaging to Jewish people and dehumanizing to Christians.[62] All three types of anti-Jewish polemic can be found in John.

Leibig and those who distinguish between the Fourth Gospel's intent and its effect are therefore entirely correct in speaking of the "anti-Semitic potential of the Fourth Gospel."[63] Not only has this gospel been read as supporting anti-Semitism, its defamatory references to "the Jews" have contributed to the development of anti-Semitism.[64] Therefore, the nuanced terms "theological anti-Judaism" and anti-Semitic potential" provide the most accurate descriptions of the Fourth Gospel's language, tone, and attitude toward Jews and Judaism.

---

61. Fuller, "The 'Jews' in the Fourth Gospel," p. 35.
62. Beck, *Mature Christianity,* pp. 283–85.
63. *Ibid.,* p. 36: "It is unfortunate that . . . the Johannine redactor did not remove all the evangelist's hostile references to the Jews. For transplanted into a new *Sitz im Leben* they acquired potentiality for a meaning which the evangelist had never and could never have intended, since he was writing for a Jewish-Christian community, the meaning of anti-Semitism."
64. See Epp's graphic description of the effect of John's use of "the Jews" in his "Anti-Semitism and the Popularity of the Fourth Gospel in Christianity," p. 41.

The Gospel of John, we conclude, develops an anti-Jewish polemic motivated by theological concerns. The anti-Semitic potential of this polemic, however, fed hostility toward Jews when it erupted with brutal consequences in later centuries.

The Task of Interpretation and Dialogue

Dialogue between Jews and Christians requires that Christians recognize the contribution of the Gospel of John and other New Testament documents to the sharpening of theological differences between Jews and Christians by means of supersessionist polemic and defamatory language. Such needless polemic and defamation of the Jewish people have contributed to the outrage of anti-Semitism in all its subtle and violent forms. Polemical attitudes and language have at times led Christians to violate the ethical principles of Christianity in their efforts to advance Christian faith.

Dialogue requires further that both shared affirmations and conflicting views be recognized. At issue for Christians is the relationship between their affirmation of the continuing authority of the Hebrew Scriptures and their confession of Jesus as the Christ, the Son of God (John 20:31). When the two are held in common, tension results and the authority of the Hebrew Scriptures is relativized. The Old Covenant is perceived as displaced by the New, resulting in the rejection of Judaism.

How can we establish a Christian interpretation of a Gospel that proclaims love for the world while fostering hatred for Jews? Sensitivity to the tension in the Fourth Gospel between the values it teaches and the stereotypes it uses can bring constructive reevaluation among both Jews and Christians. Neutralizing the "anti-Semitic potential" of the Fourth Gospel, however, will require concerted effort on six fronts:

1. Sensitive interpretation of the origin and setting of the Fourth Gospel
2. Theological critique of the Fourth Gospel's anti-Jewish elements
3. Development of a Christology that affirms Jesus' role in relation to both Judaism and the Kingdom of God
4. Reaffirmation of the importance of Judaism and its continuing contributions to the Christian faith

5. Reaffirmation of the importance of the Hebrew Scriptures as a part of Christian Scripture, including affirmation of their teachings in their own right rather than as a foil for Gospel teachings

6. Critique and repudiation of any attempt to use the Fourth Gospel to support anti-Semitic sentiments

These efforts, moreover, while based on serious theological discussion, must be communicated through sermons, popular commentaries, and religious curricula at all levels so that they will have an impact on all confessing Christians.

Ironically, at least part of the task before us is to find ways for Christians to hold firm to their confession of Jesus as the Christ and fulfill their mission as the Church while also bringing fulfillment to the prophecy of Caiaphas, "that Jesus should die for the nation, and not for the nation only, but to gather into one the children of God who are scattered abroad" (John 11:51–52, RSV).

CHAPTER FIVE

The Fantasy of Superiority: Rethinking Our Universalist Claims

Hugh Anderson

My boyhood was spent in a village of some three thousand people in the heart of the Robert Burns country in southwest Scotland. It had three Protestant churches and two sectarian groups of Brethren. But in one of the more prominent locations in town stood the Roman Catholic Chapel of St. Sophia, an impressive edifice in the Byzantine style. I had to pass it every day on my way to primary school. From early attendance at Church of Scotland Sunday School, I had already become convinced that by some decree from the highest authority, only the first day in the week was proper for going to church. I found it quite extraordinary that I should regularly see villagers enter St. Sophia's even on weekdays. Still more puzzling was the fact that at the door they appeared to dip their hands in water (I had heard rude jokes from seniors about "holy water"), then move them in an unusual way (the sign of the cross), and finally light candles and carry them into the dim recesses of the building. Strange creatures those Catholics, that they should do things so very differently from ourselves! So suspicion and a measure of distrust arose in my young mind, accompanied by a rudimentary feeling of the numinous or mysterious surrounding St. Sophia's. The sense that those others were odd was intensified in that their children were required to have their schooling from teachers and in buildings quite separate from our own.

Endemic in these village contexts was the dread of intermarriage between Protestants and Catholics and the idle gossip that arose on the rare occasions when it happened. In my village there was a further alienating factor, engendered, as I subsequently recognized, by a strong class consciousness. The Countess of Loudoun, her son the Earl and her four Lady daughters, whose residence was the enormous castle on the town's perimeter, belonged to St. Sophia's.

Misunderstanding or non-understanding of why the others should be different from us not only begets fear in us, but is all too readily transmitted later on into that most banal of all fantasies, the fantasy of our own superiority. Might not some vast eternal plan so have ordered things that impressions formed in the earliest years as to the 'strangeness' and consequent inferiority of others should be eradicated when human beings put away childish things? Of course the sad truth of our existence and our history is that this has certainly not been so, certainly not among Christians and not within Christendom.

But I believe it behooves us, both Jews and Christians, to remind ourselves that quite apart from the tragic history of Jewish-Christian relationships—within our own domains, as it were, i.e., within the boundaries of each religion—others, ostensibly professing the same faith as we, have produced terror in us, and terror has sought its release in persecution. To acknowledge this much is simply to realize that in the sphere of religion, any religion, the fissiparous tendency is a constant, and that emotions and passions run high among rival groupings. On the Christian side we need only recall the Roman Church's harrying of the Albigenses in the south of France in the eleventh and twelfth centuries, the barbarities of the Inquisition, or the often bitter intolerance of the Reformers (for instance, John Calvin's eventual acquiescence in the burning at the stake in Geneva of the heretical Michael Servetus).

I have lately been studying the life of St. John of the Cross who, together with St. Theresa, led the Reform of the Carmelite Order in Spain in the latter part of the sixteenth century. It is astonishing to read of the vengeance wrought on the Reformers by the Calced Carmelite monks and friars. The little saint, champion of the Discalced, was imprisoned in a tiny cell for months, and was only brought out weekly for the "circular discipline," the scourging of his back and shoulders by each of the Calced Carmelite Fathers in turn. It is worth noting that these cruel excesses had nothing to do with ethnic or racial hatred: they were the rotten fruit of religious or ecclesiastical prejudices. Does not much the greater guilt accrue to Christendom in this respect?

Turning to the Jewish-Christian situation, and acknowledging the limits of my competence, I propose to confine myself here to consideration of some of the main underlying causes of what has been called Christian "supersessionism," the age-old conviction among Christians that with the dawning of the new faith in Christ, the religion of Israel was rendered obsolete and no longer counted. Neither Jews nor Christians to be sure can claim to be innocent of erecting barriers *contra mundum,* and regarding themselves as the only *true* elect of God, with all the sorry misconceptions and conflicts such electionism has triggered off. On the Jewish side we would only mention, from antiquity, the extremely restrictive legislation introduced in Jerusalem by Ezra and Nehemiah in the period of the return of the Babylonian exiles (Ezra 10; Nehemiah 10, where the repudiation of the foreigner, particularly of marriage with the foreigner, is not so very different, I submit, from the dread of Protestant-Catholic intermarriage in my native village). Closer to home, at the level of personal experience, I recall that when I was minister of a church in a pleasant suburb of the city of Glasgow, I had several Jewish neighbors: next door was Dr. H., dedicated to his ancestral faith and no 'assimilationist' after the fashion of the parents of Gershom Scholem in Berlin (see his account in *From Berlin to Jerusalem*), but open, friendly, his children freely permitted to play anytime with our own; while across the street was Dr. J., closed, unfriendly, even hostile, his children prohibited from all contact with ours.

I cannot believe that Dr. J's negative, isolationist attitude resulted from any *odium theologicum.* On the whole, Jews have been far less shackled than Christians by *doctrinal* orthodoxies. And I have long been persuaded that Jews are potentially in a better position to comprehend the movement initiated by Jesus than those Christians who have minimal if any knowledge of the Jewish Bible or the mother faith.

Assuredly there are factors operative in contemporary Western culture that conspire against any improvement in the Christian condition in this regard. In a fascinating essay by Martin Marty, I lately encountered some amazing statistics concerning perspectives on the Bible in American society. A Gallup survey in 1980 found that eighty-three percent of Protestants cherished the Bible as the supremely inspired, revealed Word of God. But some forty percent of Protestants read it *never or hardly ever.* Marty, not surprisingly, thus refers to the Bible as America's "Iconic Book." When it functions iconically, especially among those for whom it remains a largely unopened book, it is commonly revered as the protector of values inherent in the culture and acts as a symbol for these values rather than as a critical corrective to them. It accords with this that in a strong Bible-believing, Protestant county in mid-America, sixty-three percent of churchgoers could not describe any real differences between the Old and New Testaments, and *knew nothing about the Hebrew prophets.*[1]

Quite aside from these disturbing contemporary statistics, we know that from the earliest age of the church, the Jewish Bible has been dismissed outright as having no significance for Christian faith and life. The supreme example was the career of the arch-heretic Marcion in the mid-second century C.E. His view of the Hebrew Scriptures stemmed from the philosophical principles beloved by the Gnostics and expressed in the mythological terms common to the Gnostic movements, that the goal of existence is to escape from bondage to matter, which is inherently evil, into the realm of pure spirit. On that premise it seemed logical enough for Marcion to hold that the God to whom the Jewish Bible bore testimony as the Creator of the material world could not possibly be the true God. According, he insisted that the only real God was the God revealed as the Father of the Lord Jesus Christ. In turn he accepted as authoritative scripture for the church only the major letters of Paul and the Gospel of Luke, and even these only as expurgated of what seemed to him to be excessively favorable references to Judaism. Marcionism has never actually died within the Christian fold. It has simply taken on constantly new forms. In his work on Marcion published at Leipzig in 1924, the eminent historian of dogma, Adolf von

---

1. M. Marty, "America's Iconic Book," in G. M. Tucker and D. A. Knight, eds. *Humanizing America's Iconic Book* (Chicago, 1982) pp. 1–23.

Harnack, described the Hebrew Bible as a fatal legacy and condemned the church for the paralysis that made her retain it.

The roots of Christian "supersessionism" clearly go very far
back in Christian history. But do they go back all the way to the
New Testament itself? Numerous recent studies have sought to
argue that case, those of Rosemary Ruether[2] and the late Samuel
Sandmel,[3] to name but two. The issue is a large and complex
one, and here we can barely touch the fringes of it. The tension
and rivalry between Church and Synagogue in their struggle
toward self-identification in the first century C.E. are clearly
enough reflected in the New Testament. The struggle was, of
course, not between two straightforward and unitary entities.
Neither Judaism nor Christianity was monolithic, then or now.
In fact, we have become increasingly aware of the immense variety and vitality of Judaism and of the wide diversity of Christian
confessions. Not only that; while long centuries of all but total
separation of Jews and Christians from each other have pat-
terned people, especially on the Christian front, to think that
the two religious movements had nothing whatever in common
from the start, but diverged radically from the moment of Jesus'
appearance in Galilee, modern studies have highlighted the fundamental religious convictions *shared* by both. On a broader
view, we do well to remember the thesis of the eminent French
Islamist, Louis Massignon, that Judaism, Christianity, and Islam
are not three different religions, but three branches of the same
religion. Within a narrower compass, Jacob Neusner speaks of
the national religion of the Land of Israel-Palestine (he calls it
"Church") as the matrix out of which were born two small
groups that were to exercise an amazing influence on world
history, nascent Judaism and nascent Christianity.[4]

The two movements have always been intensely interrelated,
but, as Neusner rightly maintains, the climactic events of the
fourth century C.E. proved a watershed in the process of self-
definition no less critical than the sack of Jerusalem in 70 C.E. The
conversion of Constantine and the recognition of Christianity as
the official religion of the Roman Empire elevated the Christian

---

2. R. Ruether, *Faith and Fratricide* (New York, 1974).
3. S. Sandmel, *Anti-Semitism in the New Testament* (Philadelphia, 1978).
4. J. Neusner, *From Testament to Torah, An Introduction to Judaism in its Formative Age* (Englewood Cliffs, N.J., 1988) pp. 15–17, 115ff.

Church to a position of power and prestige that resulted in its growing conviction of its own sovereignty and in its actual dominance of world political history for centuries. Conversely, in the course of that fateful century the social and political status of Jews in Palestine was gravely diminished. Nevertheless, the sages of the land of Israel, to their everlasting credit, responded to the rising tide of Christian triumphalism by formulating their own "symbolic system," expressed finally in the Talmud of around 400 C.E.

From the ecclesiastical triumphalism that characterized the Church after the fourth century, it was but a short step to the brand of absolutism that claims for itself a monopoly on the Truth, the sole Truth, and the whole Truth. And we can only bitterly regret the havoc that attitude has wrought and the untold suffering it has caused. No one religious system, no one theology, can comprehend or embrace the whole Truth. I do not for a moment suggest, however, in the light of that concession, that we should relapse into the sheer relativism that would make us indifferent to our religious heritage and tradition or inhibit us from celebrating such Truth as we have experienced and been able to grasp within our own particular history and in our own inward being. In one session of the present Jewish-Christian dialogue, Peder Borgen wisely cautioned us against capitulating to the cultural or religious pluralism of our age and so of forfeiting the living religious traditions that are uniquely ours and have uniquely shaped our lives. The complexity of the absolutism-relativism issue came home to me with great force on a visit to Japan in May 1986.[5]

Japanese Christians number approximately one million, about one percent of the population. In one sense they resemble the Christian communities of the first century C.E. They form a small group, not many wise by worldly standards, not many mighty, not many noble, according to the Apostle Paul's description of the Corinthian congregation. Minorities, as Jewish people above all surely know, have to fight hard for life and breath, for the freedom to be different. In so doing they most often take

---

5. I am indebted in the following two paragraphs to the essay, "A New Quest for Christology? A Current Issue for Theology in Japan," by Professor Kikuo Matsunaga, President of Tokyo Union Theological Seminary, first read at the Kansai Seminar House, Kyoto, July 22, 1985.

the firmest possible stand on their own special principles and beliefs and state the case for the universality of the Truth of their religion with uncompromising severity. A number of contemporary Japanese theologians, who have studied in Europe and more than likely have come under the influence of Karl Barth's thoroughly Christocentric theology, attribute the demise of Western Christendom to the abandonment of the absoluteness of God's revelation in Christ and acceptance of a pluralistic understanding of society, culture, and religion. They are sensitive to the fact that, in contrast to the great antiquity of Shrine Shinto and the appearance of Buddhism in Japan from Korea in the sixth century, Christianity is a late arrival on the scene. Consequently, they feel that if the Christ-centered gospel is not presented as *the* religion of salvation, there is no opportunity or need for mission, or for conversion from Shinto or Buddhism or even atheism.

Even so, Japanese theologians of orthodox persuasion, however forcefully they may advocate the absolute centrality of the person of Christ, are quite unlikely, in my estimation, to conduct a campaign of acrimony or denigration against the ancient Shinto and Buddhist traditions, which for so long have been a most extensive and integral part of the fabric of Japan's culture and whose continuing influence even Japanese Christians can hardly escape. Nor are they liable to succumb to the idea, not uncommon among Christians in the West, that, in view of the cosmic outreach of the exalted Christ, members of all other world faiths, even without knowing it, are already in Christ; they are "anonymous Christians." It is not so much the implicit arrogance but the logical conclusion of that notion that leads the Japanese preacher to ask why the Shintoist and the Buddhist should not then disregard him altogether and simply stay with Shinto and Buddhism, which (unlike Christianity) are hallowed in Japan by great age, corporate memory, and cultural formativeness.

The lesson to be learned from all this is that in seeking to assess the manner and the nature of Truth claims in religion, it is imperative that we should take full account of the historical-cultural life setting of those who make them. Within the modern Christian context, the failure to acknowledge the vast cultural gap that exists between the earliest Christian movement of the first century C.E. (roughly the period of the New Testament writings) and our own time has had the most regrettable results. New Testament texts are being lifted out of their original, immediate life-setting, are being applied directly to us and our current world situation, and are being accepted as the vehicles of present day Christian triumphalism or absolutism. For example, the theme of the universal divine glory of Christ in the Gospel of John, as we shall see shortly, has profoundly affected the language of missions, particularly in the last two centuries. And that language in turn has helped preserve and nurture the popular belief that the proper goal of Christianity is the conversion of the whole world to this *one* faith, and that therefore all other world religions are palpably inferior and must someday, somehow vanish.

Unfortunately, many in the church are, I believe, either unwilling or unable to alter or reshape the traditional missions language and lack the courage to admit that in our now "global village" of a world, we should be more and more conscious that massive groupings of people cherish their own faith and engage in their own praxis with no less conviction, sincerity, and integrity than Christians.

My aim now is to consider a few texts which have frequently undergirded the type of Christian universalism that is not prepared to see any religious or ethical validity at all in other world faiths. The veneration of Mary as the Virgin Mother of Jesus (God) in the Catholic Tradition, grounded in the Infancy narrative of Luke's Gospel, has very often effectively negated the possibility of any real grasp of the actual earthly life of Jesus of Nazareth as a Jew among Jews. It has also obscured or neglected the fact that Luke in his day wanted to commend Jesus to Gentiles living in a Hellenistic *milieu* in which they had more than a nodding acquaintance with stories of the miraculous births of divine heroes. Apposite to what we are saying here is a vivid passage in Jaroslav Pelikan's valuable work, *Jesus Through the Centuries:* "Would there have been such anti-Semitism, would there have been so many pogroms, would there have been an Auschwitz, if every Christian church and every Christian home had focused its devotion on icons of Mary not only as Mother of God and Queen of Heaven but as the Jewish maiden and the new Miriam, and on icons of Christ not only as Pantocrator but as

Rabbi Jeshua bar-Joseph, Jesus of Nazareth the Son of David, in the context of the history of a suffering Israel and a suffering humanity?"[6]

A similar question arises with regard to the distinct *Tendenz* in the Passion narratives of the gospels, gathering force from Mark and Matthew (27:25) to Luke and John, to exonerate the Romans and blame the Jews for the death of Jesus! As we know, it soon became fatally easy—with the direst consequences—to expand this *Tendenz* into a *universal* condemnation of *all* Jews for all time. Thereby were forgotten the local, specific, or particularistic circumstances for which the gospels were written, in a time when Christians were living as small sectarian communities facing the threat of extinction by the Roman Empire.

The particular texts (or rather series of texts) that probably have contributed most to such absolutism on the Christian side of the ledger are the "I am" sayings placed on the lips of Jesus in John's Gospel and the declaration of Peter in his address to the people and elders in Acts 4:12: "There is salvation in no one else, for there is no other name under heaven given among men by which we must be saved." There are of course a good many other passages of similar nature, but we can make our point by concentrating on these.

In John's Gospel we find the following statements attributed to Jesus: "I am the bread of life" (6:35, 48); "I am the light of the world" (8:12); "Truly, truly I say to you, before Abraham was, I am" (8:58); "I am the door of the sheep" (10:7, 9); "I am the good shepherd" (10:11); "I am the way and the truth and the life; no one comes to the Father but by me" (14:6). My observation of popular attitudes in various denominations of the Church over the last forty years or so suggests that the great majority of members assume that in these resounding affirmations they possess direct dominical authorization for the conviction that the universal or exclusive truth of Christianity precludes all likelihood that there is in any other world religion any vestige of light whatever. And preachers have done very little to disabuse their people of that conceit. They could help greatly by pointing out openly that what is actually going on in our world today is a far cry indeed from what was going on in the ancient world of

---

6. J. Pelikan, *Jesus through the Centuries* (New Haven and London, 1985) p. 20.

John's Gospel, which reflects the existence of a presumably small Christian sect around the end of the first century C.E. trying hard to vindicate its own peculiar sense of exclusiveness and to establish its own independent identity, particularly over against the synagogue. It is incumbent on the interpreter also to explain the distinctive character of the Fourth Gospel. In Matthew, Mark, and Luke, Jesus is very reluctant to arrogate to himself any majestic title(s). In John's Gospel, however, he quite explicitly makes these tremendous claims of himself. Now the Hebrew prophets, acting as spokesmen for God, introduced their own oracular utterances with such formulas as "oracles of *YHWH*" and "thus says the Lord." Likewise Christian prophets, active in the early communities, felt free to put in Christ's mouth their own confessions of faith. It would, therefore, help to free us from dismissive dogmatism if we construed the "I am" sayings in that light and translated them into the third person: "We in the Christian community *believe that Christ is the way and the truth and the life.*" Christians are well entitled to hold that belief still today, to celebrate it and rejoice in it, but surely without succumbing to the notion that Christ himself justifies and guarantees their infinite superiority to all other religions.

As to Acts 4:12 ("salvation in no one else . . . no other name"), it is important to notice that what is at stake in the context (see Acts 4:9) is the healing of the cripple reported in Acts 3:1–11. And the question at issue is: *"In whose name* did the Apostles Peter and Paul perform this miracle?" Peter's answer in Acts 4:12 points away from his companion and himself and turns the searchlight on the One, Jesus, in whose name they acted. "The power was in the name of Jesus," writes Krister Stendahl, "so that instead of answering all the questions of relations to other religions, the Jews and all kinds of other things, the simplest level of this verse is: we did not do it in our own name but in the name of Jesus!"[7] Nevertheless many preachers continue to import into this verse a terrific religious or theological baggage: sin's entail upon all humankind, the total depravity of all unbelievers, the coming Judgement, the utter hopelessness and lostness of all who refuse to come to Christ, heaven and hell, and

---

7. K. Stendahl, "Notes for Three Bible Studies," in G. H. Anderson and T. F. Stransky, *Christ's Lordship and Religious Pluralism* (Maryknoll, N.Y., 1981) p. 16.

much else besides. All of which unhappily often only helps fuel
the fires of bigotry and fanaticism. Our own "lightweight" or
minimalistic interpretation may be supported by the fact that in
Acts 4:12 the noun *soteria* (salvation) and the verb *sothenai* (saved)
carry the connotation of "wholeness" or "restoration to full
health."

We turn now to some more general reflections. Among Christians there is a type of *Christocentrism* which is *theologically* extremely dubious and misleading. It results from a pitiable
narrowing of perspective on the God of the Bible, from the
strange notion that God "becomes Himself," as it were, only in
that one moment when he irrupts into history in Jesus Christ.
And that makes it impossible to perceive that the God in whom
Christians believe is the God of the whole Bible, who creates
and sustains the universe and is infinitely concerned with all his
creatures. As J. A. Sanders has it, the Redeemer God of Christians is none other than the Creator of the world, the Lord of all
that is in heaven and earth and sea.[8] In our Western religious
traditions, however, so many have opted for redemption *in preference to* creation, for morbid preoccupation with sin and death
rather than life and mystic joy, for inwardness and introspection
rather than the look outward to cosmic horizons. In the face of
our exploitation and despoliation of nature and the threat of
nuclear destruction, there is urgent need to escape from captivity to stuffy "redemptionism" and to move toward what might
be termed an "ecological theology."

Such a theology will see that the goal or *telos* is not the saving
of individual souls within the parameters of *one* religion, but the
mending of a broken creation. It is incumbent upon Christians
to remind themselves that *God Has His Story Too*, if I may borrow
a phrase from the suggestive title of a book by J. A. Sanders. It
is a story whose beginning already points to the intended end.
The stress in Genesis 1:1–2:3 on the ordination of the seventh
day as a day to be specially observed is not a piece of killjoy
legislation, but a challenge to all creatures to reverence everything in the created order and to share in God's work of moving
the whole creation toward its final Sabbath rest. God's story is
also the story of His constant and patient struggle with Israel,

---

8. J. A. Sanders, *God Has His Story Too: Sermons in Context* (Philadelphia, 1979).

and of the new chapter of the struggle begun with the people drawn into the movement initiated by Jesus and those around him. The other side of the story is our own struggle with God. Rabbi Hugo Gryn of London tells of a group of rabbis in a concentration camp, filling the painful evening hours by arraigning God. They acted as prosecution, judge, and jury, and after a lengthy trial declared God guilty, guilty of forsaking His people. Shortly afterwards *they went to their evening prayers.* Perhaps only those who in the dark night of the soul have experienced God's absence can come through at length to the full light and gladness of His presence.

We have attempted to examine some of the causes and unhappy effects of absolutism on the Christian side. In relation to the missionary enterprise, it has expressed itself in the dogma that the only proper aim is to make Christians of everybody in the world, whether Hindu, Buddhist, Muslim, Zoroastrian, or those of no religion at all. It persists where there is a blunt refusal to concede the reality of the religious pluralism of the present time. The absolutist stance among Christians has perhaps found its sharpest expression in what has been termed the "demonization of the God of Israel," in the form of supersessionism that regards Judaism as a defunct religion.

It has to be said that voices of protest have been raised in the course of this century against the thoughtless arrogance which assumes that *our* Way (however much we cherish it and joyfully follow it as The Way for us) is the *only* Way for all humanity. In 1932 a report by a lay persons' commission representing seven Protestant denominations resoundingly advocated that *aggressive* missionary activity must be replaced by cooperation. The purpose of mission is not to convert people from one faith to another by setting up a Christian monopoly. We need to try to envision the emergence of the various religions out of their isolation and their gradual integration into a world fellowship in which each without rancor will bear its own peculiar testimony. It is quite possible to entertain this sweeping vision while still singing our own song of faith.

On October 28, 1965, a declaration on the relation of the Church to non-Christian religions was made at the Second Vatican Council. It read as follows: "The Catholic Church rejects nothing which is true and holy in other religions. She looks with sincere respect upon those ways of conduct and of life, those rules and teachings which, though differing in many particulars from what she holds and sets forth, nevertheless often reflect a ray of that Truth which enlightens all men. Yet at the same time she proclaims and must proclaim Christ." Perhaps a slightly patronizing statement, but still more enlightened than what we normally hear from popular or mass evangelism and television ministries.

For years, in America, Reinhold Niebuhr, though himself increasingly disenchanted both with political and theological liberalism and though latterly (mistakenly) labeled a follower of Swiss theologian Karl Barth, campaigned vigorously against Barth's "absolute Christ" idea as a sort of magical formula, beyond all validation by human reason or experience. In his admirable biography of Niebuhr, Richard Fox writes: "In his theology as in his non-Marxian Socialist politics, Niebuhr was convinced, as he put it in denouncing Barth, that we can escape relativity and uncertainty only by piling experience upon experience, checking hypothesis against hypothesis, correcting errors by considering new perspectives, not by the mere assertion of an absolute idea that is beyond experience."[9] I should add of course that Barth long continued to exercise considerable influence on American religious thought, despite the objections of Niebuhr and others against a Christocentrism which separated the realms of nature and grace by its doctrine that God revealed Himself *exclusively* in Christ, which simply encouraged a "redemption myopia" (a subject on which we have already touched).

Probably more significant for Jewish-Christian relationships than the voices of protest we have mentioned is the fact that there now is an increasingly discernible trend among New Testament scholars towards a more just and a more positive appraisal of early Judaism. There are welcome signs that earlier, mistaken assessments of the Judaism of the time of Jesus and Paul as some kind of extinct religious species, are being redressed. I refer especially to the books by E. P. Sanders and J. H. Charlesworth.[10]

---

9. R. W. Fox, *Reinhold Niebuhr. A Biography* (New York, 1985) p. 117.
10. E. P. Sanders, *Paul and Palestinian Judaism: A Comparison of Patterns of Religion* (Philadelphia, 1977) and *Jesus and Judaism* (Philadelphia, 1984); J. H. Charlesworth, *Jesus Within Judaism: New Light from Exciting Archaeological Discoveries* (ABRL 1; New York, 1988); and J. H. Charlesworth, ed., *Jesus' Jewishness: Exploring the Place of Jesus within Early Judaism* (SGAJC 2; New York, 1991).

Then, of course, there is the intensive work being done on the Apocrypha and Pseudepigrapha, led by Professor James Charlesworth, which is broadening our grasp and illumining our understanding of the richness of early Jewish life and faith.

We must admit that the proceedings of Academe are often irrelevant to the practicalities of people's everyday life. But we fervently wish that contemporary efforts to rid New Testament scholarship of its former prejudicial estimates of early Judaism as an effete and dying religion will percolate into the popular mind. It would be a much needed corrective to entrenched dogmatisms and the perennial pride that leads us to glory in our imagined superiority over all who are not like us. Surely we can glory in our religious tradition and bear the most enthusiastic witness to the faith that is in us without glorying in an unreal superiority. Let us by all means hold on as firmly as possible to the Truth that has come to us through our respective religious traditions and experience. But let us also confess, all of us, that even so "we now know only in part."

CHAPTER SIX

Jewish Fears and Christian Fears: An Israeli Point of View

Doron Mendels

When I was asked by Professor Charlesworth to attend this "thinktank," I immediately responded that as an Israeli, I neither suffer from any fears of Christians nor have I been seriously confronted with those fears at any time in my life. I am, however, conscious of anti-Semitism and in particular of what I call *neo-anti-Semitism:* the hatred towards Jews that emerged again with vehemence in the seventh decade of the twentieth century and which has been translated into anti-Israeli feelings. I was confronted with this kind of anti-Semitism in Germany in the aftermath of the Israel-Lebanon war (1984) when, evening after evening, German television was featuring the "Jewish" massacres of the Palestinians (who, one should not forget, terrorized Israel for years before the war). One of the networks in the United States even dared to call the Lebanon war "the final solution of the Palestinian problem." It was very clear that this kind of presentation tended to take everything out of context, neglecting to give a true picture of the history of the relations between Palestinians and Israelis. Needless to say, not many Germans stood up in the public to try to present a more balanced picture.

Another image that lingers in my mind is the presentation on British television of the "typical" ugly Jewish type, speaking

I wish to thank Prof. M. Zimmermann for his useful comments, and Mr. E. Argov for his help and advice while composing this paper.

to millions of English about their views on Menachem Begin during the elections of 1981. The reporter carefully chose to show an extremely negative picture of the Jews in Israel to an audience that hardly knows Israel at all. Distorted pictures of this kind aroused the Jewish population in England at the time. Was this accidental?

While travelling abroad, on occasion I have been reminded of my Jewish origin in a hostile way. The question arises: am I too sensitive? Is this just my "inherited" paranoia or is this real anti-Semitism? Does this simply reveal the real kind of relationship which Jews have with the "Christian" world? Or are all these incidents rather the products of a heightened imagination, typical of a collective Jewish consciousness?

As a non-religious Israeli, I do not feel that I have the problem of the Diaspora Jew, in that I am not confronted daily with the "Christian" world. Living in Israel in many ways has eliminated this point of direct friction with which other Jews around the world must deal. I feel myself equal to Christians and it has never occurred to me to assess somebody on the grounds of his being a Jew or a "goy." I purposely use this somewhat pejorative word here; we will return to it later on in the discussion.

The mutual fear between Jews and Christians is not a phenomenon of the recent past, and it should be examined historically. G. W. F. Hegel rightly viewed the great Hellenistic historian Polybius as the father of "pragmatical history," and I, as a "student of Polybius" think that we must refer to history to learn lasting lessons. Those of us who are theologians and historians must re-examine history for the sake of the future. We can be no less pragmatic in this respect than military historians are when they examine past battles and wars to try to better understand their own military affairs.

For two thousand years we have been confronted both in Judaism and in Christianity with what I call respectively, a "Christophobia" and "Judaeophobia." These very terms teach us something about the relationship between the two religions. Christianity certainly after the first three centuries of our era viewed Judaism from a standpoint of superiority as a result of Christianity's numerical and political power. The recognition Christianity received in 312/3 C.E. from the Roman Empire was felt by the whole of Europe, both in the west and in the east.

The presence of Judaism, which in many places was fragile, created an ambivalent situation: on the one hand the Jews had no choice but to continue living within their Christian environment, and on the other hand the Jewish spiritual leaders needed more than before, to establish rules to protect their people from the effects of Christian and other "foreign" influences. This was important because emancipation for the Jews was not yet possible. Judaism had already undergone a process of introversion, to protect itself from "Hellenistic" influences, and to help secure its own cultural and physical survival. For the Christians, even though the Jews did not threaten their existence, the presence of Jews in their midst bothered them greatly. Christians were promised that they would be the heirs of Judaism in its physical as well as its spiritual dimension, yet, to their dismay and confusion, the Jews continued to exist. Moreover, the constant presence of a Judaic entity that refused to convert to Christianity put many early Church Fathers in a dilemma and influenced their theology for generations.

Unfortunately, some Church Fathers lived at a time when the relationship between Christians and Jews in the Roman Empire was not yet clarified and was still in flux. Judaism could pose a threat to Christianity by virtue of its relations with the political regimes. This prompted the most vicious speeches against Jews by central Church figures, such as Tertullian (160–240) and John Chrysostom (354–407). We probably should add to this situation the "inferiority complex" that was imported with those adherents of Christianity who came from pagan circles and who found it virtually impossible to fulfill all the commandments of a morally strict religious framework, which was a matter of course for the adherent Jew. The Jews, for their part, contributed to this problematic relationship the famous notion of their being the Chosen People temporarily divested of their special status, needing to undergo a period of repentance in order to regain their former state. Jewish relations with Christians could thus be seen as a long trial imposed by God. Jews had to be cautious not to be tempted to take another course, the easier one, the one of conversion to Christianity. Daily Jews faced the prohibition "not to marry them." They led an introverted life within their own people, and the Christian was for them a foreigner (or just a "goy").

We can find an interesting illustration of the condition of the Jew in the Diaspora in the seventeenth-century philosopher, Blaise Pascal's work, *Pensées sur la religion et sur quelques autres sujets*, originally intended as an apologia for the Christian faith. Pascal remarked that it was a surprising phenomenon that the Jewish people managed to continue their existence for so many years, despite their constant suffering and depressed condition; but this situation, Pascal reasoned, was necessary as a proof for the Messiahship of Jesus and in order to admonish the Jew. It was also fitting, he said, that Jews should be depressed because they were after all the ones who had crucified the Messiah. Although it was somewhat of a paradox that a people could be depressed and still continue to exist, nevertheless, observed Pascal, Jews continued their existence without interruption.

In modern times, Stephan Heim revived the famous anti-Semitic tale about Ahasver, the eternal Jew. Ahasver was a witness to the crucifixion, but refused to help; for this reason he was cursed and sentenced to be an eternal vagabond until the *Eschaton* and the return of Jesus the Messiah. This tale was very popular at the time of the Reformation in Germany and demonstrates how Christian theology exploited a *topos* from popular culture that had been preserved for generations in Europe. This *topos* influenced not only the common people, but the intelligentsia as well.

Jews, on the other hand, who lived under a very severe system of ordinances, could not but despise what they saw as a pagan aspect of Christianity, which was linked to that prevalent popular culture, namely, the use of icons. Even the ascetic sector of Christianity seemed to Jews a ridiculous matter, despite the fact that the idea of asceticism was transmitted to the Western world *inter alia* by Judaism.

The segregation and seclusion of Judaism is on the one hand a "Christian" achievement and, on the other, a phenomenon that annoys Christians. In Europe in the Middle Ages, and perhaps even before that, Jews were required to put marks of disgrace on their clothes. Later, the Jews were forced to wear special "Jewish clothes" only to be faced by the leading figures of the Enlightenment with the complaint that Jews were segregating themselves and that their clothes were odd!

Christians seem incapable of showing tolerance or real understanding of the severe Jewish ordinances which are part and parcel of their religion. In seventeenth and eighteenth century Poland we hear about the Jewish "hybris which does not allow Jews to share a meal with Christians" (this is reminiscent of some Hellenistic allusions about the Jews). Indeed, the Jew was always in a delicate situation regarding food, having to be apologetic and to explain the ordinances of *kashruth*. No doubt the prohibition for the observant Jew against eating with non-Jews is a serious inhibition to any potential friendship.

Christianity seems unable to free itself from the above-mentioned inferiority complex it had towards Judaism, to which it owes its very existence. Even its name, "Christianity," derives from the Jewish concept of a Messiah *(Christos)*, and one should remember that the Messiah was the Messiah *of the Jews* (as Flusser and others have argued). However, despite that fact, or perhaps because of it, the Church, from the beginning of its existence, developed an attitude of superiority and hostility towards Judaism. This religion of love and grace created the mechanism of the Inquisition and various popular movements with the common denominator of vehement anti-Semitism and the physical elimination of Jews. Among the most notorious examples are the Crusaders who carried out terrible pogroms against Jewish communities on their way to the Holy Land. It was all done in the name of Christ, and at a period when the Jews were not hostile. At times Jews may have been hostile towards Christians, but in general they were neutral. Later we hear of various blood libels.

The dichotomy (or rather, paradox) in the Christian faith regarding the Jews has been expressed on the one hand through the attempted elimination of the Jews and, on the other, by attempts to study Judaism and regard Judaism as but a prelude to the appearance of Jesus and his community. Classic instances of the latter are the great polemics in the Middle Ages. Ironically, because most Christian theologians at the time could not handle the complicated Jewish sources, they had to press converted Jews into their service in order to argue against the Jews themselves, such as Johann Pfefferkorn (1469–1522/3). There was also an interesting attempt to develop the so-called "Jewish sciences" during the Renaissance by Pico della Mirandola (1463–1494), who was concerned with Christian "Kabbala."

A most interesting phenomenon is the fact that anti-Semitism accompanied the process of secularization in Europe in the nineteenth century. As an historical heritage of the ahistoricity of Christianity, we find both in Germany and in France of the nineteenth century an attempt to settle an account with modernism by a reexamination of the historical sources of Christianity and by encouragement of anti-Semitism. The two "best sellers" of the nineteenth century in France are no doubt *La vie de Jesu* by Ernest Renan (1863) and the anti-Semitic work par excellence, *La France Juive* by Eduard Drumont. Even the leading figure of the Enlightenment, Voltaire, said in his *Dialogue du douteur et l'adorateur* that Jesus was indeed a Jew but that his disciples were not Jews at all! Drumont translated the classical judaeophobic *topos* into modern terms using images such as "desecration of the nation." Anti-Semitism now underwent a transformation from the theological sphere and its pseudo-historical justifications to become a national hatred. A Frenchman who settled in Germany, De Gobineau, in his *Essai sur l'inegalité des races humaines* (1853–1855) was the one who added a racial definition to this national dimension.

In Germany, meanwhile, Nietzsche concluded that Judaism and Christianity are the same, saying that without the one we cannot claim the other and that, therefore, when one facet of the Judaeo-Christian entity is rejected, the remainder is worthless. It is a paradox that the man who called himself antichrist, and who longed for a Europe which would be liberated from Christian morality and which would go back to its idolatrous and pagan origins, is the very one who encouraged the belief that in spite of the bad memories of 2,000 years, there is a common denominator between the two religions. This man, against his own will, contributed to the barbarism which emerged later, as his sister and the Nazis falsified his theories, especially neglecting the points at which Nietzsche expressed admiration for the Jews. However, we cannot ignore the fact that Germany of the nineteenth century had a Wellhausen to state that Judaism was a religion that had become degenerated and that Christianity was its natural successor. It is interesting that the Nazis, who hated Christianity, could and did receive sympathy from many Christians because of one common denominator: hatred of the Jew. Nazism received a great deal of support from the ordinary people of Europe because of its anti-Semitism.

Many passages in the New Testament are so hostile to the

Jews that even today it is impossible to make many people forget what some first-century Jews did to Jesus. It should be noted that the "anti-Jewish" sections of the New Testament do not reach the Jews, who in any case do not read the New Testament. In Israel today, for example, the school children read unfortunately only one or two chapters of the New Testament, and many probably do not know their historical contexts. This ignorance no doubt has helped bring about the complete disengagement between Judaism and Christianity among non-religious Israelis.

The destruction of Nazism left behind not only a decimated Jewish people, but also a Christianity that was hurt and wounded. First of all, from the moral point of view, theologians and philosophers, as well as pastors and educators, felt the terrible moral breach that Nazism had created. It was felt that something had happened that went beyond the old concepts—a turning point after which a deep repentance was required. Christian Europe suddenly felt that her morals had been sacrificed in the Holocaust. It was no accident that the Vatican together with many clergymen, humanists, and liberals like Pope John XXIII, Jacques Maritain, and Maurice Blondel, started to emphasize the early Christian virtues such as tolerance, charity, and philanthropy. The Nazi monster had emerged out of Christian Europe. After the war Christians started to understand that the stance some had adopted during the war in fact tended towards the destruction of oneself, the Christian and moral self.

Christianity started to look into itself, and in so doing with much hardship and pain it discovered anew its bonds to Judaism. Now that there were almost no Jews left, it was perhaps easier to go back to the Jewish origins of Christianity. It was then that Judaism became an exotic thing which attracted Christians not only because of its alienness, but because of its commonness. Hence many Christians faced their heritage and asked themselves: "Are we still Christians?"

Thus we face a growing interest in Judaism, and the first bridges are built in the shadow of mistrust and the difficult past. However, at the same time, the current neo-anti-Semitism is directed not necessarily at the Jews who have remained in the Diaspora (only about ten million at present), but also at the State of Israel, i.e., Zionism. We find at times anti-Semitic remarks uttered under the umbrella of "objective" arguments based on political speculation.

This brings me to my final point. Many Christians should revise their education regarding Judaism and the Jewish people. We cannot ask the Christian church simply to remove the anti-Semitic passages in the New Testament, just as it also seems impossible to make a revision of Orthodox Jewish liturgy, which contains expressions of hatred towards the *Goyyim*. However, it is high time for the Christian world to start speaking *of* Judaism and *to* Jews as equals, instead of thinking in terms of an encounter with a minor and alien entity, "the Jew."

Thus, we will be able to face the future with an ongoing dialogue, rather than with arguments. Both Jews and Christians should fight the "barbarians" who nowadays wish to destroy the Judeo-Christian heritage and world. If nothing is done, the present generation may witness terrible consequences. Jews, however, should also act positively, because they became paranoid about their relationship with Christians as a consequence of the long and painful encounter with them. The Jews should clean and clear their language and their collective thought of the "goy" and the "stranger." Israel is in this regard an ideal meeting place between the two religions. Those Jews who accept contact with the foreign world, including the Christian one, are free of the deep phobias and hatreds of the past, should be among the ones to found a new and constructive relationship between Judaism and Christianity. We must hope for an enduring dialogue between intellectuals on both sides, but what can these intellectuals do to get deeper into the strata of society where one still finds opinions about the Jews that were prevalent in the Middle Ages? Are we now at a juncture where a sincere dialogue can permeate the sermons in churches and synagogues alike? Is it now possible for both Jews and Christians to make lasting improvements in the bridge over the two religions? I think it is imperative that we try.

For Further Reading

Almog, S., editor. *Antisemitism Through the Ages.* Jerusalem, 1980.

Dawidowicz, L. S. *The War Against the Jews, 1933–1945.* New York and Philadelphia, 1975.

Falconi, C. *The Silence of Pius XII.* London, 1970.

Hertzberg, A. *The French Enlightenment and the Jews.* New York and London, 1968.

Parks, J. *The Jew in the Medieval Community.* New York, 1976.

CHAPTER SEVEN

A Gentile in the Wilderness: My Encounter with Jews and Judaism

Martin Hengel

As the only German in this distinguished group, it is for me a particularly challenging task to participate actively in a discussion on the question—once again so painfully urgent in our own time—of mutual fear among different religious and/ or ethnic groups, especially that among Jews and Christians. We Germans, particularly of the older generation, bear throughout our lives a "mark of Cain" that we can neither deny nor remove. My fear is that even after the passing of the generation that lived through the dictatorship of Hitler, the mark will remain, affecting later, innocent generations, just as the disastrous consequences of Hitler's war may last for a century and longer.

Even if we were not personal participants in the abhorrent atrocities committed by Germans against Jews (and other peoples) between 1933 and 1945 and especially during World War II in the years 1941–1945, we would still bear the disgrace and would ever ask ourselves the haunting question: How could

I am deeply indebted to Prof. Raphael Loewe, London, and Dr. Doron Mendels, Jerusalem, for reading the manuscript, making valuable suggestions, and polishing my "Germanic" English.

these atrocities, scarcely paralleled in world history, happen in our country?

Wartime Experiences

It seems best for me, as a German, to speak quite personally and biographically, about my own experiences with Jews and Judaism. I belong to the so-called lost generation in Germany, those who were children when Hitler came to power and lost their best years of life—their youth—through the war and the inevitable catastrophe that followed it. Born on December 14, 1926, I was just six years old when Hitler came to power on January 31, 1933, a day I still remember quite well, when many people, after years of economic misery and political unrest, were expecting a time of recovery and greater security. In the spring of 1945 I was eighteen and had served in the military more than two years: first in the antiaircraft forces as a *Luftwaffenhelfer* (auxiliary air force), then in the *Arbeitsdienst* (conscript labor force), and finally as a simple soldier (wireless operator) in the Army. Many of my friends and schoolmates had been killed in the war or died later in prison camps, especially in Russia. My brother, three years my senior, disappeared in the last weeks of the war; we never heard what happened to him. Two of my cousins and a brother of my father likewise failed to return.

We lived in a rather small town in the eastern part of Württemberg, a town which in 1933 had only three or four Jewish families, who emigrated quite soon thereafter. There was therefore no Jewish community or synagogue there, and I had no experience at all with Jewish schoolmates or with the Jewish religion. The result was that I long remained rather ignorant about Jews and Judaism, knowing nothing except what I learned from the daily reading of the Bible (Old and New Testaments). My father was a self-made man who had grown up in a very poor farmer's family as the eldest of eight children: in 1925 he had founded a little textile business, which he built up slowly but steadily. The spirit in the family of five children was a pietistic Lutheran one, and I am still grateful for this background, in which our parents taught their children to read and love the Bible.

It was when I entered school that I first encountered anti-

Jewish Nazi propaganda, mixed with a distorted picture of German history and a strong nationalistic tendency: the Nazis used the national depression following the end of World War I as a vehicle for their racist ideology, which was at first not very popular. Even the youngest schoolchildren had to learn *"die Juden sind unser Unglück"* (the Jews are our misfortune), as the Jews were declared the main culprits of the German defeat in 1918 with its catastrophic consequences ("national misery," hunger, unemployment, inflation) and were later to be held responsible for world-wide depression and plutocratic capitalism, as well as for Bolshevist communism in Russia and the persecution of Christians there.

I had been educated in school and influenced by the mass media (both of which were state monopolies) to fear and to hate the Jews. I still remember a song we had to learn:

> *Geduld, verratene Brüder,*
> *schon wanket Judas Thron.*
> (Patience, betrayed children,
> Judah's throne is already tottering.)

To be sure, the Nazis were not only anti-Jewish but also anti-Christian. But first they tried—rather successfully—to conceal this, because they wanted to win the Christian voters. In 1933 not a few Christians voted for them, but afterwards (when it was too late) became members of the *Bekennende Kirche* (Confessing Church). The Nazis came to power by means of a strongly nationalistic camouflage connected with the promise to save the German people from both Bolshevist chaos and capitalistic misery, and to restore the "national honor." Strong democratic opposition was found only on the side of the Social Democrats and the Catholics (Center Party), the democratic tradition in Germany between 1918 and 1945 being, on the whole, too weak.

From the beginning, the Nazis were masters of concealment, distortion, and, at the same time, effective patriotic propaganda. Through the introduction of censorship, which began in 1933 and became steadily more repressive, it became more and more difficult to publish openly opposing opinions. The monopoly of official education and information poisoned the spirit of the youth and prepared the way for disaster. I remember very well that when I was in primary (i.e., elementary) school, between six and ten years of age, I had a rather long walk to school—about two miles—and every day I had to pass a public newsstand displaying the *Stürmer*, the worst anti-Semitic weekly, edited by Julius Streicher (who was sentenced to death at the Nuremberg Trials in 1946). I naturally read its sensational and often heart-rending stories with a bewildered interest. My parents, while they themselves had little personal experience of Jewish people, disliked racial Nazi ideology, especially this smearsheet, which was not only anti-Jewish but—in a somewhat moderated tone—also anti-Christian. My father had some business contacts with Jewish customers, but even on his part there was some anxious reluctance. (Don't have too much contact with these people, they are too successful in business.) But he deeply disliked anti-Jewish Nazi propaganda, because he knew his Bible well: "For he who touches you touches the apple of his eye" (Zech. 2:8 [12]; cf. Deut. 32:10). Like many simple, devoted Christians he expected that after the return of Christ at the millennium (Rev. 20:1–10) the Jews would become fervent missionaries of the Messiah according to Zech. 8:23 and Romans 11:12, 15. For the time being, however, they lay under the verdict of Matthew 27:28 and 1 Thessalonians 2:15, and it seemed better not to have too close contact with them. I remember that more than once he said that all peoples who persecuted the Jews had been punished by God, but also that the same could happen to those who allied themselves too closely with them. I believe that, for many Christians in prewar and wartime Germany, this uneasiness about Jews was the reason they did not really acknowledge the great injustice, crying to heaven, that was committed against the Jews from the very beginning of Nazi government and which ended in naked terror and mass murder. When they did see it, it was too late. In my homeland of Württemberg, this blindness may go back partially to a deeply irrational feeling of resentment by the rather poor, pietistic peasantry against the successful alien merchant and moneylender who belonged to another religion, possessed a superior intellectual ability, and came from an already suppressed minority.

At our home, meanwhile, we lived with the Bible. After each meal we would read a chapter around the table, each member of the family taking two verses, from Genesis 1 through Revelation 22, including—Prof. Charlesworth will be delighted to know—the Apocrypha. We boys were very fond of the books of the Maccabees, more so than of the New Testament epistles. In the 1950s, my father, who by then had a biblical scholar in the family to provide him with texts, read also Josephus and the Pseudepigrapha in German translation with keen interest, especially *Enoch* and *Joseph and Asenath.*

During the first years of Hitler's rule, my father was criticized several times for being against Hitler and Nazi ideology; yet, on the other hand, because of his strong patriotic feeling, he was impressed by the incredible political and economic success of the new government and he believed that this could not be happening without the blessing of God. In 1939, he joined the Nazi Party to safeguard his life's work, the factory he had founded in 1925 with very little capital and which he had successfully built up: he feared that it would be threatened if he did not conform at least outwardly. During the war he feared victory as much as defeat, because victory would lead to a persecution of Christians and defeat would bring the destruction of the German people. I surmise that this sort of schizophrenic situation prevailed in many Christian families.

The burning of synagogues in many towns—over fifty years ago, on November 9, 1938—came as a shock among German Christians generally; but there were very few open protests, and indeed even less concern for their suffering Jewish fellow citizens. Perhaps people remembered Psalm 74:8 ("they burned the meeting places of God in the land"), but they could not imagine that, because of Hitler's criminal policy, five or six years later German towns and churches would be burning, too. For that very year, 1938, brought Hitler's greatest triumphs: in March the "return" of Austria, and in September the "peace meeting" in Munich with Chamberlain, Daladier, and Mussolini and the agreement about the cession of the German-speaking parts of Czechoslovakia. Many believed that the "ingenious statesmanship" of Hitler had preserved the peace. I remember that on the morning after the Munich meeting, our schoolmaster—a highly cultivated son of a pastor, and by no means a Nazi—entered the classroom, deeply moved, with the words: *"Wir danken unserem Führer"* (We thank our Fuhrer). The overwhelming success of Hitler in foreign and domestic policy was, even for many Christians, only partly clouded by the organized riots of his storm troopers (the SA). Facile evasiveness all too often prompted the response: *"Das weiss der Führer nicht"* (The Fuhrer doesn't know). The incredible chain of success, political, economical, and military, lasted ten years, until the battle of Stalingrad in the winter of 1942–43. As a clever demagogue, he made masterly use of seductive persuasion, concealment, and terror, and the success of this "carrot and stick" policy, which exceeded all expectation, paralyzed any real opposition. All attempts to stop or to remove Hitler were thereby doomed to failure.

At school we were influenced, in a strongly nationalistic way, by a distorted picture of history. Other nations, such as England and America, had had much more success in building up an empire, because they had had less moral or religious inhibitions ("My country right or wrong," for instance, was still an ideal in those nations). They had also won *Lebensraum* by pushing back "inferior" races (Indians, aborigines, etc.). It was only the Germans, as "latecomers" in history, who remained a *"Volk ohne Raum"* (a people without space).

Some individual teachers even tried to inculcate hatred: "Boys, you must learn to hate," our sports instructor once shouted. He had been a fervent Catholic before 1933. Being an active member of the Center Party, he was subjected to brainwashing in a concentration camp in 1933. During the war he joined the *Waffen-SS* and was posted as missing. Another medium of subtle hate-propaganda was the cinema. My whole school class had to attend one film entitled *Jud Süß*, and we boys of fourteen were naturally impressed by what was in reality vicious anti-Jewish melodrama.

A good decision on the part of my parents sent me in 1941 (the year Hitler attacked Russia) to a private Christian boarding school of the Bohemian Brethren in the Black Forest—which at that time was still in operation but was, of course, already encountering difficulties. There, for the first time, I met a half-Jew, who was attending the school. He was a nice fellow, and I had good relations with him until he had to return home because his presence had caused severe problems for the school, which already feared for its survival. At that time, the year of the notorious secret Wannsee Conference (January 20, 1942), it had become dangerous to speak freely with respect or sympathy about Jewish people whom one knew personally. I was fifteen by then and was reading everything I could get my hands on, including Jewish authors such as Heine, Werfel, and Zweig, (who by now belonged to the forbidden literature) as well as anti-Jewish propaganda such as the *Protocols of the Elders of Zion* or Grimm's *Volk ohne Raum*. Being rather ignorant about Jews and Judaism, I could not form an opinion of my own on the larger issues, but, personally, I regretted having lost a school-mate for reasons that seemed unjust to me and which I could not explain. Then, when I had turned sixteen, just after the Battle of Stanlingrad, I was drafted into the antiaircraft forces in Karlsruhe as a *Luftwaffenhelfer*, together with other youngsters from boarding schools in the Black Forest. This new stage brought us a strong new feeling of independence, linked to more critical thinking about the Nazi Party and its ideology. I served as a radio-telephone operator, together with a soldier several years my senior who had studied economics and was a rather convinced Marxist-Leninist. With him I had endless discussions. Superior by virtue of age and knowledge, he often evinced irony in the face of my own naïveté. Through him I became acquainted with the works of some Jewish authors, which already were difficult to get.

At the end of 1943, and later in 1944, when German power was waning, we heard—from soldiers returning from Poland—whispers about concentration camps in the eastern theater of war, where Jews—and other people—were put to forced labor under inhuman conditions. When I was in the Labor-Service *(Arbeitsdienst)* in the Saar region on the western frontier, I once met two members of a small forced labor camp. Neither they nor I dared to speak to one another, for we were full of fear. Because I had sustained serious illnesses (pneumonia and diphtheria) I stayed in the southwest of Germany; even after having been drafted into the army in July 1944, shortly before "D Day" on June 6, 1944, I had to spend months in the hospital, and I re-mained a private soldier without any rank. These circumstances, I think, saved my life.

After the change in the fortune of the war in 1943, Germany more and more resembled a besieged fortress with a very mixed mood of obstinate determination, some secret opposition, sup-pressed fear, and open terror, strangely offset by moments of happiness in which all else was forgotten similar to the atmosphere described in certain ancient reports of siege conditions. The threat to one's own existence made one insensitive to the suffering of other groups, which seemed rather far away. At the same time we were astonishingly "well informed" by propaganda about the "atrocities" of the "enemy" (e.g., air raids, the burning of towns, the killing of civilians and prisoners of war), and the fearful consequences of a defeat: unconditional surrender, the Morgenthau plan, and the threat of population transfers to forced labor camps in other countries. The propaganda of the state was at pains to produce this strange, poisoned amalgam of fear, refusal to admit defeat, and desperate, futile hope.

It was only in the months after the war, from May 1945 on, that young people realized the cruel truth of what had actually happened and that the murder of millions of Jews was not the invention of allied propaganda. My most impressionable insights into the crimes of Hitler and his accomplices were gained from Eugen Kogon's book, *The SS-State*, published early in 1946. Reading this book was a watershed for me. Since then, the question has never left me: How could this happen in our country, where people were to a large extent Christians? It is a question which, although it will elicit many answers, remains unfathomable.

How could a nation with an extraordinarily rich cultural and religious tradition be led astray in such a way and fall so low? Nationalism, the idol of modern Europe, the product of the Enlightenment, is not an adequate explanation; that idol was worshipped by other nations as well. Racial anti-Semitism infected parts of our people like some pernicious, contagious mental disease. In Germany in the nineteenth and the beginning of the twentieth century, it was no stronger than elsewhere (witness the Dreyfus affair in France and the pogroms in Russia). Indeed, racism was not very popular at all. To be sure, before the decade 1932/33 the German intelligentsia (as well as the churches) underestimated the demonic, seductive fascination of Hitler, and after he came to power many expected only a short interlude. But then there followed his extraordinary political and economic success. Disillusionment would not come until shortly before the bitter end! The events of the twelve-year period 1933–1945 in Germany may be the greatest instance and most deterrent exemplification in modern history of the truth of Genesis 9:21, that "the imagination of man's heart is evil from his youth." It may warn us against all sorts of inhuman utopias, where the pseudo-idealistic purpose justifies the means. What has happened cannot yet be explained sufficiently, even less excused. It recalls Cain's answer to God in Genesis 4:13. When I think about it all, and I do so ever and again, I feel both rage (How could this happen?) and shame (Such things must never happen again!).

Postwar Experiences

In 1945, as a young man of eighteen, I had to start looking for a profession. A conflict dominated the next eighteen years: my father wanted me to become a businessman and help him reopen his little factory, which had been closed by the government in 1943. I, at my zero hour, was asking: What is needful now? What will survive? For me, it was the Christian faith. I finished school and studied theology. This decision afforded the only possibility of avoiding business and of studying at all, and even then with great difficulty; three times between 1948 and 1964 I had to re-enter the factory, and three times I left it again for my chosen vocation.

My second encounter with a Jew was when I had just begun learning Hebrew. I was sitting in a railway carriage and was reading my Hebrew textbook. On the other side sat a displaced person, a Jew from Poland, who was astonished to see a young German reading Hebrew. In the ensuing discussion, I encountered his different, Ashkenazic pronunciation. But this encounter remained an isolated episode. During my studies from winter 1947 to summer 1951 in Tübingen (and Heidelberg), I had no further personal contacts with Jews, and I got very little information about Judaism. I never attended a Jewish service and I never met a rabbi. The synagogues had been burned and no Jewish scholars lectured at our university. There was only some basic, background instruction about early Jewish history and piety for a better understanding of the New Testament, and even then—in the old Christian tradition—Judaism sometimes seemed rather to be the "contrast screen" behind early Christianity.

My personal interests were primarily in church history and I had no academic ambitions at all; I only wanted to become a good pastor. The possibility of a dissertation arose during the final examination at the university, but I wanted to enter church service and so became a vicar, first in Calw and then in Heilbronn, a town where my mother's family had been winegrowers for five hundred years and which in December 1944 had been almost totally destroyed by an American air raid. About one-tenth of the population had been killed. Seven years later it still lay largely in ruins, and I encountered severe social misery there—refugees from the East, people living in cellars, ruins, and huts. Before Hitler there had been quite an old, rather large Jewish community, but it too was destroyed, scattered. Here, therefore, I had even less opportunity for Jewish studies. The pressing social and welfare problems in the church at that time overshadowed all other concerns for me.

The same restricted situation applied when I had to return to my father's business in 1953. This gave me the first opportunity to travel in foreign countries, particularly Scandinavia. Up till then I had hardly been aware of the problem in having so little knowledge and information about Jews and Judaism, knowing few Jewish books and fewer Jewish people. I remember the impression made on me by a little book by the Christian author Helene Christaller, *Rabbinische Legenden*, which whetted my appetite for more. I had never read Talmudic literature before, except for isolated quotations in New Testament commentaries and in the Strack-Billerbeck *Kommentar zum Neun Testament aus Talmud und Midrasch*. With few exceptions, German Christian theology after the war was at first rather uninterested in Jewish thought and theology. The famous German tradition of *Jüdische Wissenschaft* had been almost totally broken. Some Christian scholars like Gerhard Kittel and Karl Georg Kuhn had let themselves be seduced by Nazi ideology, and there were only a few who tried to make a new beginning. One of these was Otto Michel, my late *doktorvater*, who sought to revive the tradition of Adolf Schlatter and later, in 1958, founded in Tübingen the Institutum Judaicum.

In autumn 1954, for the second time I left the textile business to return to theology and became *Repetent* (i.e., a student instructor) in the famous *Tübinger Stift*. During the three years since I had left Tübingen the theological climate had changed. Most of my colleagues at the "high table" of the repetents had become enthusiastic adherents of Rudolf Bultmann's theology, his New

Testament exegesis, and his program of demythologization and existentialistic-anthropological interpretation. Part of this—a heritage of the *Religionsgeschichtliche Schule*—was his overestimation of the syncretistic-pagan and gnostic background of early Christianity and the devaluation of its Old Testament and Jewish roots. To be sure, Bultmann was never anti-Jewish; on the contrary, the closest friend of his youth, with whom he exchanged many letters, was a Jew who fell in World War I, and in 1933 together with the Marburg theological faculty he strongly opposed the Aryan clause in the church. As a liberal Democrat he always had been a firm anti-Nazi. His relative distance from the Old Testament was founded in the old Protestant liberal tradition and in a marked existentialist resistance to any concept of *Heilsgeschichte*.

For me, as a young beginning *Stiftsrepetent*, Bultmann's outline of theology and exegesis involved too severe a loss of historical reality and religious experience, and I therefore decided to study the New Testament, together with its Jewish and Hellenistic background, in order to examine critically the truth of this most recent and influential form of German theology. Uneasiness about Bultmann's success led me to more intensive study of the New Testament and ancient Judaism. I must therefore always be grateful to that great critical theologian: he stimulated me to discover the treasures of the ancient Jewish sources, which helped me not only to understand my own Christian faith better, but also to enter into a progressive contact with Jewish religious thought and with Jewish people. I began to read the newly discovered Qumran texts, which were then gradually shaping the old picture of early Christianity as painted by the history of religions school; I studied the Pseudepigrapha and—without any real teacher, but more or less as an *autodidact*—Talmudic literature. In Tübingen (today a university town of about eighty thousand inhabitants and twenty-three thousand students) there had been only one synagogue until the fatal year of 1938. Later there was no rabbi or Jewish teacher to introduce me to the Talmud or the liturgy; I had to read the texts alone, or together with friends.

In the spring of 1955 I visited Palestine for the first time. Because in those early years after the war it was impossible for a German to obtain entry permission to visit Israel, I could see only the Arab regions. Jordan, the West Bank (including the old City of Jerusalem), Syria, and Lebanon. I shall never forget the sad impression of the destroyed Jewish quarter and the very narrow entrance to the "Wailing Wall." Later, in 1976 and 1978, I was able to make two visits to Israel, once for an extended period with the possibility of lecturing at the Hebrew University of Jerusalem, in Tel Aviv, and in Haifa. But in 1955 that was still an unimaginable development. In the same year I became assistant to Professor Otto Michel and cooperated in the translation of Josephus' *Jewish War* by Michel and Bauernfeind. At that time I began my dissertation on the Zealots, the Jewish liberation movement active between the time of Herod the Great and 70 C.E. But it was only seldom that I had the opportunity to have personal contact with Jews. Especially memorable was a meeting with Dr. Robert Raphael Geis, chief rabbi in Badonia, whose personality I will never forget.

But my stay at the university soon came to an end. In the spring of 1957 I had to return for very urgent family reasons, to take over commercial guidance of the family firm, about one hundred kilometers from Tübingen, and I supposed this would be a farewell forever to New Testament and Jewish scholarship. But I took with me my dissertation, of which I had finished about one-fourth, and, with an immense effort, I completed it in two years, while working in a totally different, difficult, and responsible occupation. I submitted it successfully to the theological faculty in Tübingen in the autumn of 1959. In 1961 it was published by Brill in Leiden; a second, enlarged edition appeared in 1976, and an English translation was to be published by T. & T. Clark, Edinburgh, in 1988. This book, which was written under extremely unpropitious circumstances, opened up for me the world of Ancient Judaism, and at the same time, unexpectedly, the way into New Testament and Jewish scholarship. This period, spent as a "traveller between two worlds," brought further, encouraging contacts with Jews. A Jewish customer of mine in Berlin gave me a Hebrew prayer book which thirty years later is still on my desk beside the Greek New Testament. Dr. Geis, whom I visited several times during the textile fairs in Düsseldorf, encouraged me, after the publication of my Zealots book, to return to scholarship. With this spiritual help from several friends, I left commerce after my father's death, and, after a very severe illness of my own (which was also a symptom of a deep crisis), I returned at the age of thirty-eight to the university, where in less than two years I finished my *Judaism and Hellenism* and qualified for a regular academic post in January of 1967. In 1968 I got a call to Erlangen, and in 1972 back to Tübingen as professor of New Testament and Ancient Judaism, Christian theologian, and university teacher; and as such I am especially grateful for a rich scholarly exchange and friendship with Jewish colleagues in Israel, America, England, and other countries. That is a gift which, for a German, after all that has happened, is no matter of course.

Lessons from my Life

A professor is, by definition, a student of life. I close by sketching what I feel I have learned from being a "professional student" for so many years.

The most fascinating impression I have received from many years of study of ancient, pre-70 Judaism is that period's enormously creative spiritual power and diversity: it was the most ingenious religious system in late Hellenistic and early Roman times, and one which, through its Christian branch, changed the ancient world radically. No oriental people or religion in antiquity had such a powerful and so long-term an encounter with Hellenistic-Roman civilization as did the Jews. The customary, negative picture of a sterile, numb, and parasitic "late Judaism" (which was developed by liberal Protestants and anti-Semitic ancient historians during the past century and which remains relatively influential to this day) is totally misleading. The truth is completely opposite.

Another insight gained from my studies is that early Christianity was almost wholly dependent on Jewish thought and tradition *and* on the genius of those Jews who were its creative founders: Jesus, Paul, Peter, James, John, and Matthew. What we suppose to be Hellenistic or syncretistic is mediated by Greek-speaking Judaism, which had an extraordinarily receptive and integrating power. In other words, early Christianity is essentially "Jewish," a messianic, eschatological, enthusiastic, and universalist form of Judaism, with the overwhelming experience of God's *grace and love* concentrated in the person of Jesus of

Nazareth, the Jew, as Messiah—an experience which, although betrayed by Christians a thousandfold in later history, yet remains true and powerful up to the present time.

The preparation for an experience of radical grace which Paul sustained in his lifelong encounter with Christ lay not in Greek thought but in Paul's knowledge of Hebrew scripture and his Jewish leanings. Elements of "justification by grace" are already found in Isaiah, in the Psalms, and in the Qumran Scrolls, and the central importance of faith together with the preaching of the Kingdom of God is found in the Exodus tradition (cf. Ex. 14:31; 15:18). The fundamental teaching of the church was built on basically Jewish foundations. This does not mean that Christianity and Judaism are the same; certainly not. The differences are at once fundamental and necessary, and they can be overcome only eschatologically, with the final coming of the Kingdom of God and his Messiah. But Judaism remains, historically, the mother of Christianity, and nobody can hate his mother without himself suffering extensive damage to his own personality. Even a son who, in order to "find himself," has to leave the house of his mother, should remember her in love. If Christianity lost that remembrance through a long and painful history, caused partly by the old, sometimes cantankerous domestic (or infra-Jewish) dispute in New Testament times, it is now, after the terrible experiences of our century, imperative to remember and recover this very close—once symbiotic—relationship.

As an exegete of the New Testament and a student of ancient Jewish history, I consider one of my most urgent duties this constant task of calling-to-mind (in Hebrew, *zakār*), feeling myself sometimes like a Christian *mazkîr* between Ecclesia and Synagoga.

I would end by summing up some basic conclusions from the experiences I have undergone in the course of a tumultuous life.

1. *Christians and Jews must fight shoulder to shoulder for an open and tolerant society, which is only possible in a constitutional and socially responsible democracy, with unrestricted freedom of information.* Dictatorship—whether in the form of tyrants, clans, military juntas, or political parties that monopolize information and education, practice open or secret censorship, and silence the voice of dissent—is subject to corruption by its very intolerance and disregard of human rights. People, especially young people

who have grown up in liberty, sometimes too easily forget that even "sympathetic" dictators can govern only in a climate of censorship and terror, even if subtly veiled. Consequently, any kind of dictatorship must be met by effective opposition. Our often too self-confident democracies should never forget: *Principiis obsta!*

2. *All attempts to sow hatred between religious groups, nationalities, and races must be opposed from the outset.* This does not mean renouncing every form of criticism, but criticism must be based on reasoned argument, it must be objective and not offensive, it must always differentiate between issues and persons. Demagogic defamation is inherently implausible and rebounds on its author. I well know that this is sometimes a question of temperament, but in our work as scholars we must learn to bridle it. The end does not justify the means, and truth can only be defended by arguments that are themselves self-evidently true.

3. *It helps neither Christians nor Jews to smooth away the great differences between Judaism and Christianity.* The unification of both is an eschatological aim, which lies beyond our own possibilities of realization. We may see a symbol of this aim in the role of the *Qedushah/Trishagion* in celestial worship as conceived in both Jewish and Christian liturgy.

4. *What we can achieve in the here and now, however, is a better understanding of each other.* For the Christian, surely, this means a better understanding of his own faith and its roots; for the Jew, perhaps, a better understanding of the universalistic power of prophetic promise in the Hebrew Bible and the fullness of God's grace. A special treasure is the Jewish prayer-tradition, which was of enormous importance for early Christianity. The Psalms were the prayer book not only of Israel, but also of the early Church, and the Lord's Prayer is one which Christians and Jews can both use.

Thus, it is not helpful when either side polemicizes against professing believers of the other group. Christians and Jews should have respect for each other's faith. It is no good looking for skeptical and disbelieving "allies" on the other side to defame or ridicule the faith of either Jews or Christians. A believing Jew is, for me, much nearer to me in faith than is a skeptical—let alone a cynical—pseudo-Christian. Christians and Jews now, after the cruel experience of this "enlightened" century, are in many ways dependent upon each other. I think that most Christians in Germany have learned this. They acknowledge the heavy guilt of the past and the new responsibility resulting from it. Interest in Jewish religion and history in Germany has never been stronger than at present. Millions of Germans, especially young people, have visited Israel, and their number is increasing. They may even constitute the largest block of tourists in the Holy Land. Most of them are deeply impressed by the land of the Bible and the new Jewish homeland, towards which they entertain a positive sympathy. This makes me hopeful, particularly for German Christianity. "Anti-Semitism" is in every respect totally incompatible with the Christian faith.

5. *I do not think that "Anti-Semitism" has any real future at all in Germany,* even though there are some small groups of incorrigibles and incurables, some of them old Nazis (decreasing in numbers as time marches on), and a very few young people (most of them uneducated and without influence) behaving antisocially out of a sort of irrational protest. More significant is the "Anti-Israel" feeling of some leftists, partly fostered by Marxist or Eastern propaganda, perhaps a heritage of the assimilationist ideas of Karl Marx and his followers. These will not recognize that the situation of the Jews in Israel is always under threat, and they do not see the danger of Islamic fundamentalism, which, like all fanatical fundamentalisms, is a menace to true religion and to peace between nations.

6. *To be sure, the State of Israel, throughout an existence always exposed to danger, has made political mistakes.* Every people does. We Germans especially should never forget it. Any chauvinism which has only contempt for its "inferior" neighbors will not yield positive results. But we should also not forget that the founding of the State of Israel was an indirect result of the tragedy of European Jewry. The present unrest in the Arab parts of the Holy Land is not caused primarily by the Jews, but is rather part and parcel of the continuing war declared by the Arabs on the newly founded Israeli State in 1948. They have never entered into any real, comprehensive peace negotiations. One-sided critics of Israel in the Western World seem, ultimately, to expect of her some sort of political suicide. Peace will come, however, only through genuine and lasting compromise on both sides. At the moment, fanaticized Palestinian Arabs filled with hatred seem

to be much more uncompromising and intransigent than is the Jewish majority. They seem to evince a similar irrational mentality to that which was displayed in the cruel war between Iran and Iraq. It reminds me of the murderous despair in Germany during the last years of World War II (1943–1945). Disturbances of this type will never lead to peace, but only to further bloodshed. At present, therefore, Israel needs our critical sympathy more than ever before, especially since the SCUD attacks from Iraq in 1991.

CHAPTER EIGHT

Study and Experience: Two Dimensions of Jewish-Christian Dialogue

Paul D. Hanson

College and seminary students can often be heard debating whether religious zeal has contributed more good or more ill to humanity over the course of history. Unfortunately, those taking the negative side of the debate have much evidence upon which to draw, whereas the positive evidence is often of a more ambiguous or subtle nature. The experience of the Holocaust has pressed this question upon the consciousness of every Christian, and the ongoing tension in the Middle East, whether between Arabs and Jews or between Shiite and Sunni Muslims, has established the issue of understanding between different religious communities as one that all people of conscience must address.

For Christians, a natural starting point in growth towards a deeper understanding of the person of a different faith is engagement with people of the Jewish faith, for not only is the relationship with Judaism a key factor in Christian self-identity, it can also tutor the Christian in the style of interrelationship that can foster understanding between Christianity and the other world religions as well.

The Second Philadelphia Conference on Jewish-Christian Relations gave its Jewish and Christian participants an opportunity to explore interfaith understanding within an intimate setting generously provided by Irvin J. Borowsky, Founding Chairman of the American Interfaith Institute. In my presentation to the group, summarized in what follows, I identified two levels of discussion that I regard to be essential to Jewish-Christian dialogue. Though intertwined in practice, awareness of the distinction between these two levels on the part of those engaged in dialogue safeguards against the kind of uneasiness that enters a discussion when facts and feelings are unconsciously mixed.

One of the two levels of "dialogic" discussion is cognitive in nature. It is the one on which scholars feel most comfortable. Involved on this level is the historical study of the texts and traditions of Judaism and Christianity, with an eye especially to evidence for the interrelationship between the two. In such study, Jewish and Christian scholars commonly utilize the same philological and historical methods of study, ever mindful that even such methods are influenced by the presuppositions of the individual.

Biblical studies was perhaps the first sub-discipline within which Jews and Christians discovered that they were utilizing the same tools and coming to results that could be meaningful to both communities. In the past several decades, this historical approach has been extended to the study of later historical periods, and the results have been encouraging for those who recognize the significance of rigorous scholarship within religious communities in which fear and distrust have been abetted by a legacy of misinformation, ignorance, and distortion of historical fact. Though consciousness of the subjective element present in all historical study is rightly emphasized by recent historiographic studies, the difference between the portrayal of Jesus by New Testament scholars of the Third Reich and by contemporary scholars like Geza Vermes and E. P. Sanders is the difference between scholarship controlled by ideology and scholarship that respects the integrity of the ancient sources.

In the case of the study of the first several generations of the Common Era, scholars are engaged in a battle between ignorance and knowledge. And the importance of this battle extends far beyond academic circles. The prejudices Christians have harbored against Jews over past centuries that have led to unspeakable tragedy have been fostered by ignorance or a distorted picture of the past. Within such a situation, those untrained in the complicated tools of historical reconstruction easily become unwitting pawns within the hands of demagogues in a pernicious process that can eviscerate all that is holy and good within Christian tradition.

Today we are witnessing notable breakthroughs in scholarship that are altering the course of many Christian denominations in a way that is heartening to Jews and Christians committed to accurate understanding of the past and to mutual respect. Study of Jewish and Christian sources, both canonical and extra-canonical, have led to an emerging portrait of Jesus of Nazareth that is enabling us to appreciate his relation to the Jewish parties of his time and to dispel anti-Judaic themes that have entered Christian tradition from erroneous readings of history. Similarly, scholarship has clarified our understanding of Pharisaism by integrating the New Testament references into the broad range of available sources, thus enabling a more reliable critical reading than was possible for earlier generations of scholars. Even as these two examples illustrate the solid historical foundation that is being built for understanding the origins of Judaism and Christianity, examples could be given from studies on every subsequent period down to the present to indicate the emergence of an era in which Jewish-Christian dialogue can proceed on a more factually reliable basis than was possible previously.

Factual knowledge and historical-critical study alone, however, do not ensure fair, constructive dialogue. Due to the subjective element in all historical scholarship, scholarly studies are never immune to the kind of misinterpretation that abets fear and distrust. This leads to the second level essential to any positive exchange between religious communities, what we might call the affective level. It was the clear awareness of this level that led the planners of the Second Philadelphia Conference to convene its participants directly in the wake of a large scholarly conference at Princeton Theological Seminary dedicated to the theme of Messianism in the First Century C.E. Although sound, rigorous scholarship is essential in every endeavor to engage different religious communities in serious dialogue, progress can be obstructed if the feelings of distrust, fear, hope, and yearning that are found in every heart are not lifted up out of the subconscious and subjected to careful scrutiny. Only then can the role played in our scholarly and reflective activities by attitudes and values inherited from our particular backgrounds be acknowledged and understood.

It was only natural that on the affective level our discourse largely took the form of narrative accounts of personal experiences. No amount of "pure scholarship" could contextualize the Jewish experience of Nazi Germany as vividly and accurately as the opening dialogue between Professor Martin Hengel of Tübingen University, Germany, and Professor Shemaryahu Talmon of Hebrew University, Jerusalem. A palpably somber aura descended upon the conference room as these two biblical scholars determined that on the same day that the latter and his family were being marched through Frankfurt en route to a death camp, the former's father was in that same city enrolling in the Nazi Party in the effort to save the family textile industry.

By comparison with such momentous experiences, my own story falls into the category of the trivial. But experiences of the ordinary sort also contribute to the flow of history. In fact, my story strikes me as so average as to be descriptive of the experience of many other Christians.

My childhood in Upper Michigan was characterized more by a lack of contact with Jews than either by experiences of meaningful relationships or by instances of overt prejudice. For that reason the jokes about the clever Jewish boy Ikee and his businessman "Fadder" seemed to fall outside any meaningful context. In reflecting backward, I can only explain them as so much a part of the larger culture that they were told in Wakefield, Michigan, with its Jewish population of two, in the same way they were told in Chicago or New York. Wherever they were told, however, they instilled in young minds a distorted picture of Jews as untrustworthy, especially when it came to business transactions.

What bearing did my religious education have on such anti-Jewish attitudes? Though I certainly cannot attribute sinister intentions to any of the teachers or pastors of my childhood, the Sunday School materials with which they were provided did nothing to counteract the anti-Judaism that infects the cultural traditions of the modern West; to the contrary, they participated in such anti-Judaism by portraying the Jews collectively as the hostile party that rejected Jesus and was responsible for his crucifixion. Though the crude portrayal of Jews as devils current in

Medieval and Reformation religious literature did not come to my attention until much later, it is clear that my Sunday School experience belongs to a chapter of Christendom deeply flawed by a defective theology of Judaism.

College years in a small midwestern school did little to broaden my horizons on Jewish-Christian relations. I was exposed to Judaism neither in the curriculum nor in personal relations. As if to make up for lost time, however, I was shocked into a new consciousness during the year I spent subsequent to college graduation as a Fulbright student in Germany. Especially among members of the working class whom I met in restaurants and bars, I encountered a pernicious form of anti-Semitism that struck me with added force because one of my closest friends during that year was a Jewish exchange student.

Seminary and graduate school years were conditioned by the cumulative effects of my year in Germany. My study of Judaism and Christianity alike were not conducted from a different perspective. Jewish students and teachers became tutors on a pilgrimage that continues to this day, a pilgrimage on which a Christian comes to understand Judaism as a living faith with a beauty and integrity from which all persons of faith have much to learn. Such a change in perspective profoundly influences both one's scholarly endeavors and one's personal experiences. A recent review[1] by a Jewish scholar of my book *The People Called* confirms my sense that my biblical research has been influenced significantly by my growing into a more accurate understanding of Judaism. That my response to personal experiences has been similarly transformed can be illustrated by two anecdotes.

In the fall of 1973, my wife Cynthia, my three-year-old daughter Amy, and my infant son Mark and I found ourselves in the middle of the "Yom Kippur" war in Jerusalem. We experienced the pain of trying to maintain our relationships both with our Jewish and our Arab friends at a time when many on both sides were feeling the growing animosity that accompanies war. Our Arab friends related how their rights were violated by searches and restrictions on travel. The sense of fear experienced by our Jewish friends in the face of Arab hostility became palpable as

---

1. M. Wyschogrod, Review of P. D. Hanson, *The People Called: The Growth of Community in the Bible* (San Francisco, 1986) in: *JES* 24 (1987) 450–51.

we overheard Arab youths exclaim that when the Syrian armies arrived they could embark on a campaign of shedding Jewish blood. Most shocking of all was to recognize that the people of Israel were suddenly isolated by the vast majority of the Christian world. What earlier would have appeared to me to be a political phenomenon was unmasked as evidence of the latent anti-Judaism that still plagues the Western world. We may deny that the barbarian madness of Nazi Germany lurks in our breasts, but it is hard for me to deny that many Christians still harbor a deep wish that the "Jewish problem" might be solved by an Arab military offensive against the State of Israel.

Exactly a decade later, in the fall of 1983, our family of five was located in Munich. Though unsure whether we were doing the right thing with respect to our young children, we decided to take them to Dachau to visit the infamous concentration camp. The streets along which the camps had been lined up, the ovens, the wrought-iron gates all struck our ten-year-old son with shattering force. For months he was afraid to fall asleep at night, because he would wake with a start from dreams that Hitler was out to kill him. The evil that he had seen was larger than human in form, and assurances that Hitler was dead could not lay that evil to rest.

But something else had happened that same afternoon at Dachau that provided a source of healing for Mark in his struggle with dread. As we waited for the train back to Munich, we were joined by a man whom we had seen earlier that day at the death camp. My eyes immediately focused on something I had not seen earlier, a number tattooed on his arm. My reference to that dreadful symbol opened up a remarkable story of loss of family to the Nazis, escape, flight, and survival. Yearly this man made a pilgrimage to his former prison, not out of a morbid impulse, but out of the desire to speak to shaken visitors like our son Mark about love and healing, even in the shadow of unspeakable evil. By the time our train pulled into the central station in Munich, a child in the grip of uncontrollable tears was once again a laughing, playful child, now enjoying the company of a new-found "uncle." Ṣedeqā and ḥesed, righteousness and compassion, took on a new meaning for me. Graciously, our family had been given a glimpse into the heart of Judaism and the opportunity to realize that there is a way beyond tragedy to hope.

Powerfully, our understanding is reshaped by experiences oc-
curring on what I have been calling the affective level. And ultimately, growth in wholeness occurs as our intellects and our
feelings are allowed to interact in the kind of healthful manner
in which one is not confused with the other, but where each is
accepted and scrutinized in the appropriate way. There are certain central points in biblical tradition that enable us to see the
unity underlying polarities; for me the cognitive and affective
aspects of my personal pilgrimage with Jewish-Christian dialogue coalesce around the First Commandment.

God is the only ultimate Reality, and it is idolatrous to embrace
any reality alongside God. And yet we are constantly in danger
of doing just that, not only through crude wickedness, but
through perversion of sublime aspects of our own religious traditions. When Christians transform Christology into a weapon to
diminish Jews or people of any other faith, a sublime aspect of
Christianity is turned into an ugly idol. Healing can come only
where idols are destroyed. And idols are destroyed only where
the perspective of a community is changed, where conversion
occurs.

"Auschwitz exercises a hermeneutical function," observes
Franz Mussner. "The transformation it implies constitutes nothing less than a new understanding."[2] With this observation Mussner points to an enormous task facing Christian theology. Though
space does not here allow proper exploration of this task, it is clear
to me that the Holocaust exposed a serious flaw in the way the
Christian message has been transmitted over the centuries. The
Holocaust can function hermeneutically by opening up the consciousness of Christians to the fact that anti-Judaism and anti-Semitism threaten the very heart of the Christian message. Involved
is not only an agenda for furthering Jewish-Christian dialogue,
but for reforming—indeed, delivering—Christendom itself from
a terrible and life-threatening danger. If the mission of Christianity comes to be understood in terms of destroying the faith of Jews,
Jews will not be the last victims. A process is set in motion that will
never be satisfied, but will ever seek out new victims of the need
to assert one's own understanding of God as exclusively correct
and beyond all uncertainty. Christians must therefore be retrained

---

2. F. Mussner, *Traktat über die Juden* (Munich, 1979), p. 16.

hermeneutically to recognize the implications of attitudes such as the following: "Jews who do not convert to Christianity are not saved"; "Jews bear the responsibility for the death of Jesus"; and "Judaism is a primitive, legalistic religion in contrast to the pure Christian faith which supersedes it." The combination of an historical understanding of the early history of Judaism and Christianity and one's personal experience with living Judaism *could* have a salutary hermeneutical impact on Christian attitudes. It could give Christians the courage to acknowledge that a terrible disease has gnawed at the heart of a wonderful faith and abetted terrible atrocities. To ascribe blame solely to godless Nazis is not enough, for it does not explain the paralysis of the church in Germany and other countries of the "Christian" world during the Nazi crimes. The hermeneutic to which we refer commends a new reading to passages such as the following from Matthew 5:23–24:

> So if you are offering your gift at the altar and there remember that your brother (or sister) has something against you, leave your gift there before the altar and go first be reconciled to your brother (or sister), and then come and offer your gift.

Some things must take priority over others. In the case of Christianity's interpretation of its scriptural heritage, our continuation of older methods of exegesis that rest on presuppositions which, thus far, have failed to arrest the perversion of the Christian gospel by evil ideologies betrays an idolatrous understanding of biblical religion. It is reminiscent of eighteenth- and nineteenth-century European history, when Enlightenment thought led political strategists to establish policies guaranteeing the full rights of Jews. This rational approach to curing the problem of anti-Semitism actually ushered in the most tragic stage of Jewish persecution in all of history. Disease cannot be treated superficially. We might draw on the analogy of psychotherapy. Where the deep-seated problems of the psyche go unaddressed, the surface behavior of the person may for a time appear tranquil as a result of ingenious defense mechanisms, but, far from curing the malady, they lead to the breaking out of more pernicious forms of the disease than were earlier present.

Looking below the surface in the case of serious disease is always a painful and unsettling experience. Certainly, what honest Christians are experiencing in reexamining the relation between Christianity and Judaism is painful and unsettling. But it also holds the promise of profound growth in our understanding of *both* Judaism and Christianity. A literature is growing—associated with the names Rosemary Ruether, Clemens Thoma, John T. Pawlikowski, Eugene Borowitz, Geza Vermes, and E. P. Sanders, among others—that offers an opportunity for Christians (and I speak only for Christians, even as Jews will speak for themselves) to engage anew the fundamental beliefs of their faith. I believe that a more faithful formulation of the Christian message will develop hand-in-hand with a more accurate understanding of Judaism. Though it is difficult to defer discussion of substantive aspects of this suggestion, we must leave that for another occasion. Here we must be satisfied to note the basic truth that those theological discussions that most promise to surmount old impasses and break fresh ground are those that unite rigorous scholarly investigation with attention to the affective dimensions of a healthy Jewish-Christian relationship.

1. (Top) The scholars who attended the symposium on fear sponsored by the American Interfaith Institute. Front row (seated): Charlesworth, Anderson, Borgen, Hanson, Talmon, Hengel, Murphy; back row (standing): Culpepper, Borowsky, Mendels, Segal, Fenn.

2. (Middle) When life on the earth was destroyed, only Noah, his family, and two of each species were saved by God from the flood. Noah's ark, depicted with animals looking out of the windows (see Genesis 7–8). The Verdun Altar, by Nicholas of Verdun (c. 1180). *Courtesy of Klosterneuburg Abbey, Austria, Erich Lessing, and PhotoEdit.*

3. (Right) In earliest times humans were sacrificed to God out of fear. Abraham about to sacrifice his son, Isaac (Genesis 22), according to a manuscript illuminated by a priest named Khatchatur. The Armenian manuscript of the four gospels was copied in 1455 in the monastery of Gamaghiel in Khizan by Hohannes Vardapet for Priest P'ilipof. *Courtesy of Walters Art Gallery and PhotoEdit.*

4. Moses leading the Israelites out of Egypt and the drowning of Pharoah, his men, and his horses (see Genesis 14), according to a tenth-century Greek Psalter in Paris (MS Grec 139, fol. 419v.). *Courtesy of the Bibliothèque Nationale, Paris, and PhotoEdit.*

5. The Negev Desert in which the Israelites wandered for forty years (see Numbers 33:38), often filled with fear. *Courtesy of Alan Oddie and PhotoEdit.*

6. Oasis of Kadesh Barnea and the Tell el Kadesh in northern Sinai. According to the Pentateuch Israel spent more than 35 of the 40 years in the wilderness at Kadesh Barnea. From this oasis Moses sent spies into Canaan (Numbers 13). *Courtesy of Erich Lessing and PhotoEdit.*

7. The source of Ein Harod in the Valley of Israel (Esdraelon Plain). It was here that Gideon supposedly tested his soldiers before the battle with the Midianites, the fearful enemies of Israel (Judges 7). *Courtesy of Eric Lessing and PhotoEdit.*

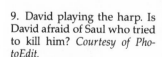

8. Top: David slaying Goliath and cutting off his head. Bottom: Abner brings David with Goliath's head to King Saul. Jonathan, out of love for David, gives him his own garments (1 Samuel 17–18). A thirteenth-century French illumination. *Courtesy of the Pierpont Morgan Library and PhotoEdit.*

9. David playing the harp. Is David afraid of Saul who tried to kill him? *Courtesy of PhotoEdit.*

10. (Left) The Old City of Jerusalem, as seen from the Garden of Gethsemane, where Jesus prayed and feared his death. *Courtesy of Israel Government Tourist Office.*

11. (Right) Jesus, being betrayed by Judas, arrested by soldiers, and scourged (see Mark 14–15), according to the Winchester Psalter (c. 1160). *Courtesy of the British Library and PhotoEdit.*

12. A northern view of Ephesus and its theater, in which there was a riot, inspired by the silversmiths who made idols and from whom Paul feared for his life (Acts 19). *Courtesy of Erich Lessing and PhotoEdit.*

13. The day of resurrection, as portrayed by Nicholas of Verdun on the Verdun altar (c. 1180). *Courtesy of Klosterneuburg Abbey, Austria, Erich Lessing, and PhotoEdit.*

14. (Right) Jerusalem and the Wailing Wall, where Jews bewail the destruction of the Temple by Roman soldiers, yearn for a life without sorrow, and plea for God to fulfill all his promises. *Courtesy of Erich Lessing and PhotoEdit.*

15. Beth Shearim, in which many devout Jews, leaders in rabbinic circles in the early Middle Ages, were buried. *Courtesy of J. H. Charlesworth.*

CHAPTER NINE

How to Respect Each Other: Lessons from Jewish-Christian Scholarship

Alan F. Segal

When I was a graduate student at Yale, Nils Dahl commented to me that Jewish-Christian scholarship was hampered by the way each scholar dealt with the presence of the other one. "Christians," he said, "always talk about Judaism. But most don't know anything about it. Jews try never to speak about Christianity, if they can help it. But it is always on their minds." This was an offhand remark, not meant as a substantive analysis. But I have not found a better observation to underscore the difficulty of any real dialogue between the two communities.

My own difficulties in studying Judaism and Christianity illustrated the problem. I was studying a group of heretics to rabbinism called "Two Powers in Heaven," at the suggestion of Nils Dahl and Wayne Meeks; I was also being guided through that study by Judah Goldin and Sid Z. Leiman. I hoped to show that the heretics could be identified either as Jews or gnostics and that there was a chronological order in the data as it existed in the rabbinic reports. I soon discovered that I would have to spend my time moving back and forth between Jewish and Christian scholarship on late classical antiquity and I discovered that I like the oscillation, even if it was constantly disconcerting.

Then came the dissertation colloquium, when the candidate presented the topic to a round table of faculty charged with judging its feasibility. After the candidate presented the dissertation proposal, it was customary for him or her to leave the room while the assembled faculty discussed the merits of the proposal and, if successful, assigned an adviser and committee to it. When I was called back into the room, I was greeted by very broad smiles, which I took to be a sign of my success. The faculty committee thought "two powers in heaven" was a good idea, but because it overlapped between Judaism and Christianity, they thought that there should be "two powers on earth," two directors—Nils Dahl and Judah Goldin. The smiles were due to their private sense of irony, not the thesis proposal.

I soon found out just how difficult it can be to try to please two excellent masters in the two fields, though I can say that neither master showed any of the traits which Nils Dahl said typified Jewish or Christian scholarship. They just had extremely high standards about what was acceptable and, unfortunately, sometimes different ideas about how Judaism and Christianity interacted.

I found many examples of the rule in my research, which necessarily cut across Christian and Jewish scholarship. The debate is so fascinating and so difficult to resolve that I have continued research in it ever since, in *Rebecca's Children*, in *The Other Judaisms of Late Antiquity*, and in my new book, *Paul the Convert*.

Jewish Silence About Christ

Professor Dahl's observation provides a good way to attack the issue of Jewish-Christian discussions. First let us take up the Jewish phenomenon, i.e., that Jews don't like to talk about Christianity even though they think about it all the time. I think this observation has some validity. Professor Charlesworth mentions that Jews don't like to mention the word *Christ*. Actually, that's not entirely true. Jews do especially like to say the name of the Christian savior when they hit their thumbs with a hammer. But, otherwise, Christianity is too much of a threat to Jewish identity to mention casually.

Among ordinary Jews I can well imagine that there is a problem using the name Christ in ordinary conversation. If I lecture on Judaism and Christianity in a synogogue, Jews are very reticent to say words with Christian overtones. But their curiosity about Christianity is great. I don't think there is any possibility that any of them will convert to Christianity (certainly not from what I say about Christianity), but I suspect that this is one underlying fear: Christianity is always interested in converts and conversion is tempting as a way to normalize one's life as a minority member over against a dominant Christian majority. Thus, Jews are especially sensitive about the specific terms of Christianity and feel no responsibility to understand it at all. It is a potential threat to Jewish identity.

I think Professor Charlesworth's chagrin at finding that Jews don't like to talk about the Christ is an example of the problem. Here is a part of gentile culture which we do not have to deal with very often. So it sounds strange to most Jewish ears. It's especially strange in synagogues, and there have been many examples of persecution of Jews in the name of Christ.

There are two possible remedies to this sensitivity. The first is to adopt a more value-neutral term, on the analogy of using B.C.E. in place of B.C. That is necessary where the theological assumption behind the chronology is just too overt to ignore. There is obviously another word for Christ and that is *messiah*. We could just use Messiah instead of Christ.

But, Christ *is* the appropriate term when dealing with the Christian messiah, so there is no reason not to use it. Christian views of the messiah, as Dahl among the many others who have studied Christology have shown us, are strikingly different from the Jewish concept of the messiah. There are important differences between Jewish ideas of messianism (even pre-Christian ones) and the Christ idea in Christianity. Using the word Christ to study Christian messianism is more appropriate than saying *the Christian messiah*. I do not think the needed remedy is to stop using the word Christ, because that term defines the Christian belief. The answer is for Jews to start talking about Christianity. With more use—just more use—our own sensitivities can be reduced.

I know that this answer seems too simple. But I recall the shock I received when my college humanities professor used the word *Yahweh* for the first time. Now I will not claim to be of the tribe of Benjamin or zealous as to the law, but I had a very good Jewish education. And when this professor (who happened to teach German, which made it worse; that was another prejudice I had to overcome) turned from the Classics to the

Bible and began to talk about the Hebrew God whose name was Yahweh, all of my Jewish education was offended. Jews do not pronounce the name of the deity. Even though I never heard the name said out loud before, I quickly recognized what the teacher intended and seriously thought for a few seconds that the class-room might be split in half by an angry bolt of lightning. When I realized that nothing happened to the professor, I concluded that his pronunciation could not be the exact, proper pronuncia-tion of the tetragrammaton. Because he was not harmed, it was only another honorific term, so I eventually came to see that the term was useful, although not right away.

I propose that this is the appropriate way to treat Jewish sensi-tivities about saying the name Christ. With habituation, a good deal of the sensitivity can be removed. Indeed, there is more need of Jews developing a talent for saying Christ when it is appropriate than for them to use Yahweh as a substitute for the divine name. And I think it will happen among Jews of good will.

Christians can help Jews over this difficult hurdle by making it clear in every way possible that the purpose of interfaith dia-logue is not to facilitate conversion to Christianity. The United Church of Christ recently made such a statement clearly, if I read their latest communication rightly. Other Christian groups should go out of their way to do the same. To be valid, the purpose of dialogue must be the converse of conversion; it must affirm Judaism as an equally valid response to the promises of the Old Testament God. A common Jewish fear is that Christians do not have honest motives in seeking out Jews for dialogue. When and if it becomes evident that Christians accept Jews for what they are and respect their faith commitments as an equally valid response to the demands of the biblical God, then the problem will just be one of habits. Until then, some Jews will always be skeptical.

Scholars in Glass Houses: The Illusion of Impartiality

As a professor I feel that something important, scholastically as well as communally, may come out of this kind of dialogue, namely, truly impartial scholarship. Interfaith dialogue has to proceed on its own terms, beginning by admitting the honest differences in perspective and trying not to fall victim to any hidden agendas of our own making. I also realize that impartial history is not possible, because the writing of history is an art of human expression. It always reflects the perspective of the writer. But that does not mean we should give up the attempt to find an impartial perspective on issues, especially such important issues as the rise of Christianity within Judaism and the difference of opinion which that engendered.

We can help make present and future Jewish-Christian historical studies more honest by avoiding obvious biases and by trying not to use the other as an example of some failing. To really understand the other perspective and to respect it on its own terms means that scholars are going to have to come to the study on their own, without bringing any preconceived agendas. This is a good deal harder than what is now passing as historical scholarship. Let me give some examples.

Jewish Analyses of Christianity

The difficulties Jews have in studying Christianity, and vice versa, are more subtle and more important than whether some people can say the word *Christ*. Because scholars are supposed to be pursuing the truth for its own sake, the work of scholars on interfaith issues shows the difficulty of interfaith dialogue most clearly. There is a considerable difficulty in reaching any agreement, even when scholars are the most knowledgeable discussants on a topic. When experts have problems looking at the material dispassionately, one can assume we will *all* have problems. So I will offer examples only from the most outstanding scholarship we have. The faults I will point out are not the faults of the individual scholar. Indeed, I have picked only the best scholars to show how difficult it is to approach the task on its own terms, without a hidden agenda. The criticism I raise is against the entire enterprise of scholarship. I would like to see scholars more aware of the benefits accruing to scholarship in the dialogue between Judaism and Christianity and more interested in consciously removing bias. If we must all have our individual perspectives in the end, we must strive to make our

perspectives as free as possible from old religious rivalries. We
owe that to our discipline as historians of religions.

Case No. 1: Susan Handelman on Paul's Methodology

Paul is a major figure in Susan A. Handelman's *Slayers of
Moses: The Emergence of Rabbinic Interpretation in Modern Literary
Theory.*[1] In this book, Handelman reverses Tertullian's question:
"What has Jerusalem to do with Athens?" Her major hypothesis
is that Jewish and European models of hermeneutics are entirely
different. The Greeks and the Church Fathers following them
were interested in an allegorical and metaphorical interpretation. The rabbis developed a thematic analogy which Handelman, following Roman Jakobsen, calls metonymy. Paul then
becomes the swing figure, the one who sets the agenda for the
future of Christian exegeses. Instead of practicing metonymy, as
in accordance with his pharisaic training, Paul, by virtue of his
conversion, turns to a new, metaphoric interpretation to express
his new faith:

> Paul, who before his conversion had been Saul, the Jew of Tarsus
> and a persecutor of the new cult of Christians, desperately sought
> to reconcile his newly adopted faith with that of his forefathers,
> and to extend it further to "those outside the law." . . . But how
> could Paul explain to the Jews this heretical abrogation of their
> Sacred text, and to Gentiles the metaphysical importance of the
> miserable Jew Jesus who had been so ignobly put to death as a
> criminal? Paul had to make both Jews and Greeks perceive that
> the Scriptures in fact spoke of something quite other than what
> appeared to be the case. He had to speak, that is, a double lan-
> guage. For this task, the most suitable interpretive methods were,
> of course, typology and allegory.[2]

Handelman is not a scholar of rabbinic or early Christian studies. And that is precisely the problem. I cannot say how
annoying I find this very unfair characterization both of rabbinic
literature and of Paul. Indeed, it is as unfair to rabbinic literature
as it is to Paul. Did rabbinic exegesis not contain metaphor, even
allegory? Rabbinic literature is full of major metaphoric play,
such as the parables of the king and even the allegorical reading

1. S.A. Handelman, *Slayers of Moses: The Emergence of Rabbinic Interpretation in Modern
Literary Theory* (Albany, 1982).
2. Ibid., p. 84.

of the Song of Songs. Granted that Paul did use allegory and metaphor, does that explain all his exegeses? He certainly reflects rabbinic training in every part of his writing, even if the conclusions to which he comes are non-rabbinic.

Handelman's conclusions are not only unlikely, they are impossible for anyone who has read either Paul or the rabbis in detail. Furthermore, Handelman misunderstands what Paul means when he talks about *letter* and *spirit* in the discussions of law. She reads 2 Corinthians 3:6 without a glimmer of recognition that *spirit* in that context has a specialized meaning as the presence of Christ in Christianity.

Handelman would be guilty only of stretching the point if her ultimate purpose were not so clear. On page 179 she says: "The wars between Jews and Greeks, so long fought on Mediterranean and European soil, have come, finally to America." This is not a passing metaphor; it is a full allegory, using the events of ancient and modern history. She is fighting the battles of the Maccabean war (which she understands in a thoroughly melodramatic way, not at all as historians of the period do) in order to say that G. Hartman and H. Bloom have renewed a Jewish genre of interpretation in contradistinction to the previously gentile method of new criticism. This is incredible ethnocentrism, not to mention a very limited way of viewing the contributions of Hartman and Bloom (even though they rely on midrash and kabbalah in a romantic way). Finally, as a historian, I want to say that the whole mistake begins with a misreading of Paul. But in this particular case I think the errors are quite a bit deeper. Even her reading of Jewish history is so blighted by lack of perception that it is not beneficial.

Case No. 2: Shaye J. D. Cohen on the Circumcision of Timothy

I see Handelman's work as representing a new ethnocentrism. In contrast to Handelman, with whose premises and conclusions I disagree, I find the work of Shaye Cohen to be real scholarship and a welcome contribution. Even though I often find myself agreeing with Professor Cohen's opinions, however, there are points at which, to my chagrin, he uses the past to promote his present agenda.

Acts 16:1–5 contains this puzzling report:

> And he [Paul] came also to Derbe and to Lystra. A disciple was

there, named Timothy, the son of a Jewish woman who was a
believer; but his father was a Greek. He was well spoken of by the
brethren at Lystra and Iconium. Paul wanted Timothy to accompany him; and he took him and circumcised him because of the
Jews that were in those places, for they all knew that his father
was a Greek. As they went on their way through the cities, they
delivered to them for observance the decisions which had been
reached by the apostles and elders who were at Jerusalem. So the
churches were strengthened in the faith, and they increased in
numbers daily.

This story is puzzling because it appears to contradict Paul's
strong opinion against circumcision given in his Letter to the
Galatians. Many scholars assume that the author of Acts has
misrepresented the facts, perhaps merely due to misinformation, or invented a story to promote a more unified church.

This passage has therefore been commented upon many
times, most recently by my close colleague, Professor Cohen.
His interpretation is that Timothy was a gentile, and that Paul
was both converting Timothy to Christianity and circumcising
him, thus accepting the opposition's view of conversion. This
argument, which seems absurd, is governed by the modern issue of the status of Jewish children in mixed marriages, which
has been inserted into this case. Cohen is using the New Testament as an historical source for setting up standards for contemporary Conservative Judaism, which is currently discussing the
issue of the patrilineal principle in Judaism. For Cohen, the
events described in Acts 16:1–5 are not only historically important but constitute an actual precedent which justifies a contemporary Jewish practice.

In the Reform movement and the Orthodox movement, there
are fewer problems with the issue of the offspring of intermar-
riages because the contemporary Reform movement's methods
of defining personal status are more liberal, while Orthodox
methods are profoundly more conservative. The Reform movement accepts rabbinic halakha as only one guide among many
for individual conscience in contemporary ethical decisions,
while the Orthodox movement has invalidated any change in
the halakha at all. The Conservative movement takes an interme-
diate position, judging the validity of a tradition on the basis of
its ancient status. The later Professor Cohen can date the halak-
hic definition of a Jew as the child of a Jewish mother, the more

latitude there is available to Conservative Judaism's practice. This is an outcome which I personally would applaud as well. Unfortunately, the facts do not cooperate. For Cohen, the story becomes a precedent for contemporary Jewish practice because it proves that the now well-established definition of a Jew as the offspring of a Jewish mother did not yet exist in Paul's day; thus the principle becomes something which Conservative Judaism can discard. This is a decision that Professor Cohen may profoundly desire because it has uniquely liberalizing implications for the definition of a Jew in the Conservative movement today. The only problem is that the story actually appears to say the opposite.

Good outcomes of twentieth-century issues in Judaism are not automatically to be embraced as good historical methodology, and they are certainly irrelevant to first-century Christian documents. To the contrary, the evaluation of historical sources must be done as disinterestedly as possible. Professor Cohen has not adequately assessed the difficulties of comparing Acts with Paul's own ideas about circumcision, preferring discussion of the Church Fathers' apologetic reading to Paul's own words of warning against circumcision for gentiles.

One thing Professor Cohen has surely shown is that the Mishnah, the earliest rabbinic document, shows the effects of its editing. The later editors may be more influential than the earlier ones. Now you don't have to subscribe to Cohen's entire program, or indeed very much of it, to know what a challenge this is to traditional Jewish scholarship.

The fact is that we now need Christianity and Philo and the other Jewish literatures to help us see what parts of rabbinic literature are antique. This is ironic, but it is necessary. So Jews have to stop thinking about Christianity and start doing something serious about studying it.

Christian Analyses of Judaism

What about Christians? Well, Christians, as Professor Dahl says, talk about Judaism all the time but, by and large, they know nothing about it.

Case No. 1: Bernhard Anderson on Deuteronomy

Professor Bernhard Anderson is one of the foremost teachers of Old Testament in this country. He has written wonderfully on issues pertaining to the Bible in almost every period. He is truly one of the most influential teachers of his generation, due to his excellent textbook, *Understanding the Old Testament*.[3] However, there are times when he slips into a polemic which has more to do with Protestant-Catholic relations than with the Hebrew Bible (I point this out to illustrate the deeply felt biases of the field, not as a reflection on him personally.):

> One of the greatest defects of Deuteronomic theology was that it considered God to be confined to a theological straightjacket, so that he had to act according to a prescribed pattern. The Deuteronomic doctrine of divine justice makes things very simple: obey Yahweh and all will go well; disobey him and hardship will come. It may be that the original version of Deuteronomy understood this truth more profoundly, but as it was worked out by the writer who left us the Deuteronomic History, it sounds suspiciously like the "success philosophy" which even today is the basis of much popular religion. Of course, the belief in divine reward (blessing) and divine punishment (judgment) had been fundamental in Israel's faith right from the very first. But, Isaiah, like the other great prophets, put into the foreground an important qualification: "If you are willing and obedient, you shall eat the good of the land" (Is. 1:19). In Deuteronomy, however, something new was added— the belief that obedience or disobedience could be measured by a code of rules set down in a book, the Book of the Torah. Joshua, according to the Deuteronomic historian, was promised success in his invasion of Canaan *if* he would study faithfully "this book of the law"—that is, the Deuteronomic Torah (Josh. 1:7–8). And, by the opposite token, he would fail if he did not heed the rules of Torah. Later on, in the period of Judaism, as we shall see, men tended to believe that they had only to devote themselves to the study and practice of the revealed commandments in order to win divine blessing and escape divine disapproval.[4]

Essentially what is wrong with Deuteronomy, according to Anderson, is that it began the process of codifying the Law in a book, which then set limits on God. This, of course, culminates in the religion of self-salvation in which man tries to dictate to God what he should do and which allows God no freedom to act. Anderson does not actually say here that the rabbinic move-

---

3. B.W. Anderson, *Understanding the Old Testament* (Englewood Cliffs, N.J., 1957).
4. Ibid., p. 319.

ment is the fulfillment of everything that he finds wrong in Deuteronomy. Nor does he say that medieval Catholicism perfected the heresy. Yet, one can hear this judgment in the back of the writer's mind.

But such ideas have nothing to do with the actual Deuteronomic Reform, which appears to have been a nationalistic reform promulgated by the court bureaucrats. Anderson's idea (based on Jeremiah 8:8 and 18:18) that the prophet Jeremiah was impatient with the Deuteronomic Reform is a convenient fiction that allows him to separate the prophetic movement from this doomed idea. But nothing could have been further from the truth. The idea of self-salvation is a kind of cipher for issues in Protestant theology.

This prevents Anderson from understanding really to what a great extent the Deuteronomic Reform was a national reformation in the vacuum left by the collapse of Assyria. He is applying theological judgments, which are never appropriate and which are anachronistic, to the time of Deuteronomy.

Case No. 2: Bultmann on Early Judaism

Rudolf Bultmann is undoubtedly the most famous New Testament scholar of the past generation. He had uncanny abilities in textual exegesis and in discovering sources and layers of tradition. When I criticize him, I do so not to demean his talents, but to show how a whole scholarly field has grown insensitive. Like most of the foregoing examples, what is striking is not that these are bad scholars but that these are some of our best.

In spite of his great talents, his misunderstanding of Judaism is profound. To begin with one of the most flagrant examples:

> Fundamentally, the Law was incapable of undergoing any further development. Since it was God's law, it was valid for all time in the exact form in which it was delivered from the time of Moses. To be sure, it contained many precepts which changing circumstances had rendered obsolete and meaningless. Yet they had still to be obeyed unquestioningly. Again, the Law failed to give guidance for the new circumstances which, despite the isolation of the people, inevitably arose through the influence of the outside world.[5]

---

5. Rudolf Bultmann, "Jewish Legalism," in his *Primitive Christianity in its Contemporary Setting*, trans. by R. H. Fuller (New York, 1956; Cleveland, 1970) p. 62.

It is hard to imagine that *any* legal tradition could be practiced in just such a way as Bultmann describes. His description has little credibility as descriptive of human endeavor anywhere. It is more incredible that a person living in Germany, which has long prided itself on efficiency and discipline, could have misunderstood the value of law so completely as did Bultmann himself. But the reasons for his description are clear. They are necessary theologically, to show that Judaism gave up its historical role just before Christianity rightfully claimed it:

> For Judaism God has become remote. He governs the world by means of angels, while his relations with man are mediated by the book of the Law. In the same way the holy people are marked off from the outside world by an elaborate ritual. Through its legalism the Jewish community achieves an artificial kind of otherworldliness. For Jesus, however, God's distinction from and transcendence over the world means that he is always the God who comes. He meets man not only in the future judgment, but already here and now in dail y life, with its challenges and opportunities. In the same way man is distinct from the world in the sense that he has no security in it. He cannot trust any tangible reality. His real life consists in his encounter with his neighbor and his response to the claims of God.[6]

These descriptions are so specious that they are not worth a detailed refutation. What disturbs me most is how Bultmann can describe Christianity and Judaism as so close phenomenologically (a description which I find exaggerated) and then say that Judaism is so far off the Christian mark. But the point here for Bultmann is that Judaism must drop out of world history before Christianity enters it. This happened, according to Bultmann, because Judaism became *legalism*.

This I find to be a true category mistake. It is tautological to fault a legal system (which is what rabbinic law is) for being legalistic; that is like accusing water of being wet. Bultmann argues that Jewish theology is too legalistic when he should be noting that the Jewish legal system is extremely interested in theological issues. For instance, it is impossible to understand how the Jewish legal system works without admitting the role given to God in understanding human motivation. The motiva-

---

6. Ibid., p. 78.

tion of the actant is assumed to be knowable because of God's supervision. Hence, the motive of the actant is of primary importance.

To be sure, there were no university teachers of Rabbinic Judaism when Bultmann trained and very little study of Jewish texts at all. This is part of the social tragedy that laid the background for Nazi anti-Semitism in the Second World War and cannot be laid at Bultmann's door personally. He may have tried sincerely to find a teacher to help him understand. Nevertheless, the enormity of the misunderstanding of Judaism speaks for itself.

Bultmann's evaluation does not merely miss the rich spectrum of opinion in the first century, when Judaism was richly diverse. He really tries to prove that Judaism had lost its historical role. If any other scholar were so wrong it would not be so disastrous. But Bultmann is commonly regarded as the foremost New Testament scholar of the mid-twentieth century. I am not criticizing the man so much as the field of New Testament studies, in which even an impossibly biased view of Judaism can continue to be so influential.

First-century Judaism is not some insignificant backwater of Christian history; it is central to it. My judgment is that no New Testament scholar can truly understand the contribution of *Christianity* unless he first really understands Judaism. Bultmann has created a straw-man Judaism, so he necessarily creates, in some way, a straw-man Christianity.

The theological biases of the previous generation have been shown in massive detail by Ed Sanders in his book *Paul and Palestinian Judaism*.[7] He shows that Christians have to stop considering Judaism as scoreboard religion, a religion of dry legalism and formulas without the love of God, as a religion which had abandoned the covenant. Yet this caricature of Judaism persists, especially in the study of Paul.

Case No. 3: E. P. Sanders on Paul as a Critic of Judaism

Here is an example (from Sanders' *Paul and Palestinian Judaism*) of how this presupposition affects Christian understandings of Paul.

---

7. E.P. Sanders, *Paul and Palestinian Judaism: A Comparison of Patterns of Religion* (Philadelphia, 1977).

It is hardly news that there was a very profound clash between Jesus and the Pharisees and that Paul's conversion instigated a dialectic no less violent. But later Christian animosity has badly distorted the true nature of this confrontation. Pharisees are described as hypocrites or as uncaring legalists and inhuman externalists who imposed on others burdens which they themselves would not bear. Most of which is inaccurate, unhistorical and purely polemical. If Pharisees were such, how is one to explain their tremendous power over people for whom they had only the authority of competence? In fact, the Pharisees were superb moral guides. But there precisely lay the problem which Jesus and Paul saw so clearly.

Apart from the damage such caricatures have done to Judaism, and the relationship of Christianity to it, there is another very serious result within Christianity itself. When Christianity is no longer aware of what Jesus and Paul were fighting against in Pharisaic Judaism, it can hardly be conscious of a similar presence within itself. The debate did not concern good law as over against bad law or even internal and sincere law as over against external and hypocritical law. The challenge of Jesus and of Paul was this: obedience does not lead to God, but God leads one to obedience. The question is not God *or* law, covenant *or* commandment, faith *or* works, but, granting both, in which direction does the arrow fly from one to the other? It must be emphasized that this is not a debate between Judaism and Christianity but a conflict *within them both* and a conflict ever ancient and ever new. So, according to Jesus and Paul, it was the gift of God's presence that made a good life possible, not a good life that made the reward of God's presence inevitable. Paul's way, as everyone knows, was to proclaim human righteousness as God's free gift and that one is justified by receiving it in faith. Jesus' way was to announce the Kingdom's advent as demanding decision and response, life and action, *but* never articulating such action in detail within the parables themselves. His own life is, of course, one such actualization.[8]

This is an extremely sensitive and important discussion. In it, there is a very good understanding of the previous ways in which Judaism has been victimized by over-zealous scholars of Christianity. If Christianity represents an advance, Judaism must represent somehow a lesser evolutionary stage. In spite of the

---

8. Ibid., pp. 80–81.

writer's good intentions we see the implicit judgment against Pharisaism and Judaism in his second paragraph.

But, so far as I can see, Judaism did not lack the sentiments which are ascribed to Jesus and Paul by J. D. Crossan. In Rabbinic Judaism, God's role as prior judge makes law possible, his role as motivator of human hearts is acknowledged everywhere. Judaism is not a simple religion of self-salvation. Though it acknowledges that good works are what God wants, it does not say that the "do-gooder" is automatically saved.

Furthermore, God's merciful role is always stressed in Judaism, as the liturgy for the High Holiday season constantly reminds me. In the liturgy of Rosh Hashanah and Yom Kippur, the community prays for God's mercy, and accuses itself of sins. It assumes itself guilty of many serious sins, even though almost everyone in the community can claim not to have committed *all* the crimes that are enumerated in great detail; the community as a whole takes responsibility for them. The entire community presents its *works* and finds them unworthy; they are never sufficient. They must rely on God's grace, mercy, and forgiveness. Furthermore, the dominant theme of the High Holiday services is precisely that God is merciful and will forgive, if man atones and repents sincerely:

> Our Father our King, be gracious unto us and answer us, for we have no (significant) deeds; lo, we are unworthy; deal thou with us in charity and loving-kindness and save us.

I think Jewish scholarship has a remarkable amount to learn from Christianity. The time when we can read Mishnah and Talmud, confident that everything in them is a true and accurate reflection of first-century conditions, is over. Studies have shown that the texts of Rabbinic Judaism crystallized centuries after the major texts of Christianity. We must be careful and insightful readers of Christianity, in order to understand what Judaism was in the first century, even if we must constantly correct for the anti-pharisaic and sometimes anti-Jewish biases we find in Christian writings.

Likewise, the time when Christians could make easy raids on Judaism to explain abstruse parts of the New Testament is over. One cannot just import Mishnaic and Talmudic references to explain the New Testament. In fact, it is easier to do the opposite.

And with this new caution we should also caution ourselves not to make facile comparisons or merely use the other community's traditions for our own benefit. The renewed dialogue, when seen as a necessity for historical studies, implies that we have to respect and understand the other community's traditions for what they are before we begin to read them for our own purposes.

It is my firm belief that we can get beyond even these subtle theological colorings to a more objective discussion of the relationship between Judaism and Christianity. I do not think that it will be easy, or it would have already been done. But I do think it is possible to get closer to a neutral description of the two faiths than we have already achieved.

I think that the dialogue is important not only for reasons of brotherhood; there are real historical insights to be gained by consulting each other's traditions in more straightforward ways. Neither community recorded all the information necessary for understanding itself. But, luckily, each community recorded some of the other's missing pieces. What is at stake in learning to read each other's history more fairly—or failing to do so—is a better understanding of our own tradition. In this regard, I feel that we scholars must show the way. I also feel that scholarly conferences are important settings for Jewish-Christian dialogues. What we do is important, for we have students to teach. And our students teach others. Scholars of religion are not in an ivory tower. Our historical studies have consequences, for the faith of this and future generations, of which we can only be dimly aware.

Now, I am not so naive as to believe that it is possible to write neutral history. I think a Jew writing on Christianity will necessarily find other things of interest than a Christian will, and vice versa. But I do think we should clear the air of hidden agendas. Only then will we find that we have an enormous amount to teach each other about ourselves. And then Jews may feel more comfortable speaking about Christianity, while Christians may have more observations to make about Judaism.

CHAPTER TEN

Overcoming Fear

Peder Borgen

A long and painful story of tension, persecution, and hatred between Christians and Jews parallels the history of Western civilization. Among these tragic events, however, there have also been moments of heroism, bonds of kinship, and expressions of love. Unfortunately, hatred and alienation have far too often prevailed.

These many conflicts demonstrate that humanity has not yet managed to overcome fear and hatred in group-relationships. A frightening picture appears when one surveys the tensions, rivalry, conflicts, and acts of cruelty that have taken place—and still take place—among the different ethnic groups, nations, and social classes. Co-operation is a rare phenomenon in comparison with strife, which at times even takes the form of cruel deeds beyond imagination.

In many situations the problem is aggravated when a majority group wishes to control, dominate, or exploit a minority group. At times the majority, through their control of the governmental powers, attempts to extinguish the minority. In other cases, a powerful minority may terrorize a majority in order to stay in power and keep their privileges.

Such conflicts have taken place at the various cultural levels, in the various cultural and religious settings around the world, in the various economic and social systems, and at various times in history. Some examples are the conflicts between Tamils and Sinhalese peoples in Sri Lanka; among Muslims, Christians and Jews at various places in the Middle East today; between the Armenian people and their Turkish and Russian conquerors; between the main Church and heretics in Medieval Europe; between whites and Indians, black people and white people in America; between white and black peoples in Africa (particularly in South Africa), and among many tribes and ethnic groups in Africa as well as other places around the globe.

The sufferings of many Jews throughout the centuries witness in a concentrated manner to this destructive force among human beings. These many events of discrimination, of fear, and sometimes of despair, challenge us today not to give up and flee into fatalistic resignation. They call us to overcome fear, to act as responsible human beings, to heal wounds, and to work for reconciliation and cooperation.

Jews in Egypt in Antiquity

In January 1985, the Rockford Institute Center on Religion and Society and Temple Emanu-El of New York City sponsored a conference on "Jews in Unsecular America." The conference resulted in the book *Jews in Unsecular America*, edited by R. J. Neuhaus. At that conference Rabbi David Novak of the Jewish Theological Seminary of America made the statement that "we cannot reduce anti-Semitism to Christianity, even though there have been Christian manifestations of anti-Semitism."[1]

To illustrate this, it is of importance to examine the conflicts that existed before Christianity came upon the historical scene. The history of the Jews in Egypt can provide us with relevant material on this point.

After Alexander the Great had conquered Egypt, Macedonians ruled that country in the form of the Ptolemaic dynasty. Although the Ptolemaic kings made Alexandria the capital and ruled over Egypt as a sovereign country, they were felt by the Egyptians to be foreigners and intruders into their country. The Ptolemies opened the country to an influx of people from many nations. Many were hired for service in the army. The native Egyptians reacted with hatred. Many Jews immigrated and became an important factor in the army as well as in other professions. The Egyptian priest Manetho wrote an anti-Semitic book

---

1. R. J. Neuhaus, ed., *Jews in Unsecular America* (ES 6; Grand Rapids, Mich., 1987) p. 93.

against the Jews.[2] For him, the Jews had polluted the purity of Egypt at the time of Moses. They were lepers, and a mixed group who for various maladies had to be banished from the country. Hence, Moses and the Jews were forced to leave Egypt.

The Jews, in stark contrast, wrote their own history in order to stress the sufferings of their ancestors when they were a minority group in Egypt. Pharaoh and the Egyptians became the embodiment of evil. The Jews celebrated annually the fact that God through the agency of Moses had punished the Egyptians and through His own might had destroyed the Egyptian army in the sea. For the Jews, then, the Exodus was an event of redemption and deliverance.

The situation of the Jews in Egypt worsened in the Roman period. One reason for this was that the very large community of Jews in Alexandria was caught in the middle between the privileged "Greeks" and the underprivileged native Egyptians. In the year 38 C.E., a terrible pogrom took place in the city. The Alexandrian "Greeks" desecrated the synagogues by setting up in them images of the Roman emperor Gaius Caligula.

The Roman governor Flaccus denounced the Jews as foreigners and aliens; they had no rights in the city. He permitted the mob to plunder the houses of the Jews and destroy their synagogues. Jewish leaders were scourged and killed. The Jews, who used to live in various parts of the city, were driven together into only one section. They were even pressed out to the dung hills.

What were the reasons for this tragic event? The causes were complex; they were partly legal and economic, partly social and religious. The Jewish community had been pressing for equal legal and economic rights with the "Greek" full citizens. The "Greeks," on their side, felt threatened by the expanding Jewish community. Socially and culturally each group felt itself superior to the other. The "Greeks" wanted to group the Jews together with the native Egyptians. The Jews fought against this. Eventually, the situation became a struggle between Jewish monotheistic religion and the polytheistic cults of the "Greeks" and the native Egyptians.

2. W. G. Waddell, *Manetho, with an English translation*, (LCL; Cambridge, Massachusetts and London, 1940); see also P. M. Fraser, *Ptolemaic Alexandria*, vol. 1 (Oxford, 1972) pp. 505–10.

Already this history of the Jews in Egypt, and especially the pogrom in Alexandria in 38 C.E., raise this basic question: Is it possible for two or more groups to live peacefully together with equal rights when they have different identities, different lifestyles, and different numerical strengths? The many tragic episodes of discrimination, persecution, and exploitation throughout the centuries make it difficult to answer in the affirmative. Nevertheless, there must be a way by which dynamic and peaceful interrelationships among groups can grow sufficiently strong so as to remove fear and keep destructive forces under control.

Jews and Christians

Is it possible for Jews and Christians to overcome their fear of and conflict with each other? The many tragic events in history make such an effort seem hopeless and such a goal utopian. But some glimmer of encouragement can be gained from history as well as from present developments. There are examples of peaceful relationships developing and of relationships characterized by mutual respect and cooperation. Christians and Jews today should not give up searching for ways to overcome fears and to find means of removing misconceptions and discrimination. They should cultivate fellowship and seek areas of cooperation.

There is a close kinship between the Jews and the Christians. Both worship the God of Abraham, Isaac, and Jacob as God the Creator of the world and of all humankind. By the spread of Christianity the sacred books of the Jews have had a larger impact on peoples around the world than they probably would have had if Christianity had not moved into the heart of many nations.

Ironically, however, that kinship has occasionally caused conflicts to be intense and fierce. When the Christian movement expanded and (directly or indirectly) became allied with the political authorities, Jews at many places and at various times in history were subject to humiliation, persecution, and pogroms. At times these events were at the hands of Christians; at other times they merely received the encouragement and support of Christians. On occasion some church leaders took the initiative. And at times, unfortunately, there were outbursts of hatred and cruelty on the part of Christians at the grass-roots level.

These events in history are researched by historians; but they must be brought into the consciousness of the public. We must not be caught up in a psychosis of guilt and fear. We must avoid mutual hatred and accusation, yet face the horror, acknowledge it as such, and learn from the evil events how to promote and encourage mutually beneficial forms of interaction. By this means, similar events can be avoided in the present and in the future.

It must then also be made clear that tension and, at times, conflicts and terror take place within the sphere of Christianity itself, and within Judaism itself. One example of such conflict is the conflict between Catholics and Protestants in Northern Ireland, although admittedly the causes are complex. Correspondingly, there are in Israel small extreme and militant Jewish groups that cause conflicts within the Jewish community.

As for the many events in history in which Christians have followed the path of hatred and have persecuted Jews, it is tragic that those Christians have forgotten what earlier Christians had experienced when in minority situations. Several times during the first two centuries Christians at various places suffered persecutions by the Romans; many were killed. And even earlier, when Jesus and his followers were a minority movement among Jews within Judaism, they became involved in intramural conflicts in some of the Jewish communities.[3]

The language used by suffering minorities against those who persecute them is understandably harsh and polemical. Such language can easily be taken out of its original context and used in a generalizing way when the minority group has grown into a majority; then the language will be used to justify hatred and persecution. In this way the language of conflict in the intramural strife between the small minority of Jews who confessed Jesus as the Messiah and the majority who did not, became the language used by some *gentile* Christians to express their own enmity with "Jews" in their own environment. The language originally used by some Jews against other Jews thus became the language used by some non-Jews against all Jews. In several cases this language developed into anti-Semitic terminology and stereotypes.

---

3. See especially Acts 8:1–3, 9:1–2; Gal 1:13–14; 1 Thes 2:14–15; Acts 21:27–31; 22:12–15.

The lesson to be learned from this is that minorities which grow into a majority position should not retaliate, but should take care that their own sufferings, experienced when they were minorities, should not be suffered by others who are now in minority positions. It is tragic that so many Christians at various times and places have failed to learn these lessons from the experience of their religious ancestors, and have chosen instead to nourish anti-Semitic emotions and commit cruel actions.

Today there is not much open conflict between Christians and Jews in Europe and America. Underneath the surface, however, much fear and distrust exist. Is it possible to overcome this fear? It is a challenge that we need to meet both through vigorous and creative dialogues and through appropriate actions. Misconceptions and misunderstandings need to be analyzed and cleared up. Our common heritage needs to be revitalized. At the same time we need to be realistic about points of disagreement and about the different convictions held as basic by each side. Despite those differences, fellowship can develop to such a degree that harassment, hatred, fear, and persecution can be removed. In certain areas also joint action can prove beneficial to both parties in today's world.

Guilt

The concept of guilt has played a central and tragic role throughout history. Too often, Christians have viewed guilt as a collective entity and have blamed the whole of the Jewish nation for the death of Jesus. This understanding of guilt must be totally abolished. Only *some* Romans and *some* Jews took part in the execution of the Jew named Jesus. Therefore, *other* Jews—in past and present—are not to be blamed for the action of some persons in a particular historical situation.

More differentiated understandings of guilt must be applied both ways, however. Just as the Jews collectively are not guilty of the execution of Jesus and some of his first disciples, so Christians who have not taken part in anti-Semitic activity are not guilty of persecutions of Jews at different places and times in history.

The experience of some Norwegians during the Second World War may clarify this point. Non-Jewish Christian citizens and

Jewish citizens of Norway fought together in their common defense against the Nazis. Some were tortured and killed in Norway, others, both Jews and non-Jews, met death in concentration camps in Germany and Poland. The Christian Norwegians who were killed by the Nazis were not guilty of the killing of Jewish Norwegians who were killed by the same Nazis, just as the Jewish Norwegians were not responsible for the killing of the Christian Norwegians. And some Norwegian Christians risked punishment and death to help and support Jews.

When persons by default or permissiveness did not voice protest or do whatever was possible in situations in their own time and place in which Jews suffered persecution and death, then those persons do share in the guilt for the evil deed. Similarly, during World War II, when persons from fear and timidity did not speak up and act to help other fellow citizens who were tortured to death by the Nazis, they shared in the guilt. We who live in relatively safe and secure situations today must be very cautious, however, in placing blame too soon on persons in an occupied country, where all faced the threat of torture and death all the time.

A formulation made by Rabbi David Novak at the above-mentioned conference in New York, January 1985, should be quoted at this point:

> We have to deal with crimes against the Jews on ethical criteria and not automatically on theological criteria. That, primarily, is what we Jews have always said. For example, on the question of deicide, we are perfectly willing to admit the fact that some Jews were involved in the unjust murder of Jesus of Nazareth. But that does not entail guilt on my part. Visiting the iniquity of the fathers on the children in Jewish theology, specifically, is divine and mysterious; every man dies for his sin, not for somebody's else's. . . .
> If we Jews have argued this way against the deicide charge for generations, we cannot pull the same kind of logic on Christians. Therefore, political/ethical argumentation that is related to theological discussion is required. The notion of saying that this crime, the Holocaust, is the direct result of, was caused (incidentally, the original word for *cause* in Hebrew and Greek meant "guilt") by, Christianity is morally illegitimate."[4]

---

4. Neuhaus, ed., *Jews in Unsecular America*, pp. 95–96.

Novak called for Christians to jump off the Holocaust-guilt bandwagon and for Jews to let them jump off.[5]

Dialogues

In the joint effort to remove misconceptions and to bring destructive stereotypes and myths out into the open so as to break their evil spell, many forms of action are needed. One important form is that of scholarly research and dialogue. Such dialogues ought to have limited and well-defined agendas and objectives, jointly agreed upon by both parties. In this way mutual respect and trust can be strengthened, step by step. Areas of disagreement should be defined, as well as areas of general agreement and areas of common concern.

Such a step forward might be accomplished if a group of Christian and Jewish scholars would put down in two parallel columns, so to speak, evil and derogatory statements and symbols used in past and present when negatively characterizing persons from the other side. In this way the many current anti-Semitic statements and symbols will be brought into the open, so that Christians today can openly reject the use of that language and do away with the attitudes and actions reflected therein. And the derogatory characterization of Jesus, as well as some negative ideas and halakoth on Gentiles in Jewish tradition, can openly be faced as obstacles.

Some topics may be felt to be so existential to one party or the other that it may be difficult to take them up in dialogue. Attempts ought to be made, however. Some such difficult topics may even be found in our common belief in God the Creator of all mankind and Him being revealed in a particular nation, the Jewish nation, among all the nations. The disagreement will manifest itself as soon as we try to answer the question: What event and what phenomenon in the history of this particular nation provide the decisive basis and criterion for understanding God and His revelation? The different points of departure on the Jewish side and on the Christian side will lead to different perspectives on how God acts in the chosen people and nation relative to other peoples and nations. Although a dialogue on

---

5. Ibid., p. 95.

these questions might lead to formulations of basic disagreements within the framework of much common ground, topics such as these are important and should not be ignored when Jews and Christians meet.

Today the concept of two covenants is often used to characterize Jews and Christians and their mutual relationship. The concept of covenant is a heritage that Jews and Christians share, and it may be a topic worth dealing with in research and in dialogues. When one talks about two or more covenants, however, many different ideas and vague and diffuse language easily enter into understanding and practice. Thus, thorough analysis is needed. Some such questions are: Who are the parties among whom the covenants are established? What is/are the basis/bases for the covenants? How are people involved in different covenants to regard each other? How are those in the one covenant interpreting the nature of the other covenant? What are the rules to be followed to guide us in our mutual relationship and interaction?

Another topic that needs to be discussed in this connection is our understanding of the fact that Jesus and his disciples were Jews who lived and worked among fellow Jews in Eretz Israel. They interpreted the sacred writings of their own people and were existentially involved in the question of the relationship between Israel and other peoples.

A topic of a more general nature is the observation that Christians and Jews in many situations have stressed and, when necessary, fought for religious freedom. Thus, it might be fruitful to deal with this issue both as a universal principle and as a principle to be applied to concrete and specific situations around the world. Here, much work needs to be done, and can be done.

Through dialogues, encounters, joint research, as well as through publications and joint action in areas of common concern, distorted pictures can be corrected and rendered more adequate, and elements of trust can be cultivated and can grow. A cautious attitude on both sides may help us to be realistic in our pilgrimage together through these difficult and existentially sensitive areas. But cautious attitudes should not prevent us from acting with determination in our effort to increase mutual understanding and make manifest our will to overcome fear.

Finally, as an example of practical solidarity in times of crisis,

I would like to mention that on the outer wall of the United Methodist Church to which I belong in Trondheim, Norway, there is a plaque put up by Jews from the Synagogue and Christians from the Church. The plaque was placed there in memory of the period during the Second World War when the Jews had a secret synagogal room on the top floor of the church building. The synagogue building had been confiscated and debased by the Nazis. When the Jews had to flee to Sweden, or were arrested, then the Torah Scrolls and other sacred items were hidden in the church building. After the war ended, the Jewish community had the Synagogue remodelled and re-dedicated, and they then received back the Torah and other items that had been safely hidden in the Methodist Church. In this way, continuity of worship in the Synagogue before and after the War was established.[6]

Actions such as this one offer a basis for hope and serve as encouragement in our efforts to overcome fears.

---

6. See further on this in a forthcoming issue of *Explorations*.

CHAPTER ELEVEN

Clement of Alexandria's Philo-Judaism: A Resource for Contemporary Jewish-Christian Dialogue

W. Barnes Tatum

Since the Holocaust there has been considerable scholarly discussion about the role of Christian theological anti-Judaism in shaping the cultural context for the emergence of modern racial anti-Semitism. A major stimulus in this discussion was Rosemary Ruether's controversial and now well-known claim that a theological anti-Judaism—as evidenced in the NT writings themselves—developed as the "left hand" of a christological interpretation of Jewish Scripture. Referring to the early Christian community, she states:

> On the one hand, the Church argues that the true meaning of the Scriptures is that of a prophecy of Jesus as the Christ. And, on the other hand, it developed a collection of texts "against the Jews" to show why the authority of the official Jewish tradition should be discounted when it refutes this christological midrash of its own Scriptures.[1]

Dr. Tatum's paper, while not presented at the Second Philadelphia Conference, nonetheless constitutes a significant contribution to the dialogue occasioned by that event. Thus, we are pleased and honored to include it in these proceedings.

The research for this study was initiated in an NEH Summer Seminar on the "Classical and Christian Roots of Anti-Semitism," directed by Louis H. Feldman, at Yeshiva University in New York City during the Summer of 1987.

1. R. Reuther, *Faith and Fratricide: The Theological Roots of Anti-Semitism* (New York, 1974) p. 65. For a collection of essays written in response to Reuther, with a concluding statement by Ruether herself, see T. Davies, ed., *Anti-Semitism and the Foundations of Christianity* (New York, 1979).

Ruether documented this anti-Judaic polemic in the writings of the Church Fathers. In particular, she appealed to the *adversus Judaeos* literary tradition expressed in the works of Justin Martyr, Origen, Tertullian, Cyprian, Chrysostom, and Augustine. But like other interpreters who have subjected the Church Fathers to scrutiny in this matter, she omitted from consideration Clement of Alexandria, presumably because he failed to express the common Christian invective against the Jews and Judaism.[2]

What *does* Clement of Alexandria say about the Jews and Judaism?[3] If Clement escapes the often virulent anti-Judaic attitudes and views of the Church Fathers, this would be of especial significance, given the locale in which he labored and by which he has become known—Alexandria, in Egypt.

The claim that "anti-Semitism originated in Egypt"[4] has a certain credibility. With the writings of the Egyptian priest Manetho in the third century B.C.E., there appeared a Graeco-Egyptian literary polemic against the Jews, furthered by the later writings of Lysimachus, Chaeremon, and Apion.[5] Also on at least three

---

2. Many recent surveys of the Church Fathers' views on the Jews and Judaism ignore Clement of Alexandria or dismiss him from consideration. Marcel Simon (*Verus Israel* [Oxford, England, 1986; French edition, 1964] p. 248) cites with frequency such early Christian thinkers as Justin Martyr, Origen, Tertullian, Augustine, and Jerome, but mentions Clement only in passing. Demetrios J. Constantelos ("Jews and Judaism in the Early Greek Fathers 100 A.D.–500 A.D.," *GOTR* 23 [1978] 145–56) excludes Clement from an admittedly selective review. David Rokeah (*Jews, Pagans, and Christians in Conflict* [Jerusalem, 1982] pp. 12, 13) presents in his introduction brief sketches of Justin Martyr, Tatian, Origen, Minucius Felix, Tertullian, Arnobius, Ambrose, and others, with Clement confined to two footnotes. J.G. Gager (*The Origins of Anti-Semitism: Attitudes Toward Judaism in Pagan and Christian Antiquity* [New York, 1985] pp. 160, 172) concentrates on such anti-Marcionite writers as Justin Martyr, Tatian, Origen, and Tertullian with only cursory references to Clement. Brief but helpful discussions of Clement in relation to the Jews and Judaism are found in the following: R. Wilde, "The Treatment of the Jews in Greek Christian Writers of the First Three Centuries" (Ph.D. diss., Catholic University, 1949) pp. 169–180; and H. Schreckenberg, *Die christlichen Adversus-Judaeos-Texte und ihr literarisches und historisches Umfeld (1.–11. Jh.)* (Frankfurt am Main/Bern, 1982) pp. 211–13.

3. Among the many studies in individual Church Fathers relative to their attitudes toward the Jews are the following: B.Z. Bokser, "Justin Martyr and the Jews," *JQR* 64 (1973–74) 97–122, 204–11; W.H.C. Frend, "A Note on Tertullian and the Jews," *StPatr* 10 (1970) 291–96; N.R.M. de Lange, *Origen and the Jews* (Cambridge, England, 1976); J. Neusner, *Aphrahat and Judaism* (Leiden, 1971); K.W. Noakes, "Melito of Sardis and the Jews," *StPatr* 13 (1975) 244–49; A.A. Bell, Jr., "Anti-Judaism in a Fourth Century Christian Historian: *De Excidio Hierosolymitano* of Pseudo-Hegesippus" (NEH Summer Seminar, Yeshiva University, 1987); and W.R. Ribando, "A Critique of the First Book of St. Cyprian's Treatise 12 on *Testimonies Against the Jews* (NEH Summer Seminar, Yeshiva University, 1987).

4. V. Tcherikover, *Hellenistic Civilization and the Jews* (Philadelphia, 1959) p. 358.

5. The existence of a Graeco-Egyptian literary tradition against the Jews is undeniable, as attested by Josephus in his treatise *Contra Apionem*. Scholars, however, have sometimes

occasions ill will between the sizeable Jewish community in Alexandria and other segments of the local populace erupted into what have been called "anti-Semitic pogroms"[6] or expressions of anti-Semitism in "a violent form."[7] In 38 C.E., the Alexandrian Jews endured mob attacks on their synagogues during the governorship of Flaccus. In 66 C.E., they were slaughtered at the instigation of Tiberius Julius Alexander coincidental with the outbreak in Palestine of the Jewish war against Rome. In 115–117 C.E., the Jews of Alexandria apparently were virtually annihilated in retaliation for the Diaspora revolt led by the messianic pretender Lukuas-Andreas. But even with a greatly diminished Jewish population in Egypt and in Alexandria, papyri fragments dating from the late second or early third century CE testify to a continued anti-Semitic or anti-Judaic sentiment.[8]

The recent attempt by Birger Pearson to reconstruct the contours of the relationship between Jews and Christians in Alexandria of the first century C.E. relied in part on the so-called *Letter of Barnabas*.[9] This Christian writing with its strong anti-Judaic thrust has been called "a tract against Jews," indeed "the first of a series of writings *adversus judaeos*."[10]

Remarkable it would be, therefore, if Clement, among all the Church Fathers, somehow avoided being imbued with anti-Judaic feelings and ideas.

The way Clement of Alexandria regards himself in relation to the Jews and Judaism constitutes the principal focus of the present study. The thesis herein developed is this: *that the thought of Clement of Alexandria not only generally lacks anti-Judaic or anti-Semitic sentiment but, within limits, discloses strong philo-Judaic or*

---

disputed whether the anti-Judaic passages of Manetho cited by Josephus are actually by Manetho. See W.G. Waddell, trans. and ed., *Manetho* (LCL; Cambridge, Mass., 1940) pp. xiv–xxviii.

6. L.H. Feldman "Anti-Semitism in the Ancient World," in D. Berger, ed., *History and Hate: The Dimensions of Anti-Semitism* (Philadelphia, 1986) p. 22.

7. A. Segré, "Antisemitism in Hellenistic Alexandria," *JSS* 8 (1946) 128.

8. Fragments no. 529 and 520, in V. A. Tcherikover, et al., eds., *Corpus Papyrorum Judaicarum* (3 vols., Cambridge, Mass., 1957–1964) vol. 3, pp. 116–21.

9. B.A. Pearson, "Christians and Jews in First-Century Alexandria," in W.E. Nickelsburg and W. McRae, eds., *Christians Among Jews and Christians* (Philadelphia, 1986) pp. 206–16. Also see B.A. Pearson. "Earliest Christianity in Egypt: Some Observations," in B.A. Pearson and J.E. Goering, eds., *The Roots of Egyptian Christianity* (SAC; Philadelphia, 1986) pp. 132–59.

10. J. Alvarez, "Apostolic Writings and the Roots of Anti-Semitism," *StPatr* 13 (1975), esp. pp. 72–74.

philo-Semitic tendencies.[11] In establishing this thesis, the present study falls into three parts: (1) brief comment on Clement's life and literature as the context and the text for his philo-Judaic tendencies; (2) consideration of his philo-Judaic tendencies; and (3) recognition of the limits of his philo-Judaism.

Life and Literature

Modern interpreters, following the testimony of Eusebius,[12] have located Clement in Alexandria during the closing years of the second century C.E.—from ca. 180 until 202/203.[13] Clement assumed residency there as a student of Pantaenus, the head of the Christian academy or catechetical school. Clement departed the city, never to return, at the time of the persecutions under Septimius Severus. Such details of his sojourn in Alexandria as his relationship with Pantaenus—and later with Origen—and his formal roles within the school and church have been debated for the past century. But Clement's stay in Alexandria itself has been beyond dispute.[14]

There is yet another fundamental certainty with regard to Clement. He has bequeathed to later generations three major works and one lesser: the *Protrepticus*; the *Paedagogus*; the *Stromata*; and a homily, *Quis Dives Salvatur.*[15] The literary and theo-

---

11. The voluminous writings on anti-Semitism, modern and ancient, reflect a persistent concern for the issue of definition. See, for example, S.J.D. Cohen, "'Anti-Semitism' in Antiquity: The Problem of Definition," in Berger, ed., *History and Hate*, pp. 43–47. In Cohen's study on the thought of Clement of Alexandria, the terms "anti-Semitism" and "anti-Judaism" are used synonymously to mean hostility toward Jews as a group and toward their religion without regard to individuals. Conversely, the terms "philo-Semitism" and "philo-Judaism" are used synonymously to mean appreciation for Jews as a group and toward their religion without regard to individuals. Philo-Semitism in the ancient world has been a particular interest of Louis H. Feldman. He was responsible for the first treatment in any language of philo-Semitism in Greek and Roman authors: "Philo-Semitism among Ancient Intellectuals," *Tradition* 1 (1958) 27–39. Shaye J. D. Cohen, as expressed in a recent article, prefers to speak of "respect for Judaism" rather than "philo-Semitism": "Respect for Judaism by Gentiles According to Josephus," *HTR* 80 (1987) 409–30.
12. *HE*, 5.10.1–11.5.
13. For example, J. Ferguson, *Clement of Alexandria* (TWAS 289; New York, 1974) pp. 13–17.
14. W.H. Wagner ("A Father's Fate: Attitudes Toward and Interpretations of Clement of Alexander," *JRH* 6 [1971] 209–31) provides a sweeping survey of how Clement the man and his ideas have been assessed over the centuries.
15. The English translation adapted for this study is the translation by W. Wilson, "Clement of Alexandria," in *Fathers of the Second Century* (*ANF* 2; reprinted, Grand Rapids, Mich., 1986) pp. 163–629. The translation has been selectively revised with reference

logical relationships among the three major works have occasioned ongoing discussion.[16] That all three were written in their entirety in Alexandria remains a possibility.[17] Or, as André Méhat has argued, at least the *Protrepticus* (ca. 195), the *Paedagogus* (ca. 197), and the *Stromata* 1–5 (ca. 198–201) were written in Alexandria, while the *Stromata* 6–7 (ca. 203) was written shortly after Clement's departure.[18]

The only overtly autobiographical statement by Clement appears in the opening section of the *Stromata*, a passage also cited by Eusebius,[19] where Clement lists anonymously those teachers who had transmitted to him the doctrine derived from the apostles Peter, James, John, and Paul. He identifies one of these teachers as ". . . a Hebrew in Palestine" (. . . *en tē Palaistinē Hebraios*, *Strom* 1.1, 11.2).[20] The four works of Clement preserved today are also mentioned by Eusebius along with several other writings no longer extant or preserved only in fragments. One of these presumably "lost" books was identified by Eusebius as being against the Judaizers (*pros tous Ioudaizontas*).[21] Whatever philo-Judaic tendencies Clement exhibits in his thought, therefore may be due at least in part to his "Hebrew" mentor; and

to the Greek text originally edited by O. Stählin, *Clemens Alexandrinus*, 4 vols. (GCS; Leipzig, 1905–36). References given herein to the writings of Clement are in accordance with the division and enumeration of the Greek text adopted by Stählin.

16. The traditional point of view, as summarized by Walter Wagner ("Another Look at the Literary Problem in Clement of Alexandria's Major Writings," *CH* 37 [1968] 251–60) considered the *Protrepticus* to serve as exhortation for possible Christian converts, the *Paedagogus* to serve as instruction for simple Christians, and the *Stromata* to serve as esoteric teaching for gnostic Christians. Wagner himself, however, considered the three works in the light of ancient ethical literary forms, particularly the forms in Stoic ethics. He concluded: "The three works are consequently not a trilogy in the sense of the traditional thesis but are best viewed as ethical treatises which, considered as a whole, satisfy the requirements of writings on particular and absolute duties. The major writings are a thoughtful, fundamentally complete and consistent attempt to present an ethic in Christ."

17. This position was carefully presented by R. B. Tollinton, *Clement of Alexandria*, 2 vols. (London, 1914) vol. 1, pp. 324–33.

18. This proposal by Méhat was cited and endorsed by Ferguson, *Clement of Alexandria*, pp. 16–17. For excellent commentary on Clement, especially on his *Stromata*, consult A. Méhat, *Étude sur les 'Stromates' de Clement d'Alexandrie*, (Patr Sorb 7; Paris, 1966).

19. *HE*, 5.11.1–5.

20. Among those proposed as the "Hebrew" teacher of Clement are Theophilus of Caesarea and Theodorus the Gnostic. See Ferguson, *Clement of Alexandria*, p. 14.

21. *HE*, 6.13.3. A footnote in the LCL edition of Eusebius suggests that the phrase *pros tous Ioudaizontas* can be translated "*to*," rather than "*against* the Judaizers." Accordingly, the work need not be less philo-Judaic than Clement's other writings. But Clement in other contexts (e.g., *Strom* 4.1,1.3) does use the preposition *pros* with the meaning of "against."

whatever conclusions may be established about his philo-Judaism would be put to the test by the discovery of his treatise
against the Judaizers.

Philo-Judaic Tendencies

Clement of Alexandria, once called "a gentleman among the
Fathers" by Morton S. Enslin,[22] has a genuine appreciation of
Judaism. Three areas of his thought reflect strong philo-Judaic
tendencies: the relationship between the Greeks and the Hebrews; Moses and the Mosaic law; and the history of the Hebrews. The *Stromata* represents the principal—albeit not
exclusive—repository for his thoughts on these topics.

The Relationship Between the Greeks and the Hebrews

Clement knows the ethnographic traditions of his day, as suggested by his repeated references to Herodotus (*Strom* 1.14,65.1;
1.16,75.1; et al.). He discloses his own probable Greek origin by
viewing humankind in Greek fashion. There are Greeks, and
there are non-Greeks (i.e., barbarians). As he succinctly states,
"of humans all are Greeks and barbarians" (*kai tōn anthrōpōn
pantes Hellēnes te kai Barbarui, Strom* 5.14,133.8).

On occasion Clement offers both descriptive and evaluative
comments about the different "nations" (*ethnē*) or "races" (*genē*)
among the barbarians:

> Of the nations, the Celts and the Scythians wear their hair long,
> but do not deck themselves. The bushy hair of the barbarian has
> something fearful in it; and its auburn color threatens war, the
> hue being somewhat akin to blood. Both these barbarian races
> hate luxury. . . . But I approve the simplicity of the barbarians;
> loving an unencumbered life, the barbarians have abandoned lux-
> ury. Such the Lord calls us to be—naked of finery, naked of vanity,
> wretched from our sins . . . aiming only at salvation. (*Paed*
> 3.3,24.2–25.3)

One of the identifying characteristics of a nation is its language. Clement twice defines the meaning of a "dialect" (*dia-*

---

22. M. S. Enslin, "A Gentleman Among the Fathers," *HTR* 47 (1954) 213–41.

lektos, Strom 1.2,142.3; 6.15,129.1). After acknowledging the differences of opinion about the exact number of "nations and tongues" (*ethnē kai glōssas*), he concludes that there are "seventy-two generic dialects, as our Scriptures hand down."[23] He continues with the observation that the Greeks claim to have "five dialects" among themselves and, moreover, that "the languages of the barbarians, which are innumerable, are not called dialects but tongues" (*Strom* 1.21,142.1–4).

Among the barbarians Clement places that nation or race that he variously refers to simply as "barbarians," or more definitively as "Hebrews" (*Hebraioi*) or "Jews" (*Ioudaioi*).[24] Although not entirely consistent, Clement uses the term "Hebrews" when identifying them as a people with a common history and shared cultural characteristics. Clement does use the term in one strikingly pejorative, although not hostile, passage where he illustrates a kind of fear: the kind "accompanied with hatred, which slaves feel towards hard masters, and the Hebrews felt who made God a master, not a father" (*Paed* 1.9,87.1). But generally he uses the term descriptively without negative connotations. Examples abound: "the language of the Hebrews" (*Strom* 6.15,130.3); "the Hebrew dialect" (*Strom* 6.15,129.1); "the Hebrew philosophy" (*Paed* 2.1,18.1); "the Hebrew scriptures" (*Strom* 1.19,93.1); "the Hebrew prophets" (*Strom* 1.17,87.2); "the ancient kings of the Hebrews" (*Paed* 2.8,61.2); and "the land of the Hebrews" (*Paed* 2.10,115.2).

Clement often uses the expression "Jews" when speaking about this people in conjunction with a NT text, particularly those passages where Paul speaks about the "Jews" and the "Greeks" parallel to one another. For instance, having cited Galatians 3:26–28 and 1 Corinthians 12:13, Clement introduces a quotation from Galatians 4:1–5 with these words ". . . the apostle

---

23. There are only 70 nations according to the table in Genesis 10; and Deuteronomy 32:8 may read that God divided humankind in accordance with the number of the "sons of Israel" (namely 70; Gen 46:27). The number 72 may be an extension of the tradition that 72 translators were responsible for the Septuagint (*Epistle of Aristeas*).

24. For a broad survey of the use of the term "Hebrews" and "Jews," consult A. Arazy, "The Appellations of the Jews (IOUDAIOS, HEBRAIOS, ISRAEL) in the Literature from Alexander to Julian," 2 vols. (Ph.D. diss., New York University, 1977). Arazy's comments on Clement are quite limited (vol. 2, pp. 238–39). But he sees within Christian sources between the destruction of the Temple in 70 C.E. and the Council of Nicaea in 325 C.E. a general tendency "to romanticize the appellation of the Jewish ancestor 'Hebraios'" in contrast to "the scornful appellation 'Ioudaios'" (vol. 2, pp. 242–43).

himself shall testify, calling as he does the Jews heirs according to the first covenant . . ." (*Paed* 1.6,33.4).

Clement also uses the expression "Jews" when referring to these people as his contemporaries. He directs his words in the *Stromata* primarily to Christians of Greek, or non-Jewish, background. But three of the books therein open with revealing comments about how Clement views his relationship not only with non-believing Greeks but with non-believing Jews; for he preserves the parallelism between the Greeks and the Jews so common in the letters of Paul:

> In addition, it will in my opinion form an appropriate sequel to defend those tenets, on account of which the Greeks assail us, making use of a few Scriptures, if perchance the Jew may also listen and be able quietly to turn from what he has believed to Him on whom he has not believed. (*Strom* 2.1,2.1)

> After which sketch, the brief explanation of the Scriptures both against the Greeks and against the Jews will be presented. (*Strom* 4.1,1.3)

> The Greeks, then, clearly learning, from what shall be said by us in these pages, that in profanely persecuting the God-loving man, they themselves act impiously; then, as the notes advance, in accordance with the style of the *Stromata*, we must solve the problems raised both by Greeks and barbarians [= Jews] with respect to the coming of the Lord. (*Strom* 6.1,1.4)

Although Clement in these introductory statements has in view primarily the Greeks, who unlike the Jews persecute Christians, he has not abandoned the possibility that his words might have a salutary effect on the Jews. One specific objection apparently leveled at Christians by Greeks and Jews was the diversity of sects among the Christians. Clement defends Christianity against this charge by pointing out the multiplicity of sects among the Greeks and the Jews themselves. His defense contains what may be the only polemical "you" addressed to the Jews in his extant writings:[25]

> To whom we say, that among you who are Jews, and among the most famous of the philosophers among the Greeks, very many sects have sprung up. (*Strom* 7.15,89.3)

---

25. Me'hat, *Étude sur les 'Stromates,'* p. 398.

Elsewhere Clement associates "Jews" negatively with ignorance (*Strom* 2.5,21.1) but positively with frugality (*Paed*
2.1,17.1). And he refers to "the Jewish writings" (*Strom* 6.6,53.1),
interpreting scripture "in a Jewish sense" (*Paed* 1.6,34.3), and "a
custom of the Jews to wash" (*Strom* 4.22,142.3).

Clement of Alexandria, therefore, sharply delineates between
the Greeks, on the one hand, and the barbarians among whom
are the Hebrews or Jews, on the other. This demarcation provides the conceptual framework for his argument about the relationship between the Greeks and the Hebrews. *Clement exhibits
philo-Judaism by his claim that the Greeks have appropriated much of
their philosophy and culture from the Hebrews.* This claim of dependence of the Greeks upon the Hebrews had its beginnings, as
might be expected, in Hellenistic Jewish apologetics[26] and appeared in Christian apologetics prior to Clement.[27] Although
Clement makes such a claim in the *Protrepticus* (e.g. 6.70.1) and
the *Paedagogus* (e.g. 1.8,67.1), his sustained argument in this
regard runs through most of his *Stromata*.[28] Clement commences
his argument by citing and then interpreting a saying of Jesus
from John 10:8:

> But, say they, it is written, "All who were before the Lord's advent
> are thieves and robbers." . . . But the prophets, being sent and
> inspired by the Lord, were not thieves but servants. . . . Well, be
> it so that "the thieves and robbers" are the philosophers among
> the Greeks, who from the Hebrew prophets before the coming of
> the Lord received fragments of the truth, not with full knowledge,
> and claimed these as their own teachings. . . . (*Strom* 1.17,81.1–2;
> 87.2)

As he proceeds, Clement periodically reminds his readers of
this thievery by the Greeks. The stolen property includes such

---

26. Clement himself refers his readers to Philo as one who subscribed to the view that
the Greeks were dependent upon the Jews for much of their philosophy (*Strom*
1.15,72.5). As an example from Philo's own writings, see his *Quis rerum divinarum heres*
43.214. Norman Roth ("The 'Theft of Philosophy' by the Greeks from the Jews," *CF* 32
[1978] 53–67) traces this theme from the works of Hellenistic Jewish apologists into
medieval Jewish literature.

27. See, for example, Justin Martyr, *1 Apol* 44.

28. S. Lilla (*Clement of Alexandria: A Study of Christian Platonism and Gnosticism* [Oxford,
1971] 31–41) considers at some length "why" Clement spends so much time on the topic
of the theft by the Greeks. Lilla claims that Clement is responding to Celsus, who had
claimed that Greek philosophy represented the culmination of a long process anterior
not only to Christianity but also to Judaism.

philosophical teachings as faith as the foundation of knowledge (*Strom* 2.4,12.1–19.4), the realm of ideas as a place containing all things universally (*Strom* 5.11,73.3), the creation of the world (*Strom* 5.14,92.1–4), and the devil as an evil spirit (*Strom* 5.14,92.5–93.3). The stolen property also includes those virtues which serve as the foundation of morals: temperance, courage, justice, and wisdom (*Strom* 2.18,78.1–96.4).[29] The Hebrews could find consolation, however, in the awareness that the Greeks stole from one another as well as from other barbarians such as the Egyptians and the Indians (*Strom* 6.2,41–27.5; 6.4,35.1–38.12). Clement finally concludes his argument with these words:

> That the Greeks are called pilferers of all manner of writings, is, as I think, sufficiently demonstrated by abundant proofs. (*Strom* 6.5,39.1)

These summary remarks indicate that a plagiarism of the magnitude of that perpetrated by the Greeks required them to have access to the writings of their victims. The Greeks must have had access to the literature of the Hebrews—specifically to the Hebrew Scriptures. Clement had anticipated this problem. In his account of the translation of the Septuagint during the rule of Ptolemy Philadelphus, Clement divulges that there had been an earlier translation of the Hebrew Scriptures into Greek (*Strom* 1.22,148.1–150.5).[30] The Greeks, therefore, had opportunity. The Hebrews became their victims.

Moses and the Mosaic Law

Clement often personalizes his demonstration of the Greeks' robbery of the Hebrews by making it a transaction involving Plato, or Pythagoras, and Moses and the Mosaic law (e.g. *Strom* 1.15,68.2). For Clement, Moses represents the founder of the Hebrews. He speaks about "the age of Moses" (*Strom* 1.14,59.5) or "the epoch of Moses" (*Strom* 1.21,101.1) as that period when the Hebrews were established as a people. *Clement further exhibits*

---

29. Louis H. Feldman ("Philo-Semitism," pp. 27–39) has persuasively shown that temperance, courage, justice, and wisdom, as the four cardinal virtues, represented qualities of the Jews that elicited praise from pagan authors.
30. Clement's claim of a pre-Septuagint translation of the Hebrew Scriptures into Greek was quite likely based on the *Epistle of Aristeas* 314.

philo-Judaism by his portrayal of Moses as worthy of honorific designations and by his presentation of the Mosaic law as a beneficent means of establishing virtue.[31]

Clement recognizes Moses' foundational role among the Hebrews by narrating in detail the circumstances of his life. In the *Stromata,* he presents sequentially Moses' birth and upbringing (1.23), his leadership during the exodus and wilderness wandering (1.24), and his mediation of the law (1.26–28). Throughout his writings, Clement bestows upon Moses a variety of complimentary epithets. These include: "gnostic" (*Strom* 5.11,74.4); "truly wise" (*Strom* 1.26,168.4); "all-wise" (*Strom* 5.12,78.2; of God in *Prot* 1.1.2); "sage" (*Strom* 2.5,21.1); "theologian" (*Strom* 1.22,150.4); "philosopher" (*Strom* 1.24,158.1); "prophet" (*Strom* 1.22,150.4; *Paed* 1.11,96.3); "king" (*Strom* 2.5,21.1); "legislator" (*Strom* 1.26,168.4); "politician" (*Strom* 1.24,158.1); "general" (*Strom* 1.26,168.4); "hierophant" (*Prot* 2.25.1; of God in *Prot* 2.22.7); "interpreter of sacred laws" (*Strom* 1.122,150.4); "one skilled in military tactics" (*Strom* 1.24,158.1); "truly holy" (*Prot* 6.69.2); "just" (*Strom* 1.26,168.4); and "God-beloved" (*Strom* 1.26,168.4).

Clement begins his exposition of the mediation of the law through Moses by quoting (as he does with some frequency) those passages in Galatians (3:19, 23–24) where Paul affirms that the Law was "instituted because of transgressions" as a "schoolmaster (*paidagōgos*) to bring us to Christ" (*Strom* 1.26,167.2). But whereas Paul tended to stress the more negative functions of the law, such as revealing and stirring up sin, Clement moves beyond Paul and emphasizes the Law's more positive possibilities. Clement associates the Law with the categories of the "good" (*agathos*), the "noble" (*kalos*), and "virtue" (*aretē*). He states:

> In a word, the whole system of Moses is suited for the training of such as are capable of becoming good and noble men. . . .
> (*Strom* 1.26,168.3)
>
> . . . so also we shall say that legislation, inasmuch as it presides

---

31. For a thorough assessment of the varying views on Moses among non-Jews in the Mediterranean world, see J.G. Gager, *Moses in Greco-Roman Paganism,* SBLMS 16 (Nashville, 1972).

over and cares for the human flock, establishes the virtue of persons, by fanning into flame, as far as it can, what good there is in humanity. (*Strom* 1.26,169.1).

But it is the highest and most perfect good, when one is able to lead back any one from the practice of evil to virtue and well-doing, which is the very function of the law. (*Strom* 1.27.173.1).

Understandably, Clement repeatedly underscores the beneficence of the law and refers to the law as "benefactor" (*euergetēs, Strom* 1.27,171.1). Furthermore, he draws a parallel between the work of the Law and that of the physician, perhaps taken from Plato,[32] thereby ascribing to the Law the titles of "savior" (*sotēr*) and "healer" (*iatros, Strom* 1.27,171.2). For Clement, unlike Paul, the Law is not just a "schoolmaster" preparing the way for Christ. Rather the work of Christ as "the Schoolmaster" (*ho Paidagōgos*) expresses itself through the Law. Clement declares that ". . . both the law and the gospel are the energy of one Lord" (*Strom* 1.27,174.3).

Neither is this section of the *Stromata* (1.26–28) nor elsewhere in his writings does Clement suggest that the Law was imposed on the Hebrews, or Jews, through Moses because of their sins. This silence stands in sharp contrast, for example, to the constant refrain in Justin Martyr's *Dialogus cum Tryphone* where Justin reminds Trypho of the reason for the Law: the "hardness of heart" (*sklērokardia*) of Trypho's people and their fathers.[33] Also, Clement does refer to those outward signs of Jewishness, sanctioned by the Law, which elicited such derision from many ancient writers: circumcision, dietary practices, and sabbath observance.[34] But he refrains from polemical comments about circumcision (*Strom* 6.15,124.1); dietary practices (*Strom* 7.6,33.1; 7.18,109.1–110.3); and sabbath observance (*Strom* 5.14,107.1; 6.16,137.4–145.7). Moreover, Clement uses the tabernacle and its furnishings to illustrate allegorical interpretation (*Strom*

---

32. Ferguson, *Clement of Alexandria*, p. 119.

33. 27.4; 43.1; 46.7; 67.4; et al. Theodore Stylianopoulos should be mentioned as one who has explored the theme of the "hardness of heart." See his *Justin Martyr and the Mosaic Law*, SBLDS 20 (Missoula, 1975) esp. pp. 41–45.

34. For the primary sources, see the monumental, three-volume work edited by Menahem Stern, *Greek and Latin Authors on Jews and Judaism* (Jerusalem, 1974–84). Recent interpretations of the evidence include: Feldman, "Anti-Semitism," pp. 15–42, and J.L. Daniel, "Anti-Semitism in the Hellenistic-Roman Period," *JBL* 98 (1979) 45–65.

5.6,32.1–40.4); and he gives a "gnostic" exposition of the Decalogue (*Strom* 6.16,133.1–148.6; also *Paed* 3.12,89.1).

The History of the Hebrews

The thievery by the Greeks from the Hebrews, the robbery by Plato of Moses, presupposes the antiquity of the Hebrews as a people. Clement devotes a section of the *Stromata* to a meticulous demonstration of that antiquity (1.21), a section Raoul Mortley acknowledges has been given "very little scholarly attention."[35] Clement introduces this section with these words:

> On the plagiarizing of the dogmas of the philosophers from the Hebrews, we shall treat a little afterwards. But first, as due order demands, we must now speak of the epoch of Moses by which the philosophy of the Hebrews will be demonstrated beyond all contradiction to be the most ancient of all wisdom. (1.21, 101.1)

Clement begins with a tedious and somewhat labyrinthine establishment of the date of Moses and the exodus from Egypt of the "Jews" (not "Hebrews," contrary to common usage) by synchronizing Moses and the exodus with other ancient peoples and happenings. Moses was a contemporary of Amosis, the Egyptian pharaoh, and of Inachus, from whom the oldest of the Greek states took its rise.[36] As a result, Clement confidently declares that Moses antedates the deification of Dionysus, the appearance of humankind according to Greek reckoning, and the presence of poets and philosophers among the Greeks.

Clement proceeds with his historical presentation along several lines. He traces the history of the Hebrews from Moses through the judges and kings and through the life of Christ until the destruction of Jerusalem by the Romans. Periodic summary statements refer to Moses. Clement also traces, in more limited

---

35. R. Mortely, "The Past in Clement of Alexandria," in E.P. Sanders, *Jewish and Christian Self-Definition*, 3 vols (Philadelphia, 1980–82) vol. 1, p. 188. Mortley thinks that Celsus' critique of Christianity might in some way underlie Clement's historical presentation in the *Stromata* 1.21. He suggests that Celsus' critique was developed over against the "Gnostic face" of early Christianity; and, therefore, Clement here attempts to distinguish his own view from that of Valentinian Gnosticism.

36. This synchronization of Moses with Inachus was widely attested at the turn of the common era as shown in a helpful study by Ben Zion Wacholder, "Hellenistic World Chronicles," *HTR* 61 (1968) 451–81.

scope, the histories of the Babylonians, the Persians, the Macedonians, the Egyptians, the Greeks, and the Romans. Inter-
spersed lists allow Clement to mention Adam twice (*Strom*
1.21,140.2; 144.3) and the death of Commodus a number of
times. He calculates these years to the death of Commodus: from
the first games of Domitian at Rome, 111 years (*Strom* 1.21,139.2);
from the death of Antony and the establishment of the Roman
empire, 222 years (*Strom* 1.21,140.7); from Vespasian, 121 years
(*Strom* 1.21,140.7); from Augustus, 222 years (*Strom* 1.21, 144.3);
from Adam, 5,784 years (*Strom* 1.21,144.3); from Julius Caesar,
236 years (*Strom* 1.21,144.5); from Romulus the founder of Rome,
953 years (*Strom* 1.21.144.5); from the destruction of Jerusalem
by the Romans, 128 years (*Strom* 1.21,145.5); from the birth of
Christ, 194 years (*Strom* 1.21,145.5); and from Inachus and
Moses, 3,142 or 2,831 years (*Strom* 1.21,147.4).

Clement concludes his demonstration of the antiquity of the
Hebrews, within the context of universal history,[37] with a reference to the genealogy that opens the First Gospel:

> In the Gospel according to Matthew, the genealogy which begins
> with Abraham is continued down to Mary the mother of the Lord.
> "For," it is said, "from Abraham to David are fourteen genera-
> tions; and from David to the carrying away to Babylon are four-
> teen generations; from the carrying away to Babylon to Christ
> are likewise fourteen generations."—three mystic intervals. . . .
> (*Strom* 1.21,147.5–6)

Moreover, in his presentation of the history of the Hebrews,
*Clement exhibits philo-Judaism by his treatment of the crucifixion of
Jesus and, more generally, by his use of documentary sources both
scriptural and non-scriptural.*

Clement twice refers to the earthly ministry of "Christ" or
"our Lord" within the context of his historical argument for the
antiquity of the Hebrews. Admittedly he speaks of the crucifixion in rather oblique (if not docetic) terms as "reigning in Jerusalem" (*Strom* 1.21,126.1) or "the time he suffered" (*Strom*
1.21,145.4); but he avoids assigning the responsibility for that

---

37. Thomas Finan ("Hellenism and Judeo-Christian History in Clement of Alexandria,"
ITQ 28 [1961] 86–114) outlines what he sees as Clement's response to "the problem of
reconciling Christian universalism . . . with the fact of an independent tradition of pro-
fane history. . . ."

death to the "Jews." Elsewhere in his major writings Clement also avoids attributing responsibility for Jesus' death to the "Jews," or to any particular group, although he does implicate Judas (e.g. *Strom* 6.13,105.1–2). A fragment of his "missing" work on the Passover, however, does contain this seemingly accusatory notation: "And on the following day our Savior suffered, He who was the Passover, propitiously sacrificed by the Jews."[38] Again, Clement's general silence in this matter relative to the Jews stands in contrast to repeated statements by such near contemporaries as Justin Martyr and Tertullian. Both of the latter hold the Jews responsible and accountable for the death of Jesus, and both express this sentiment within and without their *adversus Judaeos* writings.

Justin Martyr, for example, writes:

> . . . the Jews took counsel about Christ Himself, taking counsel to crucify and slay Him. . . . (*Dial Trypho* 72.3)[39]

> . . . the Jews who are in possession of the books of the prophets did not recognize Christ even when he came, and they hate us who declare that he was crucified by them as predicted. (*1 Apol* 36)[40]

Tertullian similarly affirms:

> Therefore, since the Jews still contend that the Christ is not yet come, who in so many ways we have approved to be come, let the Jews recognize their own fate,—a fate which they were constantly foretold as destined to incur after the advent of Christ, on account of the impiety (*impietatem*) with which they despised and slew Him. (*AdvJud* 13.24)[41]

> Now, since you join the Jews in denying that their Christ has come, recollect also what is that end which they were predicted

---

38. The English translation and the Greek text of this fragment, preserved in the Paschal Chronicle, are those found respectively in *ANF* 2, p. 581, and Stählin, *Clemens Alexandrinus*, vol. 3, p. 217.

39. English translation and Greek text: A.L. Williams, trans., *Justin Martyr. The Dialogue with Trypho* (London, 1930); G. Archambault, *Justin Dialogue avec Tryphon*, 2 vols. (TD; Paris, 1909).

40. English translation and Greek text: C. Richardson, ed. and trans., *Early Christian Fathers* (LCC 1: Philadelphia, 1953) pp. 225–89; L. Pautigny, *Justin Apologies* (TD; Paris, 1904).

41. English translation and Latin text: S. Thelwall, trans., *The Writings of Tertullian* (*ANF* 3; Grand Rapids, Mich., 1986) pp. 151–73; H. Tränkle, *Q.S.F. Tertulliani Adversus Iudaeos* (Wiesbaden, 1964).

to bring on themselves after the time of Christ, for the impiety (*impietatem*) wherewith they both rejected and slew Him. (*Adv-Marc* 3.23.1)[42]

The extraordinary richness of Clement's education becomes apparent with even a cursory glance at the quotations in his writings. It has been claimed that he cites 348 authors.[43] Among the Greek authors cited are those whose writings contain references to the Jews. He refers to Alexander Polyhistor because his work *On the Jews* preserves texts of letters reportedly from Solomon to neighboring kings (*Strom* 1.21,130.3). He also quotes a passage from Megasthenes' book *On Indian Affairs*, which contains one of the earliest references to Jews in Greek literature (*Strom* 1.15,72.5). In his account of the pre-Septuagint translation of Jewish Scripture from Hebrew into Greek, Clement reports the words of Numenius the Pythagorean: "For what is Plato, but Moses speaking in Attic Greek?" (*Strom* 1.21,150.4). And Clement reports the claim of Clearchus the Peripatetic to have known a "Jew" who had been associated with Aristotle (*Strom* 1.15,70.2).

Clement was also dependent on Hellenistic Jewish literature.[44] His familiarity with the Septuagint has long been established,[45] as has been his reliance upon Philo.[46] He often cites Philo and acknowledges dependence on Philo's *De vita Mosis* for his own presentation of the life of Moses (*Strom* 1.23,153.2). He also identifies Josephus "the Jew" as one who had composed a history of the Jews (*Strom* 1.21,147.2). But Clement relies on other Hellenis-

---

42. English translation and Latin text: P. Holmes, trans., *The Writings of Tertullian*, ANF 3, pp. 269–475; E. Evans, ed. and trans., *Tertullian Adversus Marcionem*, 2 vols. (Oxford, 1972).

43. Ferguson, *Clement of Alexandria*, p. 17.

44. For a collection of the literary remains of many Hellenistic Jewish writers cited by Clement, consult the following: C.R. Holladay, ed. and trans., *Fragments from Hellenistic Jewish Authors*, (SBLTT Pseudepigraphia Series 1; Chico, Calif., n.d.); and J.H. Charlesworth, ed., *OTP* 2, pp. 775–919.

45. O. Stählin, *Clemens Alexandrinus und die Septuaginta* (Nürnburg, 1901).

46. Salvatore Lilla (*Clement of Alexandria*, p. 233) offers this concluding comparison between Clement and Philo: "Clement has produced a process of Hellenization of Christianity which is closely parallel to the process of Hellenization of Judaism which is characteristic of Philo's work. . . . He wanted to transform his religious faith into a monumental philosophical system, to which he allotted the task of reflecting absolute truth." Also see the comments on the relationship between Clement and Philo in the works of Harry A. Wolfson: *Philo*, 2 vols. (Cambridge, Mass., 1947); and *The Philosophy of the Church Fathers: Faith, Trinity, Incarnation* (Cambridge, Mass., 1956).

tic Jewish writers as well. Demetrius and Eupolemus each wrote a book *On the Kings in Judea* (*Strom* 1.21,141.1; 1.23,153.4). Ezekiel was a composer of such "Jewish tragedies" as *The Exodus* (*Strom* 1.23,155.1). And there were Aristobulus and Artapanus (*Strom* 1.22,150.1; 1.23,154.2).

Clement uses scriptural texts, OT and NT, in ways that deviate from the anti-Judaic practices of other Church Fathers.

One characteristic of patristic exegesis involves what has been called a "schizophrenic" application of OT prophetic texts.[47] The texts that express God's judgment on God's people for their disobedience are applied to "the Jews"; but the texts which promise God's forgiveness are applied not to "the Jews" but to God's future church. In the *Paedagogus*, however, Clement includes an important section intended for Christians that brings together under rhetorical headings (complaint, invective, reproof, etc.) some thirty-one scriptural passages, most of which are OT "judgment" texts (1.9,76.1–81.2). These passages Clement applies not to "the Jews" but to Christians, to illustrate "the mode of God's loving discipline, with the aid of prophetic testimony" (*Paed* 1.9,75.3). Thus, not only "forgiveness" but also "judgment" are the lot of Christian believers.

Certain scriptural texts lend themselves to use in patristic exegesis as "judgment" against the "Jews." The OT story of Aaron and the golden calf (Exodus 32, esp. vss 4, 19–20) became foundational evidence both for the waywardness of the Jews and for their rejection by God (already in Acts 7:39–41).[48] This episode plays a central role in the anti-Judaic polemic of both Justin Martyr[49] and Tertullian.[50] Although Clement refers to this incident, he omits mention of the golden calf and highlights the excessive eating and revelry (*Paed* 1.11,96.3–97.1; but 1.10,90.2).

Matthew 27:25 and 1 Thessalonians 2:14–16 are statements of judgment against the Jews for their involvement in the killing of Jesus. Tertullian uses both texts in his diatribes against the Jews.[51] Clement cites neither text. John 8:44 is a saying on the

---

47. Ruether, *Faith and Fratricide*, pp. 131–37; also see Simon, *Verus Israel*, pp. 156–78.
48. L. Smolar and M. Aberbach, "The Golden Calf Episode in Post-Biblical Literature," *HUCA* 39 (1968) 98–116.
49. *DialTrypho* 19.4–5; 20.4; 73.6; 132.1.
50. *AdvJud* 1.6.
51. *AdvJud* 8.18; *AdvMarc* 2.15.3; 5.15.1–2.

lips of Jesus, addressed to "the Jews," which declares: "You are of your father the devil." Clement cites this verse; but he applies the text not to "the Jews" but to "false prophets" (*Strom* 1.17,84.6–85.2).

The Alexandria of Clement was a city, as noted earlier, with a history of anti-Judaism or anti-Semitism. The writings of Apion and the *Letter of Barnabas* give expression to this polemic against Jews. Clement knows and uses both sources in his *Stromata* but does not endorse their anti-Judaic perspective.

With regard to Apion, Clement says:

> Apion, then, the grammarian surnamed Pleistonices, in the fourth book of the *Egyptian Histories*, although of so hostile a disposition towards the Hebrews, being by race an Egyptian, as to compose a work against the Jews, when referring to Amosis king of the Egyptians, and his exploits, adduces as a witness, Ptolemy of Mendes. (*Strom* 1.21,101.3)

Clement uses Apion's work in establishing the date of the exodus from Egypt under Moses. He mentions the anti-Judaic nature of that work to enhance the credibility of its use by him. But Clement does not report the particulars of the calumny.

Clement also makes reference to, and quotes, *Barnabas* several times.[52] But he does not use those passages which assert that the Jews have been abandoned by God.

Alexandria had a tradition of anti-Judaism, literarily and socially. Clement, however, in his writings displays strong philo-Judaic tendencies in his treatment of the relationship between the Greeks and the Hebrews, of Moses and the Mosaic law, and of the history of the Hebrews. At least literarily, in his attitude towards the Jews and Judaism Clement does appear to be "a gentleman among the Fathers."

Clement's Philo-Judaic Limits

When Clement juxtaposes the Greeks and Hebrews, Plato and Moses, and Philosophy and the Law, he subordinates the former to the latter. But Clement writes as neither a Greek nor a Jew, but as a Christian. He takes seriously Paul's statement that "in

---

52. *Strom* 2.6, 31.2; 2.7, 35.5; 2.15, 67.3; 2.18, 84.3; 2.20, 117.3–4; 5.10, 63.1–6.

Christ" there is "neither Jew nor Greek" (Gal 3:28, e.g. in *Paed* 1.6,31.1). Clement makes explicit what was implied by Paul: that Christians constitute a third "race" or "people." Following a reference to Jeremiah 31:31, Clement affirms that God

> made a new covenant with us; for what belonged to the Greeks and Jews is old. But we who worship God in a new way, in a third form (*tritō genei*), are Christians (*Christianoi*). For clearly I think, God showed that the one and only God was known by the Greeks in a Gentile way, by the Jews in a Jewish way, and in a new and spiritual way by us. . . . Accordingly, then, from the Hellenic training and also from that of the law, are gathered into one race (*hen genos*) of the saved people those who accept faith. . . . (*Strom* 6.5,41.6–7; 42.2)

For Clement, the Word who spoke through Plato and Philosophy, through Moses and the Law, has appeared in Jesus "the Instructor" (*ho Paidagōgos*, esp. *Paed* 1.2,4.1–6.6). The Instructor leads to salvation, to eternal life, to the highest glory, those Christians of faith who through Him become a true "gnostic" (*gnōstikos*), assimilated to God, perfect and without passions (*Strom* 6.12, 13, 14). Without such Christian faith, there is salvation for neither Greeks nor Jews.

The limits of Clement's philo-Judaism, therefore, are circumscribed by his christology or, more precisely, by his exclusionistic soteriology: Jews cannot attain salvation without Christian faith. With the recognition of these limits, two final observations about Clement himself and a concluding comment about Clement's omission from consideration by Rosemary Ruether are appropriate.

Although Clement does not affirm that Jews may be saved without Christian faith, he exhibits a kind of philo-Judaism in his reflections on the so-called descent of Christ into Hades based on 1 Peter 3:18–19; 4:6 (*Strom* 6.6,44.1–53.5). Clement emphasizes how Christ through his descent extended the offer of salvation both to those Gentiles who were righteous according to Philosophy and to those Hebrews who were righteous according to the Law. Although Clement suggests that Christ may have descended to preach either to all the righteous or only to the righteous Hebrews, he is inclined to the view that Christ himself preached only to the Jews with the apostles' having descended to preach to the non-Jews.

Although Clement does not affirm that Jews may be saved without Christian faith, he exhibits a kind of philo-Judaism in his reflections on the different ways of obtaining Christian knowledge and thus salvation (*Strom* 6.15,119.1–5; cf. Romans 11.17–24). Clement uses an image drawn from horticulture, outlining four ways of engrafting an olive tree, which parallel four ways of gaining knowledge. The second way of engrafting, which involves cutting the wood and inserting a cultivated branch, applies both to students of Philosophy and to the Jews, who have the Old Testament. By setting forth the possibility for such engrafting for Jews, therefore, Clement clearly does not consider the Jews to have been finally rejected by God.

Rosemary Ruether, in surveying the negative views of the Church Fathers toward the Jews and Judaism, omitted from consideration Clement of Alexandria. She omitted him with good reason: Clement does not assess the Jews and Judaism negatively. His christological interpretation of the OT does not have as its "left hand" a theological anti-Judaism. Furthermore, his exclusionistic soteriology has as its "right hand" an inclusive possibility not only for Greeks but also for Jews.

CHAPTER TWELVE

Eighteen Months in Catholic-Jewish Relations (April 13, 1986–September 11, 1987)

Eugene J. Fisher

In Jewish tradition, the number eighteen has special meaning. Eighteen is the sum of the numerical value of the letters of the Hebrew word for "life" *(hayyim)*. As I speak, the past eighteen months in the relationship between the Jewish people and the Catholic Church have been dramatic ones, with event after event challenging the deepest religious sensitivities, historical memories, and spiritual aspirations of both communities. They have seen the development and denoument of a drama of passion and controversy, marred by much inflated rhetoric and prophecies of doom. It has been a drama of life itself. We have emerged from it, Catholics and Jews, with a deeper understanding of one another and a renewed commitment to dialogue and reconciliation.

How does one tell a story such as this one—a story in which each event evokes not only other contemporary events but also the scenes and images of an often troubled history stretching back almost two millenia in time to the period of our very origins? The first century was a period in which two Jewish religious movements, Rabbinic Judaism and Early Christianity, movements with surprisingly similar yet surprisingly different religious views, both emerged from the rubble of the destruction by imperial Rome of the Jewish temple and city of Jerusalem to offer to the Jewish people and to the world their related yet distinct interpretations of the sacred history of biblical Israel and its One God, the God of Abraham and Sarah, Isaac and Rivkah, and Jacob and Rachel?

The present story begins long after those foundational experiences. It begins in the Grand Synagogue of Rome, a structure whose predecessors date back to long before the apostles Simon-Peter and Saul-Paul came to that city to preach and to die at the hands of the pagans who then ruled it. On April 13, 1986, Pope John Paul II became the first bishop of Rome to visit a synagogue since the time of Simon-Peter. There, he prayed with the Jewish community the Hebrew Psalms. He listened reverentially as Jews read the Hebrew Scriptures and expounded their meaning according to ancient rabbinic traditions. And he affirmed clearly that the covenant entered into between God and the Jewish people was and is "irrevocable," as Scripture testifies. The Pope's unambiguous acknowledgment of the spiritual validity of contemporary Judaism and of its continuing role in salvation history articulated the central significance of his visit.

It was an historic moment, pregnant with theological implications, and one which seemed to seal symbolically the fact that the movement toward reconciliation between Jews and Catholics begun by the Second Vatican Council is irreversible and in keeping with the central tradition of the teaching of the Church. Yet even as we celebrated together this solid beginning of a new relationship between our communities, controversies born of the misunderstandings of the past were developing that would severely test the strength of our dialogue: the process of beatification of Edith Stein was moving toward its conclusion; a small group of Polish nuns were working on the interior of an abandoned theater across the street from the infamous death camp at Auschwitz-Birkenau; and Kurt Waldheim, former secretary general of the United Nations, was being proposed as president of Catholic Austria.

All three actions touched on the Holocaust and thus on a memory sacred to the Jewish people today. Jewish nerves, rubbed raw by centuries of persecution, and the Jewish soul, scarred by the agony of the loss of one-third of its entire people just forty years ago, cried out with sincere anguish, an outcry of pain and accusation that threatened to rend the still delicate fabric of the new relationship Catholics and Jews have been weaving in patient dialogue for the past twenty years in this country and throughout the world.

The first two events are properly taken together and separately from the third, though the hurts experienced in them did intensify the emotions of this summer. Rabbi Daniel Polish has attempted to articulate how Jews perceived—and why they reacted the way they did to-the news (not always accurately presented in the media, it may be added) of Edith Stein's beatification and of the establishment of a small Carmelite convent so close to the site of the major Nazi death camp in Poland.[1]

Rabbi Polish first captures the sense of perplexity among many Catholics to the Jewish outcry in the two cases: Are not, Catholics ask, the beatification of a Catholic and the establishment of a convent internal Church matters? Should not these symbolic gestures on the part of the Church to join its voice to that of the Jewish people in prayerful memory of the six million be acknowledged by Jews as sincerely motivated Catholic efforts to heal the wounds of the past and to heed the Jewish people's own call to the world to remember the Shoah?

"How difficult we must seem to Catholics to make sense of," Polish comments. "In both cases we (Jews) responded paradoxically to what one could construe as expressions of fellow-feeling, even solidarity." Polish has it right. Catholics are confused, and hurt, by Jewish rebukes in these matters, and especially by the tendency on the part of some Jewish commentators to call into question the sincerity of the *intentions* of Catholic authorities, often without even first asking what the Catholic motivation might have been but simply presuming an evil intent.

Such rhetoric, with its presumption of guilt until proved innocent is, I think justifiably, found highly offensive by many Catholics. It reached its peak this past summer during the Waldheim controversy, which we shall discuss later on.

But before lapsing into righteous indignation on our part, we Catholics need to listen a bit more carefully to understand the very real *fears* that underlie the Jewish rhetoric that has caused us so much pain over the last eighteen months. These fears—and as a Catholic I can say this only with a profound sense of

---

1. D. F. Polish, "The Pain of Legacy: Jews and Catholics Struggle to Understand Edith Stein and Auschwitz," *EcumTr* (in press).

sadness and contrition—are all too solidly founded in our history. Again, Rabbi Polish helps us to move beyond harmful rhetoric to the deeper sensitivities involved: "At the heart of the Jewish response to the beatification of Edith Stein is the perception that it has the effect of legitimizing efforts to promote conversion among the Jews."

From a Jewish point of view, Polish writes, it is very difficult to distinguish between the Catholic Church's veneration of a Jewish convert and the blatantly proselytizing activities of extreme fundamentalist groups such as the "Jews for Jesus" and the "Messianic Jews." Catholics would quickly respond that such Jewish fears are groundless. As the Bishops' Committee for Ecumenical and Interreligious Affairs of the National Conference of Catholic Bishops stated on the occasion of the beatification itself:

> Catholic respect for the integrity of Judaism and for the ongoing validity of God's irrevocable convenant with the Jewish people is solidly founded on our faith in the unshakeable faithfulness of God's own word. Therefore, in no way can the beatification of Edith Stein be understood by Catholics as giving impetus to unwarranted proselytizing among the Jewish community. On the contrary, it urges us to ponder the continuing religious significance of Jewish traditions, with which we have so much in common, and to approach Jews not as potential "objects" of conversion but rather as bearers of a unique witness to the Name of the One God of Israel. (April 24, 1987, Secretariat for Catholic-Jewish Relations, National Conference of Catholic Bishops).

Rabbi Polish, however, sees the beatification as potentially playing into the hands of the "Jews for Jesus" types, whom, he notes "have taken to propounding the specious idea that one can profess Christian faith and still remain a Jew. . . . The notion of investing that school of thought with the authority of the Pope is profoundly disturbing" to Jews.

Since the responsibility of resolving the age-old question, "Who is a Jew?" lies with the Jewish community and not with the Catholic Church, the matter cannot properly be one for debate between Catholics and Jews. (It might, however, be pointed out that there does exist Orthodox *halachic* opinion that one who is born Jewish does not cease to be a Jew, albeit an apostate Jew, simply by conversion to another faith, even Christianity.)

Likewise, with all respect, I would suggest that Rabbi Polish may here be misinterpreting or, rather, *over*-interpreting the intent of the Holy Father's repeated insistence in his homily during the beatification ceremony on May 1, 1987, that Edith Stein died as "the daughter of a martyred people . . . a Jew . . . a daughter of Israel" and "at the same time" a Catholic martyr who was sent to Auschwitz by the Nazis in reprisal for the strong public protest issued by the Catholic bishops of the Netherlands against the deportation of Dutch Jews.

The Pope's careful phrasing acknowledged clearly the uniqueness of the Jewish tragedy as well as the obvious fact that to the Nazis neither Jewish nor Catholic tradition held any authority. To the Nazis, Edith Stein was simply one more Jew to be executed with bureaucratic efficiency—no more, no less than the rest of the six million. Catholics, then, according to the Bishops' statement cited above, "see the beatification of Edith Stein as a unique occasion for joint Catholic-Jewish reflection and reconciliation. In honoring Edith Stein, the Church wishes to honor all the six million Jewish victims of the Shoah. . . . Catholic veneration will necessarily contribute to a continuing and deepened examination of conscience regarding sins of commission and omission perpetrated by Christians against Jews during the dark years of World War II" (Bishops' Committee for Ecumenical and Interreligious Affairs, National Conference of Catholic Bishops, April 24, 1987).

This Catholic intent and predicted effect, one may say, is almost precisely the opposite of that feared by the Jewish community as articulated by Rabbi Polish. It is at this point as well that our consideration in dialogue of Edith Stein merges with our differing perceptions of the Auschwitz Convent, Polish accurately reflects widespread Jewish opinion, I believe, when he states that Stein's beatification and the move by the Carmelites into the abandoned theater across from Auschwitz are seen "as part of a pattern of Catholic actions . . . leaving the impression that the Catholic Church is trying to appropriate the Holocaust as its own."

Such an allegation, with its almost conspiratorial overtones, will come as a very real surprise to Catholics, not the least among them Catholics involved in dialogue with the Jewish community. Polish explains that for Jews the Shoah is a *tremendum*,

"filled with import as any event in our millenia-long experience."
Just as the Exodus, the Babylonian exile, and the destruction of
the Jerusalem temple were part of the sacred history of the Jewish people, "so do we perceive this tragedy wrought upon the
body of our people as an intrusion of God, ineffably, into human
history . . . a sanctum for us."

As the Catholic Church appropriated into itself the sacred
scriptures and sacred story of the people of Israel, Polish argues,
and as it has continued to absorb "the very location of temples,
shrines and sacred graves of the various native traditions and
cultures it has displaced" over the centuries, so too is it "appro-
priating the holocaust—this sancta of the Jewish people—to itself." The essence of Catholic tradition, a tradition symbolized
by the crucifix, Polish states, is to discern the transcendent
meaning and "redemptive potential" of suffering. Having been
born in an appropriation of the Jewish experience of suffering
and redemption, Polish implies, it may be "inevitable" for the
Church (and not necessarily with invidious intent) to wish to
take as its own this latest chapter in the ongoing Jewish story.
But in the process the particularity of that story as Jewish is once
again lost, once again put to another, Christian purpose.

Polish's brief article touches the deeper levels of the concerns
raised by the Jewish community in the Edith Stein and Auschwitz Convent controversies. The latter problem, of course, has
been happily resolved, through dialogue, with the agreement of
Cardinal Franciscus Macharski of Cracow to move the convent
farther away from the death camp.

Here again Rabbi Polish is, I believe, mistaken in assessing
conscious conspiratorial motivation to the Carmelites' original
intention, which was a move simply, in accordance with traditional Carmelite spirituality, to offer the expiation of a life of
prayer and silence at the site of this greatest evil of our age.

In neither case would these very sincere Catholic expressions
of reverence for Jewish victims have had the dire effect—the
subsuming of the Shoah into Christian categories—that Polish
and many in the Jewish community for whom he speaks seem
to fear. Rather, they would and were intended to have the effect
of supporting the Jewish particularity of the Shoah against those
who would trivialize the Shoah, such as the Communist government of Poland, which seeks to universalize it, and the neo-Nazi

revisionists who seek to deny it. They would have and will stand as perpetual challenges to the Christian conscience and reminders of the evils of anti-Semitism and, indeed, of the ancient Christian "teaching of contempt" so strongly condemned by the Second Vatican Council and repeatedly by Pope John Paul II.

Further, I would argue that Rabbi Polish's case essentially rests upon an assumption that, while widely shared in the Jewish community today, does not adequately present the facts regarding the Jewish origins of the Church. With this point we reach to the very heart of the age-old dialogue and disputation between the Church and the Jewish people. For in denying that born Jews converted to Christianity can in any way be considered to be any longer "Jewish," Rabbi Polish effectively denies the Jewishness of Christianity's founders—Jesus, the twelve apostles, and Paul—and even that of Jesus' mother, Mary. They are not, he very clearly implies, part of the Jewish story. Rather, they formed a group of outsiders who "took over a gamut of Jewish theological constructs and made them its own." Even the sacred scriptures, Polish asserts, "were claimed by the Church, which later asserted that it alone had the ability to interpret them."

But in point of fact the founders of Christianity *were* Jews, members of one of a number of Jewish movements of the time which sought to interpret the traumatic events of the last decades of Second Temple Judaism in the light of their *own* religious—which is to say Jewish—heritage. Only one other Jewish movement of the period ultimately survived the devastation of the destruction of the Second Temple. That was rabbinic Judaism, which Rabbi Polish so ably and so profoundly represents. The counter-question is thus raised between us: "Who is a Christian?"

There is not time in a retrospective such as this to go into the complex theological implications raised by these considerations. They are mentioned here only to illustrate how deeply the events of the past eighteen months have cut into the collective psyches of the Jewish and Catholic communities. Pope John Paul visited the Rome Synagogue to acknowledge the Church's debt to God's people, Israel. There, he affirmed Israel's right to its own title, destiny, and validity from the point of view of Catholic faith, which affirms and joins itself to—but does not claim to replace—

the Jewish people in its understanding of God's call to both the Church and the Jewish people.

But the events of the intervening months, so modest in themselves—the honoring of a victim of Nazi genocide, the establishment of a very small convent (six nuns) and a meeting with the president of Austria—struck chords far deeper than an objective historian or sociologist could have anticipated. Evoked for Jews were bitter memories of ghettos and pogroms, forced conversions and massive expulsions, charges of deicide and blood libel, crusades and inquisitions, all culminating in the Holocaust, a trauma on the body and an attack on the soul of the Jewish people that has only begun to heal, a phenomenon that challenges all that Jews themselves have believed for three millenia, beliefs clung to in the midst of Christian persecution and Christian oppression—events designed, Jews felt, to force them to deny the sacred heritage of their covenant with God.

The intensity of Jewish reaction to the Papal audience with Kurt Waldheim, then, is not to be marvelled at. At stake was, for Jews, survival—not just of themselves as a people, but of the vision of God and of the meaning of human history that it is their sacred duty to proclaim to the world.

Nor should American Jews be surprised at the intensity of American Catholic reaction to the level of rhetoric emanating from the Jewish community in its protests against the Waldheim audience. Catholics, no less than Jews, are an immigrant people in this country. Our experience, like that of Jews, has been one of a religious and ethnic minority, barred from many neighborhoods and schools, clubs and occupations because of our persistence in holding on to our faith and to our religious institutions, especially the papacy.

The Jewish community, I am sure, saw itself as a David taking on a Goliath in denouncing the Pope and in raising various charges against the Papacy, such as the so-called "silence" of Pope Pius XII. Only in the present generation have American Catholics begun to feel free of the "dual loyalty" charges precipitated over the years by our relationship to the See of Rome. (Protestant, nativist America told us quite clearly in many ways that we could only be acceptable as full "Americans" when we forsook "the whore of Babylon.") In the face of stinging columns and full-page newspaper ads attacking the papacy, we Catholics felt ourselves to be a David without a slingshot up against a very angry Goliath. We feared—and, like Jews, not without historical justification—that the Jewish protestations, however legitimate, might trigger a new wave of nativist bigotry against *us*, that Jews might somehow be playing into the hands of forces inimical to both of our communities.

Such fears are very difficult to articulate when one feels oneself to be under attack. Cardinal John O'Connor of New York revealed his great sensitivity to the subtler complexities of the issue when he asked Catholics to be restrained in their responses to the situation. Largely, that and other calls by the American hierarchy were heeded over the hot months of the summer of 1987. Unchecked, the situation could have become much grimmer on our shores than it did in fact.

In retrospect, the miracle of the summer, for all its painfulness, may be that the lines of dialogue and the close bonds developed through dialogue over the last decades on the local level, synagogue to parish, friend to friend, not only remained firm but may have been strengthened by the process. That is the real story that the media, for all its talk of "religious summitry" and negotiations (who "won" more concessions at Castelgondolfo and Miami, etc.), missed entirely.

Communicated to Rome by the American bishops, I firmly believe, it was the significance and steadfastness of those who remained in dialogue that made possible the truly remarkable and unprecedented series of events that have capped this incredible period in the history of Catholic-Jewish relations.

I say this because there are those within both the Catholic and the Jewish communities, and certainly in the media, who want to write the story of this summer as a story of winners and losers—that it was the harshness of the most bitter of Jewish attacks that caused the Holy See to "cave in" to Jewish "pressure." It has been mainly those in our communities who have been least involved in the ongoing dialogue, and who may therefore be said to have a stake in diminishing its significance, who have tried to push this false interpretation of the events.

There are also those in both communities, and in the media, who would tell us that with a master stroke of public relations skill and personal charisma, the Pope charmed the Jewish leadership, dispelling the furor while conceding nothing to Jewish concerns regarding either Waldheim or the State of Israel.

(As an aside it may be asked how the Waldheim affair and the State of Israel are linked. They are not, except insofar as each has become symbolic of Jewish self-identity, so that some would see movement on the latter to be responsive to concerns about the former. Other Jews, however, disagreed with this linkage from the beginning and regarded it as inappropriate and likely to reduce perception of the moral questions about Waldheim to the level of a political ploy. In my opinion, they were right.)

Both of the above spurious interpretations seek to trivialize the significance of the events of the summer. What happened, I can attest as a participant, was much deeper than any "bargaining table" model can possibly discern. What happened was a spiritual event, inexplicable on purely pragmatic grounds. Neither side conceded, nor was asked to concede anything. What took place was that through religious dialogue, tough and challenging on both sides, Jewish and Catholic leaders were able to cut through the rhetoric of outrage and defensiveness to touch, for a moment, each other's hearts. In Buberian terms, what took place in Rome and Castelgandolfo was an I-Thou encounter wrongly interpreted by non-participants and the media as an I-It negotiation of instrumentality. But how, save through poetry, can those of us who were there, whose hearts were touched and changed, explain an essentially spiritual encounter? The bare facts can only hint at these deeper realities.

We were, to be sure, quite close to despair by the first week in August. In fact, it was on the very day that Bishop William Keeler, the chair of the Bishops' Committee for Ecumenical and Interreligious Affairs, whose full role in the events may never be known, had set up a telephone conference with staff and Bishop Ernest Unterkoefler of Charleston, S.C., to discuss cancelling the Miami meeting between the Pope and Jewish leaders, that we learned from Rabbi Mordecai Waxman, chair of the International Jewish Committee for Interreligious Consultations (IJCIC), that he had received a phone call from Cardinal Johannes Willebrands of the Holy See's Commission for Religious Relations with the Jews. Cardinal Willebrands' call was to invite IJCIC representatives to Rome for a full-day meeting to discuss all substantive issues of the current agenda, with meetings with Cardinal Casaroli of the Secretary of State and then with the Holy Father to follow the next day.

Soon thereafter, we learned from the Apostolic Nunciature in Washington that the Pope would be responding to the gift of a book sent to him by Archbishop John May of St. Louis, President of the NCCB.[2] The letter was to address very movingly the Pope's own profound understanding of the meaning and significance of the Shoah. Drawing on his earlier remarks to the tiny remnant of the Jewish community of Warsaw on June 14, 1987, the Pope hailed the Jewish memory of the Shoah "as a warning, a witness, and a silent cry . . . before the eyes of the Church, of all peoples and of all nations." He acknowledged "the indifference and sometimes resentment" harbored by Christians against Jews in various periods, and called for joint "historical and religious studies" on the Shoah by Catholics and Jews working together, a theme to which he was to return both in Castelgandolfo and, more formally, in Miami.

The meetings took place, as scheduled, in Rome. I must say that the discussions were marked by a candor, bluntness, and sense of urgency not always typical of exchanges on such a level. The Jewish agenda was set forth strongly and with no sense of inhibition, leaving a deep and lasting impression on the Catholic participants, certainly on myself. Ongoing structures for better communications between the Holy See and world Jewry were worked out and the Commission announced its intention to prepare a document on the Shoah and anti-Semitism.

On the Catholic side, though the point is not in any way to be "paired" with anti-Semitism, which is a unique and uniquely dangerous phenomenon, the pain and hurt of the Catholic community at aspects of the summer's rhetoric attacking the papacy and raising the spectre of renewed anti-Catholicism, especially in the United States, was communicated to the Jewish leaders.

The meeting with the Pope, of course, was the high point. The meeting was unusual, first of all, in the informality of its format. We sat in a circle around a small table bearing a text of the Hebrew Scriptures. The meeting opened with a brief recita-

---

2. The book is a collection of addresses by *John Paul II on Jews and Judaism, 1979–1986*, co-edited by Eugene Fisher and Leon Klenicki (Washington, D.C., 1987). The Pope called the book a "significant undertaking."

tion of a psalm in Hebrew and Latin, followed by summaries by Cardinal Willebrands and Rabbi Waxman of the previous day's intense discussions and agreements. The Pope welcomed us in his turn and remarked on the significance of Jewish-Catholic dialogue, citing the area of science and human values as one of many areas of shared concern on which we need to work together for the sake of all humanity.

Then the floor was open. The nine Jewish delegates, one after another, spoke their hearts personally, respectfully, yet forcefully to the Pope. His response was not on the level of details or explanations or defensiveness, but directly to the heart of the concerns. He recalled his youth in Poland and his Jewish classmates and friends who perished in the death camps, the virtual destruction of the great Jewish community of Poland. He reaffirmed his Warsaw statement and his belief that the Jewish witness to the Shoah constitutes one contemporary aspect of the "particular vocation" of the Jewish people today, "showing you to be still the heirs of that election to which God is faithful." In that Warsaw address, which he termed "spontaneous,"[3] the pope not only acknowledged the uniqueness of the Jewish tragedy, but also acknowledged as a Pole that "one might say that you suffered it also on behalf of those who were to have been exterminated." Such an acknowledgment of the priority of another people's suffering over one's own is truly remarkable, and offers a sure guide to those Catholics who may be restless with the Jewish community's compulsion to tell their story while the generation of tl e survivors, now aging, is still alive to witness to it. For my part, I believe it is our responsibility as Catholics to tell our own story, which is related to yet different from that of the Jews, since Catholics can be numbered among both the victims and the executioners in those terrible years.

The Pope then offered a meditation on the Exodus of the Jewish people from Egypt as a source of hope, of the possibility of goodness emerging out of even the awesome evil of the Shoah. I think that Rabbi Polish, had he heard the Pope grappling in such an authentic manner with the deepest implications of the Holocaust, would have been reassured in his concerns regarding

3. While given on June 14, the Warsaw address was not published in *L'Osservatore Romano* until August 3.

the Church's alleged intention to "appropriate" the Shoah into its own categories. There was no hint of such a move in the Pope's unrehearsed allocution. To the contrary, as in Warsaw, the Pope sought only to "unite his voice" with the primary witness of the Jews, and to put the weight of his office and his personal integrity behind it.

A number of years ago a Catholic thinker deeply influenced by Martin Buber published a small volume which had great significance in my life. It was entitled *The Miracle of Dialogue*. I have not read it in many years and do not know whether I would agree with all its points today. But the meeting at Castelgandolfo that I was privileged to attend testifies to the aptness of the title. Deeply involved as I have been in discussing (and arguing and pleading and praying) with both Catholics and Jews on all levels over a summer of the most intense dialogue between our two peoples that has occurred certainly in the last two decades since the Vatican Council and perhaps in two millenia, I can only marvel at the workings of the Spirit. Somehow, through all the pain and confrontation, a moment of true dialogue was reached, impossible though that would have seemed to any "objective" observer in, say, the first week of August. That is a true miracle.

Many hurts and confusions remain, however. The path we have embarked upon together, to study the Shoah and anti-Semitism, is fraught with sensitivities. The process will be a lengthy one, but in the end a healing one. As Cardinal Willebrands stated in the name of the Church during his address to the Jewish leaders on the night before their meeting with the Holy Father in Miami: "The task facing us is a hard thing. But it is the right thing to do. And we shall do it." That statement encapsulates, for me, the central meaning of the last eighteen months of Catholic-Jewish relations.

The addresses exchanged by Rabbi Waxman and the Holy Father in Miami serve to distill much of what has been communicated between us over this past eighteen months. I would urge careful study of both texts in Jewish-Catholic dialogue groups across the country, in order to understand the essence of what has occurred. The eighteen months of controversy has given renewed life to our relationship and perhaps moved us a qualitative step toward reconciliation and the potential of joint witness and collaboration in *tikkun olam*, the mending of the world. Of that only time will tell. The great saying of *Pirke Aboth* sums up our present challenge: "It is not your part to finish the task, yet you are not free to desist from it" (2:15). To that I say, "Amen!"

CHAPTER THIRTEEN

Redefining the Role of Jews and Judaism in Christian Theological Education: A Continuing Challenge

John T. Pawlikowski

In the early stages of the Christian-Jewish dialogue, education was one of the primary concerns. This was especially so on the Christian side of the table. Certain studies focusing on the representation of Jews and Judaism (as well as other religious and racial "outgroups") in Protestant and Catholic educational materials were undertaken respectively, at Yale University by the late Dr. Bernhard Olson[1] and by a team of Catholic sisters through the sociology department of St. Louis University.[2] These studies were instrumental in launching the process of constructively reframing the churches' understanding of the theological relationship between themselves and the Jewish people. This process continues today.

In the initial years of this effort, the focus was almost entirely on removing from the Christian consciousness venerable negative characterizations of the Jewish community that have been shown by sound scholarly research to have no factual basis.

Fr. Pawlikowski's paper, while not presented at the 1988 Symposium on Fear, provides valuable practical insights on how the results of Jewish-Christian dialogue may be implemented. We are pleased and honored to include it in these proceedings.

1. B.E. Olson, *Faith and Prejudice* (New Haven, Conn., 1963).
2. J.T. Pawlikowski, *Catechetics and Prejudice: How Catholic Teaching Materials View Jews, Protestants and Racial Minorities* (New York, 1973). For an update on the Jewish findings, cf. E. J. Fisher, *Faith Without Prejudice* (New York, 1977).

Among those negative images are the "deicide" charge, the blood libel accusation, the characterization of the Pharisees as "hypocrites," and a host of more modern social stereotypes. To a large extent, at least in mainline Christianity, this effort has achieved its major objectives.

Early on in the dialogue, the Jewish community also developed an interest in the educational reform, as evidenced in the studies sponsored by the American Jewish Committee at Dropsie College in Philadelphia.[3] The results of this investigation, however—which never appeared in book form—did not have the same overall impact in Jewish educational circles as their Christian counterparts had among Christians. To be fair, this was due in part to the nature of the results, which revealed little stereotyping of Christianity in Jewish materials in comparison with the Christian texts. The major problem uncovered in the Jewish materials was *omission* of information on Christians and their churches which, while troubling in a pluralistic society, is hardly on par with classical anti-Semitism. Recently, there have been efforts in some Israeli texts to improve the depiction of Christianity,[4] particularly the image of Jesus as a faithful interpreter of the Jewish Torah. And Hebrew Union College continues to require that its rabbinical candidates for the Reform movement do some study of the New Testament. On the whole, however, interfaith education remains an underdeveloped area on the Jewish side.

Turning back to the issue of Christian responsibility in the area of education in the light of the Christian-Jewish dialogue, it is important to recognize that we in the churches are now entering the second, and more difficult, phase of the process. Ridding our teaching materials, particularly at the primary and secondary school levels, of the classic stereotypes of Jews and Judaism (which by and large, we have done well) was comparatively easy. We must now face up to the implications of Karl Barth's oft-quoted remark that dialogue with Jews is in many respects the most fundamental of all dialogues in which the Christian churches are engaged. Barth did not mean to disparage the continuing importance of inter-Christian ecumenism nor to

---

3. B.D. Weinryb and D. Garnick, *Summary of Findings. The Dropsie College Study of Jewish Textbooks: Jewish School Textbooks and Intergroup Relations* (New York, 1970).
4. P.E. Lapide, "Jesus in Israeli Schoolbooks," *JES* 10.3 (Summer, 1973) 515–31.

deny the significance of the Church's outreach to religious traditions other than Judaism. Rather, he was making the point, which remains as valid today as it was in Barth's time, that in thoroughly rethinking its relationship with the Jewish people Christianity will necessarily come face-to-face with its own basic self-identity—which so often in the past has been predicated directly on the displacement of the Sinai covenant by the covenant in Christ. Christian-Jewish dialogue, in this difficult second phase upon which we are now embarked, if it works well, will in the end enable Christianity to relate more constructively not only to the Jewish people but to communities of other faiths as well.

Theological education remains the key to success or failure in this second phase. Movement must begin here if the more popular levels of Christian education are to change significantly. The process of cleansing Christian texts of unwarranted negative images of Jews and Judaism could happen at the primary and secondary levels rather independently of theological education. The expression of a fundamentally new Christian self-identity vis-à-vis the Jewish people, however, cannot be developed by Christian educators at the primary and secondary levels alone. Because of the extreme interfaith and *intra*faith sensitivity involved, such radical reconstruction should be initiated and guided by national and international leaders in theological education at the highest levels of experience, understanding and expertise.

The challenges facing Christian theological education in this dawning second phase of the dialogue come from several quarters. The first originates in the realm of recent biblical scholarship, both in terms of the Hebrew Scriptures (or "First Testament") and the Christian Scriptures (or "Second Testament").

With regard to the Hebrew Scriptures, there is ample evidence that a major shift of emphasis is underway. More and more scholars are recognizing the value of studying these texts in their own right and not merely as a backdrop for the New Testament. The view, which has prevailed in most Christian churches for centuries, that the "Old Testament" materials are intended merely as a "foil" or a "prelude" to the inherently superior teachings of Jesus is gradually receding. Surely the Hebrew Scriptures remain important for an adequate understanding of the New Testament. And the debate whether the term "Old Testament" should be dropped from the Christian vocabulary continues unabated, with some Jewish scholars such as Jon Levenson insisting that Christians and Jews will always see these Scriptures with different eyes.[5] But it is now becoming apparent to scholars that the Hebrew Scriptures have revelatory insights that Jesus implicitly shared without explicitly commenting upon them publicly in his preaching and ministry. Thus, for today's Christian, it may be said that without deep immersion into the spirit and content of the Hebrew Scriptures the Christian theological student is left with a truncated version of Jesus' message and hence an emasculated version of biblical spirituality.

We also see some signs that Christian scholars beyond the world of biblical studies are catching up with these developments and beginning to incorporate them into their expressions of Christian faith. One example is the constructive use of the Hebrew Scriptures by certain liberation theologians, particularly Gustavo Gutierrez and Jose Miguez Bonino, in framing their understanding of God and Christ for the contemporary Christian. While their formulations remain questionable in certain respects from the standpoint of the Christian-Jewish dialogue, their willingness to take seriously the original covenantal traditions and, in the case of Gutierrez, to turn to Job as a faith model for our day, represent important advances. This is even more so with respect to the positive use of The Book of Genesis for a theology of human responsibility in certain recent Catholic social statements, particularly Pope John Paul II's *Laborem Exercens* and the U.S. Bishops' Pastoral Letter on the U.S. Economy.

Despite these recent signs of an incorporation of the new heremeutical approach to the Hebrew Scriptures on the part of Christian biblical scholars into a broader theological framework, this remains largely virgin territory. The major areas of Christian theological education—systematics, ethics, spirituality, and preaching—still remain virtually untouched by this new biblical outlook on the role of the Hebrew Scriptures in Christian identity. Even in the traditionally "Catholic" areas of liturgy and sacramental theology, where the use of the Hebrew Scriptures has

---

5. Cf. J.D. Levenson, "Why Jews Are Not Interested in Biblical Theology," in J. Neusner, B.A. Levine, and E.S. Frerichs, eds., *Judaic Perspectives on Ancient Israel* (Philadelphia,

been more frequent over the years, the controlling rubric has still been the ultimately prejudicial one of "foreshadowing." If the Hebrew Scriptures are to move to center stage in the faith expression of Christians—as they were for Jesus himself—then those scriptures must begin to assume the status of primary— not merely peripheral—resources in the overall theological curriculum. We might not be prepared to say with James Sanders that "Without Torah the Christian gospel is hollow, gutless, and nothing but a form of hellenistic Palestinian cynicism"[6] or with Andre LaCocque that the New Testament is merely one among several possible commentaries on the Hebrew Scriptures which remain the central core of faith for the Christian[7]; but surely we must be prepared minimally to embrace the words of Raymond Brown, who has written that

> Too often for Christians the proclamation of the word means the proclamation of the Jesus story. Yet that story can be easily misconstrued and distorted if one does not recite the story of Israel.[8]

Clearly the new message is beginning to break through the formidable barriers of Christian tradition. The recognition is growing that the New Testament remains inadequate in outlook in some areas when taken by itself as the basis of Christian faith.

The contemporary dialogue with Jews and their tradition has begun to impact even more profoundly on New Testament interpretation. It is no exaggeration to say that, however quietly, a genuine revolution is well underway in New Testament scholarship that is beginning to influence theological education as well. This revolution is being fueled by our enhanced understanding of Hebrew and Aramaic and a greater exposure to Jewish materials from Judaism's Second Temple period (the "intertestamental" period, in more conventional Christian terms). We are presently witnessing a rapid end to the dominant hold of early "Religionsgeschicte" which strongly emphasized the Hellenistic setting of Pauline Christianity as well as its later modified incarnation in Rudolf Bultmann and some of his disciples such as Ernst Kasemann and Helmut Koester. This exegetical approach to the New

---

1987) 281–307. Also cf. R. Brooks and J.J. Collins, eds., *Hebrew Bible or Old Testament? Studying the Bible in Judaism and Christianity* (Notre Dame, Ind., 1990).

6. J.A. Sanders, "Rejoicing in the Gifts," *Explorations* 3.1 (1989) 1, 4.

7. A. LaCocque, *But As For Me: The Question of Election in the Life of God's People Today* (Atlanta, 1979).

8. R. Brown, *Biblical Exegesis and Church Doctrine* (New York, 1985)p. 138.

Testament had the effect of eroding Jesus' concrete ties to biblical and Second Temple Judaism. The scholars associated with this approach tended to portray Jesus in excessively "universalist" terms which, whether intended by them or not, frequently paved the way for theological anti-Judaism.

In the last decade or so we have seen a profound shift in New Testament scholarship. This movement has been led by the likes of W. D. Davies, E. P. Sanders, James Charlesworth, Douglas Hare, Daniel Harrington, Robin Scroggs, and others. The list continues to grow. While certainly not in agreement on all aspects of Jesus' relationship to Judaism, these exegetes share the conviction that Jesus must be returned to his Jewish milieu if we are to properly understand his message. The title of one of James Charlesworth's books says it all: *Jesus Within Judaism*.[9] Arthur J. Droge, in a review of E. P. Sanders' volume *Jesus and Judaism*, speaks of the impact of this movement in rather blunt terms: "Like Professor Sanders, I take this to be a positive development—a sign that New Testament studies is finally emerging from its 'Bultmannian captivity.'"[10]

No doubt we will continue to see significant refinements in the positions advanced by these exegetes, particularly on specific points such as Jesus' relationship to Pharisaic Judaism. Major source problems will guarantee ambiguity in some areas indefinitely. But there is little question that the growing consensus among New Testament scholars has transformed the churches' understanding of Jesus' links to Judaism when compared with that of even a decade ago. Robin Scroggs has summarized the principal facets of this scholarly consensus in a way that is worth quoting at length:

1. The movement begun by Jesus and continued after his death in Palestine can best be described as a reform movement within Judaism. . . . There is no evidence during this period that it attempted to break with its matrix.
2. The Pauline missionary movement, as Paul understood it,

---

9. J.H. Charlesworth, *Jesus Within Judaism: New light from Exciting Archaeological Discoveries*, ABRL 1 (New York, 1988); see also J.H. Charlesworth, ed., *Jews and Christians: Exploring the Past, Present, and Future* (SGAJC 1; New York, 1990) and *Jesus' Jewishness: Exploring the Place of Jesus Within Early Judaism* (SGAJC 2; New York, 1991).
10. A.J. Droge, "The Facts about Jesus: Some Thoughts on E.P. Sanders' *Jesus and Judaism*," *Criterion* 26.1 (Winter, 1987) 15.

is a Jewish mission which includes Gentiles as the proper object of God's call to his people.

3. There is, . . . prior to the aftermath of the war against the Romans, no such thing as Christianity. . . . Believers in Jesus did not have a *self-understanding* of themselves as a religion over against Judaism.

4. After the war, the two communities gradually separate.

5. The later writings of the New Testament all show signs of this movement toward separation, but they also always demonstrate some form of dialogue with the Jewish matrix.[11]

This understanding of the profundity of Jesus' debt to Judaism is beginning to appear even at the level of church leadership. Cardinal Carlo Martini of Milan, a biblical scholar of prominence in his own right, is among those Christian leaders who have spoken out clearly and decisively on this matter. Martini has written that "Jesus is fully Jewish, the apostles are Jewish, and one cannot doubt their attachment to the traditions of their forefathers."[12]

There is another phase to this process of legitimate "re-Judaization" of the New Testament. It involves the actual translating and annotating of the original Greek text. Many students in theological education today are not sufficiently skilled in Greek to rely to any significant degree on the original text. This is certainly true for the people whom they will teach later in academic or in less formal, pastoral settings. Hence, English versions of the New Testament, which increasingly are published with notes and introductions, have become crucial to the effort of restoring Jesus to his authentic Jewish context. Many previous and current translations fail in this task, even leading the reader at times to an anti-Jewish interpretation of Jesus' message. For the past several years, however, a group of prominent New Testament scholars and outside consultants under the leadership of Professor James Charlesworth and the sponsorship of the American Interfaith Institute has been at work on an English version of the New Testament that will finally show the pro-

---

11. R. Scroggs, "The Judaizing of the New Testament," *CTSR* 76.1 (Winter, 1986) 42–43.
12. Card. C.M. Martini, "Christianity and Judaism: A Historical and Theological Overview," in Charlesworth, *Jews and Christians*, p. 19.

nounced Jewish character of Jesus and early Christianity. It will be available soon.

There is also need for major revisions in other theological disciplines as a result of this exegetical shift. By and large most of the other areas still are operating on the basis of the older exegetical approach developed by Bultmann. This approach, evident especially in systematic theology, accounts for a widespread, often subtle theological anti-Judaism in the work of many contemporary Christian systematic theologians, including several central figures in liberation theology, such as Leonardo Boff and Jon Sobrino.[13]

The revolution in understanding the Jewish-Christian relationship, launched by the biblical exegetes, must begin to penetrate the whole of theology. Until we reach this point, the theological student will become increasingly frustrated over basic conflicts in the way the relationship is presented in New Testament courses and the way it is described in the remainder of the theological curriculum, in which Christian self-identity still is largely based on the sense of the church as the total replacement for the outmoded, spiritually inferior, convenanted people of Israel.

Significant work has been done by Christian theologians in several countries specifically on restating the relationship between the church and the Jewish People theologically in light of the new exegesis. Prominent names include Paul van Buren,[14] A. Roy Eckardt,[15] Franz Mussner,[16] Bernard Dupuy, O.P.,[17] Marcel

---

13. Cf. J.T. Pawlikowski, *Christ in the Light of the Christian-Jewish Dialogue* (New York, 1982) pp. 59–73.

14. P. van Buren, *Discerning the Way* (New York, 1980); *A Christian Theology of the Jewish People* (New York, 1983); *A Theology of the Jewish Christian Reality, Part III: Christ in Context* (San Francisco, 1988). Also cf. "The Context of Jesus Christ: Israel," *RIL* 3.4 (Summer, 1986) 31–50.

15. Cf. A.R. Eckardt with A.L. Eckardt, *Long Night's Journey Into Day: Life and Faith After the Holocaust* (Detroit, 1982); A.R. Eckardt, *Jews and Christians: The Contemporary Meeting* (Bloomington, Ind., 1986); A.R. Eckardt, "Salient Christian-Jewish Issues of Today," in Charlesworth, *Jews and Christians*, pp. 151–77.

16. F. Mussner, *Tractate on the Jews: The Significance of Judaism for Christian Faith*, trans. by L. Swidler, (Philadelphia, 1984) and "From Jesus the 'Prophet' to Jesus the 'Son'," in A. Falaturi, J.J. Petuchowski, and W. Strolz, eds., *Three Ways to the One God: The Faith Experience in Judaism, Christianity and Islam* (New York, 1987) pp. 76–85.

17. B. Dupuy et al., *Juifs et Chretiens: Un vis-à-vis permanent*, Publications Des Facultes Universitaires Saint-Louis, 42 (Brussels, 1988).

Dubois, O.P.,[18] Rosemary Ruether.[19] Pope John Paul II has also contributed significantly to this reconstruction through his theology of "intimate bonding" between Jews and Christians at the very core of their identity, which he has developed in several of his major addresses.[20] I have also contributed to the discussion in several works.[21]

Certainly, among these various Christian contributors to this historic process, no consensus has been reached as to how the new theology of the Jewish-Christian relationship should in fact be expressed in the churches. But there is general agreement that the old "displacement" or "supercessionist" theologies, which fundamentally denied any constructive role to the Jewish covenant after the Christ Event, simply must go. So must any Christian perspective which regards the Jewish covenant as simply "preparatory" to the covenant in Christ. In the new thinking, the Jewish covenant is not displaced nor is it a mere preparatory stage of a process now fulfilled. Rather, it retains its integrity and continues to hold an important place in the process of human salvation, however difficult it may be at this juncture to articulate precisely the meaning of its role in contrast to that of Christianity.

Another point that needs to be raised regarding the area of systematic theology in theological education has to do with the growing importance of feminist thought and its portrayal of Jesus' relationship to Judaism. In a study of Christian theological education prepared by Joseph Hough and John Cobb we find the following statement:

> The church inherited from Judasim a way of thinking of deity from which feminine elements had been largely excluded. In the origins of the new movement, social conventions were strained. Jesus treated women with notable respect as persons. Women

---

18. M. Dubois, "Christian Reflections on the Holocaust," *SIDIC* 7.2 (1974) 10–16 and *Recontres avec le Judaisme en Israel* (Jerusalem, 1983).
19. R. Ruether, *Faith and Fratricide: The Theological Roots of Anti-Semitism*, with intro. by G. Baum (New York, 1974); also cf. *Disputed Questions: On Being a Christian* (Nashville, 1982).
20. Cf. E. Fisher and L. Klenicki, eds., *Pope John Paul II on Jews and Judaism, 1979–1986* (Washington, D.C., 1987).
21. Cf. J.T. Pawlikowski, *Christ in the Light of the Christian-Jewish Dialogue* and *Jesus and the Theology of Israel* (Wilmington, Del., 1989).

played important roles in the earliest Christian communities, and
Paul saw that in Christ there is neither male nor female.[22]

Certainly this viewpoint, which has become rather standard fare
in feminist theological circles, has truthful aspects to it. But the
seemingly monolithic view of Judaism at the time of Jesus that
lies behind such a statement needs to be critiqued. Several Jewish and Christian feminist authors have taken issue with what
they regard as perilously close to a repetition of some of the
classical, stereotypical ways of relating Jesus to the Jewish community of his day. The Jewish community of this period was a
far more complex reality, as the new exegesis has demonstrated.
The evidence is not overwhelming that Jesus broke with *all* Jewish movements of the time in the way he welcomed and affirmed
the dignity of women. We must be wary of building our much
needed feminist and liberation Christian theologies once more
on the backs of Jews. Not only would this be false and unhistorical, but it would rob such theologies of some useful positive
resources from the Jewish biblical and Second Temple traditions.

Finally, in terms of systematic theology, there is need to pay attention to what some Jewish scholars are saying about the nature
of first-century Judaism and about the relationship of the Jewish
community to the new emergent church. When Jacob Neusner, for
example, posits the notions, correctly in my judgment, about the
multiplicity of Judaisms throughout Jewish history, including in
the first century C.E., Christian scholars ought to take notice.[23]
For if Neusner is correct, then it will prove much more difficult to
speak about the theology of the Jewish-Christian relationship in
a way that assumes a certain basic homogeneity in first-century
Judaism. If this basic homogeneity is in fact missing, then we
ought to speak in more modest and nuanced terms about the relationship. And when Irving Greenberg[24] describes Pharisaic-rab-
binic Judaism as a more advanced stage of Judaism (in comparison
to biblical Judaism with which Christianity has most in common

22. J.C. Hough, Jr. and J.B. Cobb, Jr., *Christian Identity and Theological Education* (Chico,
Calif., 1985) p. 63.
23. J. Neusner, *Death and Birth of Judaism: The Impact of Christianity, Secularism and the
Holocaust on Jewish Faith* (New York, 1987).
24. I. Greenberg, "The Relationship of Judaism and Christianity: Toward a New Organic
Model," in E.J. Fisher, A.J. Rudin, and M.H. Tanenbaum, eds., *Twenty Years of Jewish-
Catholic Relations* (New York, 1986).

in his judgment) or Hayim Perelmuter[25] speaks of Jews and Christians as two new, distinctive "sibling" groups, coming out of biblical Judaism, then—inevitably—the nature of discussion about the theological dimensions of Jewish-Christian relationship is affected.

Other implications for theological education flow from the developments in Christian-Jewish relations over the last several decades. I would like now to examine some of them briefly. All, in the final analysis, are rooted in the sense of a permanent link between the church and the Jewish people, a link that affects the church at the level of fundamental identity.

The first such implication is the incorporation of Jewish resources, both biblical and extra-biblical, in a central way in the theological curriculum. If we truly believe what the churches have increasingly been saying in a variety of documents, then it is impossible for us to express the theological and ethical meaning of the Christian covenantal relationship itself without explicit reference to the ways in which various Jewish scholars have interpreted covenantal responsibility throughout the ages, including the present day. This includes the little-known Oriental Jewish tradition, whose significance for the encounter has increased with the enhanced emphasis on a multicultural approach to Christian theology. Contemporary Jewish reflections on the meaning of such basic religious issues as the significance of the God of the covenant today or Jewish deliberations on such pressing ethical issues as abortion and peace assume an indispensable status. It is no longer a question of including such Jewish materials in a course because of an interreligious sensitivity or a commitment to pluralism, as important as these values might be; they need to be included across the board because in the light of the renewed theology of the Christian-Jewish relationship they have become integral church resources, not merely materials from a parallel religious community to be incorporated in a peripheral way.

When one considers the Jewish community in the twentieth century, the experience of two events—separate but still profoundly related—stand out in the shaping of its ethos. These

---

25. H.G. Perelmuter, *Siblings: Rabbinic Judaism and Early Christianity at their Beginnings* (New York, 1989).

events are the *Shoah* (the Holocaust) and the rebirth of the State of Israel. While significant, even profound differences remain among Jewish scholars regarding the ultimate significance of these two events for contemporary Jewish self-identity, virtually all regard them as central questions.

There is no question that Christian anti-Semitism provided an indispensable seedbed for Nazism. That particularly virulent and widespread strain of anti-Semitism was responsible for making Jews the primary and special victims of the Third Reich's wider onslaught against humanity and for eliciting the support, whether active or passive, of thousands of ordinary Christians. Yet, in the final analysis, the Nazi plan was profoundly anti-Christian as well. The Nazi leaders envisioned themselves as heads of a new social order, freed finally from the moral restraints of both Judaism and Christianity and "cleansed" of all unfit human groups including the Jews, the Gypsies, the mentally or phyically impaired, and German-born homosexuals, with subjugation of the Slavic peoples, especially the Polish nation.

The Nazis were convinced it was now possible to reshape human society, perhaps humanity itself, to a degree never thought possible in the past. Death now became viewed as a means of resolving the basic problems of human existence. As the late Israeli historian Uriel Tal had maintained, the "Final Solution" was intent on responding to a universal crisis of humankind. It sought to produce an all-encompassing transformation of human values. At the heart of this transformation was the loosening of the "shackles" of the classical vision of God with its attendant notions of moral responsibility, redemption, sin, and revelation. David Tracy is quite correct in insisting that the fundamental challenge raised by the Holocaust, for Christian and Jew alike, is our continued ability to speak of a divine presence in history:

> As far as I am aware, the ultimate theological issue, the understanding of God, has yet to receive much reflection from Catholic theologians. And yet, as Schleiermacher correctly insisted, the doctrine of God can never be "another" doctrine for theology, but must pervade all doctrines. Here Jewish theology in its reflections

on the reality of God since the *tremendum* of the Holocaust, has
led the way for all serious theological reflection.[26]

David Tracy has also pursued other theological implications of
the Holocaust for Christianity. Outside the fundamental challenge it presents in terms of the God reality, the most decisive
impact of the Holocaust according to Tracy, is to be found in the
area of theological methodology. After the Holocaust, neither a
purely metaphysical approach to theology nor a mere emphasis
on historical consciousness as abstract concept will suffice. Such
concrete historical events as the Holocaust and the emergence
of the State of Israel thus assume central importance for the
Christian theologian.[27] Since methodological choices influence
basic curricular design, the significance of Tracy's remark for
theological education is obvious.

Several other Christian theologians view this return to concrete historical methodology in theology as the primary impact
that the contemporary Christian-Jewish dialogue has had on the
church's self-awareness. Names deserving mention in this regard are Johannes Baptist Metz, Rosemary Ruether, Rebecca
Chopp, and Elisabeth Schüssler-Fiorenza.

Metz has addressed the issue in several works. In *The Emergent
Church*, he assigns Jews and Christians to "an alliance belonging
to the heart of *saving history.*" But immediately he warns that
this new alliance must not "serve as a screen for a triumphalistic
metaphysic of salvation which never learns from catastrophes
nor finds in them a cause for conversion. . . ."[28] Speaking somewhat more generally in an essay in a volume of *Concilium* devoted to the Holocaust, Metz adds that the experience of the
Shoah necessitates a shift in Christian theology from a "system
concepts" approach to a "subject concepts" approach. He writes:

> This demand for a subject-based rather than a system-based kind
> of Christian theological concern is not the expression of a privatis-
> tic or individualistic form of theological consciousness. It is the
> natural consequence of "historical consciousness" in the field of

26. D. Tracy, "Religious Values after the Holocaust: A Catholic View," in A.J. Peck, ed.,
Jews and Christians after the Holocaust (Philadelphia, 1982) p. 101.
27. D. Tracy, "The Interpretation of Theological Texts after the Holocaust," unpublished
lecture, International Conference on the Holocaust, Indiana University, Bloomington,
Fall 1982.
28. J. Metz, *The Emergent Church* (New York, 1981) pp. 19–20.

theology—demanded of us, expected of us and granted to us in
the face of Auschwitz. Even this . . . demand may show that here
. . . it is not a matter of a revision of Christian theology with
regard to Judaism, but a matter of the revision of Christian theology itself.[29]

Rosemary Ruether has turned her attention primarily to the
implications of the long history of Christian anti-Semitism of
which the Holocaust, in her estimation, is the climax. What has
produced that history, as it has produced other forms of church
collaboration with human exploitation (such as colonialism, sex-
ism, and gender discrimination) is the erroneous assumption at
the very outset of Christian history that Christ's triumphalistic
resurrection has moved the church beyond the realm of human
history, that it was now superior to all other communities, religious or otherwise. Christians were on God's right side whereas
the "rejectionist" Jews, still mired in history, stood on God's left.
Hence Ruether's oft-quoted remark that theological anti-Judaism
is the left hand of Christology.

Ruether joins other Christian theologians involved in the dialogue in rejecting any claims about the messianic age having
appeared with the coming of Christ. The realities of the human
condition will not permit such an assertion. If Christianity continues to insist that the term "Christ" signifies the messiah of
Israel's hope, then it must likewise appreciate that

> from the standpoint of that faith of Israel itself, there is no possi-
> bility of talking about the messiah having come (much less of
> having come two thousand years ago, with all the evil history that
> has reigned from that time until this) when the reign of God has
> not come.[30]

Ruether argues that Judaism cannot envision a separation between the coming of the Messiah and the appearance of the
messianic age. The two are simultaneous. Christianity adopted
the traditional Jewish belief in a messianic era of the future. The
problem is that the church transposed into the realm of human

---

29. J. Metz, "Facing the Jews: Christian Theology after Auschwitz," in E. Schüssler-
Fiorenza and D. Tracy, eds., *The Holocaust as Interruption* (*Concilium* 175.5; Edinburgh,
1984) p. 27.
30. R. Ruether, "An Invitation to Jewish-Christian Dialogue: In What Sense Can We Say
that Jesus Was 'The Christ'?" *Ecumenist* 10 (January/February, 1972) 17.

history what for Jews remained future. Christianity declared that evil had been overcome decisively through the Christian Event. The end result of this was a false solution to the ultimate crisis facing human existence, the crisis that divides the historical from the eschatological. Both Christian anti-Semitism and the Western nations' penchant for political totalitarianism and imperialism have their roots ultimately in this unwarranted assumption by the church of eschatological fulfillment.

Elisabeth Schüssler-Fiorenza also takes the "return to history" theme as a central implication of the *Shoah* for subsequent theology. We cannot speak of the suffering of the victims of the Holocaust as a "theological metaphor" for all human suffering. Instead, that suffering "must be named in its political particularity. The ideological heart of Nazi-fascism was racism, its ideological catch-word was *"Untermensch,"* the less than human, the subhuman being."[31] Nazism represented an extreme example of the Western capitalistic form of patriarchy, with origins in Aristotelian philosophy and subsequent mediation through Christian theology. The same ancient philosophical system, imported into Christian theology by Thomas Aquinas and others, that first subjugated women as people with "subhuman" nature, combined with religiously rooted bigotry and a new bio-theology to produce the Nazi cataclysm in Europe.

For Schüssler-Fiorenza, overcoming biblical and theological anti-Judaism becomes the first step in the complicated, rather wrenching process of cleansing Western society of its patriarchal basis. In an essay co-authored with David Tracy, she writes:

> Christian biblical theology must recognize that its articulation of anti-Judaism in the NT goes hand in hand with its gradual adaptation to Greco-Roman patriarchal society. Christian as well as Jewish theology must cease to proclaim a God made in the image and likeness of Man. It can do so only when it mourns the "loss" of women's contributions in the past and present and rejects our theological "dehumanization." Moreover, white Christian and Jewish theology must promote the full humanity of all non-Western peoples and at the same time struggle against racism wherever it is at work. In short the memory of the Holocaust must

---

31. E. Schüssler-Fiorenza, "The Holocaust as Interruption and the Christian Return into History," in Schüssler-Fiorenza and Tracy, *The Holocaust as Interruption*, p. 36.

"interrupt" all forms of Western patriarchal theology if the legacies of the dead are not to be in vain.[32]

Yet another theologian who views the major significance of the Holocaust as the summons for Christian theology to return to the concrete historical matrix of its original Jewish roots, in which the human person in history—especially the victimized and suffering human person—becomes the focal point of theological discourse and education, is Rebecca Chopp. She lays particular stress on the profound connection she detects between Holocaust literature and the liberation theology. She terms this relationship unique among Western religious writings. Both groups of writings create new theological space, which in turn forces upon Christianity a fundamental reworking of its theological framework. Holocaust literature and liberation theology, as she interprets them, both agree on one foundational assumption:

> . . . the challenge to contemporary thought and action is the challenge of massive suffering. Christianity and Christian theology can no longer be content with addressing suffering on an individual level from Christian texts, symbols and traditions but must criticize, interrupt and transform both action and reflection in light of past, prevailing and potential events of massive suffering. Liberation theology and Holocaust literature interrupt and disrupt Christianity and Christian theology with the question and the quest "who is the human subject that suffers history?"[33]

She goes on to add that both liberation theology and Holocaust literature force us to understand history not merely in terms of abstract notions of evolution or process, but primarily in terms of the suffering realities of that history caused by various forms of human exploitation. The history that now must serve as the basis of theological reflection is not abstract history, but the history of human victims. The voices and the memory of the tortured, the forgotten, and the dead must become primary resources for Christian anthropology. And, while Chopp does not herself explicitly articulate this position, one could take her viewpoint in the same direction as Schüssler-Fiorenza and Tracy

---

32. *Ibid.*
33. R. Chopp, "The Interruption of the Forgotten," in Schüssler-Fiorenza and Tracy, *The Holocaust as Interruption*, p. 20.

take the feminist argument—that biblical anti-Judaism, with its inevitable dehumanization of concrete Jewish persons, paved the way for Western colonialism to which liberation theology has been responding.

To conclude the treatment of the Holocaust, let me say a word or two about its implications for Christian spirituality. Jaroslav Pelikan, in a plenary addres to the ninth National Workshop on Christian-Jewish Relations in Baltimore (May 1986), remarked that Christian renewal today ultimately comes down to one fundamental reality: the church must once and for all surrender its longing to be saved from history. Expressing this same idea some years earlier, the Austrian Catholic philosopher Friedrich Heer insisted that the church's failure to challenge the Nazis in any effective way was symptomatic of how the church had dealt with other manifestations of evil, in particular, war and the possibility of a nuclear holocaust. For him, the main problem sprang from the church's withdrawal from history:

> The withdrawal of the church from history has created that specifically Christian and ecclesiastical irresponsibility towards the world, the Jew, the other person, even the Christian himself, considered as a human being—which was the ultimate cause of past catastrophes and may be the cause of a final catastrophe in the future.[34]

As Heer sees it, anti-Semitism is the product of a long-standing and deep-seated cancer within Christianity that began to grow in its classical period. The disregard on the part of Christians for the well-being of the Jewish people throughout history, especially between 1918 and 1945, can only be understood as part of a general disregard for humanity and the world. He attributes this attitude to the dominance in Christian theological thinking of what he calls the "Augustinian principle." This attitude views the world under the aspect of sin and ultimately leads to a sense of fatalism and despair about the world. Heer is convinced that this fatalistic tendency constitutes as much a danger today as it did during the incubation of Nazism. In fact, he argues, millions of contemporary Christians share the responsibility for preparing the suicide of the church and of humankind in a new

---

34. F. Heer, *God's First Love* (New York, 1970) p. 406.

holocaust which may be brought about by nuclear warfare while the churches remain silent bystanders. He writes:

> There is a straight line from the church's failure to notice Hitler's attempt at a "Final Solution" of the Jewish problem to her failure to notice today's and tomorrow's endeavors to bring about a "Final Solution" of the human problem. The murder of millions of Jews during the Hitler era anticipated the murder of millions and perhaps hundreds of millions of human beings who would die if the great war returned—a war that could only end in mass murder and genocide.[35]

The only cure for this centuries-long pattern in Christianity, according to Heer, is to relinquish the "Augustinian principle" and replace it with a return to Christ's own piety rooted in the Hebrew Bible, and to even older roots—namely, the original faith of Israel in which people felt themselves to be both God's creatures and responsible partners in the development of the earth.

To conclude this overview of the impact of the Christian-Jewish dialogue on theological education, I will briefly mention several other areas of potential importance. The first is that of Israel. As David Tracy and others have correctly insisted, grappling with this issue in present-day Christian theology is one way of taking history seriously and *concretely*. Focus on Israel will also help in the recovery of the biblical land tradition, which, as W. D. Davies and Walter Brueggemann have been telling us of late, Christianity too readily abandoned.[36] Though Christians and Jews may continue to disagree on some implications of the land tradition, its recovery by the churches will help the Christian community develop a new rootage in the earth and in earth's history. Such a reappropriation of the land tradition in fact represents another dimension of the revolt against the excessive Bultmannian personalism which Droge so roundly criticized, a critique with which Brueggemann would basically identify.

There is likewise much to be gained from a study of the Second Temple/rabbinic notion of "oral Torah." This innovative way of ensuring creativity and change in a living religious tradition is, in my judgment and in that of W. D. Davies, the foundation

---

35. F. Heer, "The Catholic Church and the Jews Today," *Midstream* 17 (May, 1971) 29.
36. Cf. W. Brueggemann, *The Land* (Philadelphia, 1977) and W.D. Davies, *The Gospel and the Land* (Berkeley, Calif., 1982).

for the Christian notion of tradition as a basic source of revela-tory meaning. Too often churches have used tradition in a retro-gressive rather than a creative manner. A proper understanding of "oral Torah" as an instrument of constructive change can help change this pattern. It can prove very useful in developing a dynamic approach to the notion of tradition in theological edu-cation.

The basic goal of the above reflections has been to establish the relevance of the Christian-Jewish dialogue for theological education—in a sense, to prove the wisdom of Karl Barth's post-World War II remark. We still have much to do to incorpo-rate the results of the dialogue into Christian theological curric-ula. Some signs of progress are evident. The 1985 Vatican *Notes* on teaching and catechesis affirm the centrality of Jews and Juda-ism in Christian education.[37] And the Catholic bishops' Secretar-iat for relations with Jews has produced a major curricular guide for theological education.[38] But much work awaits us. Clearly the impact of such efforts, if the churches stay the course, will be a major redefinition of Christian identity in several respects, with implications for every area of theological inquiry.

37. Cf. "Notes on the Correct Way to Present the Jews and Judaism in Preaching and Catechesis in the Roman Catholic Church (June 1985)" in H. Croner, ed., *More Stepping Stones to Jewish-Christian Relations* (New York, 1985) p. 221.
38. Cf. E.J. Fisher, *Seminary Education and Christian-Jewish Relations: A Curriculum and Reference Handbook*, 2nd ed. (Washington, D.C., 1988).

CHAPTER FOURTEEN

The Fear of the Lord:
A Fear to End All Fears

Roland E. Murphy

My topic is dictated by the fact that it is the only aspect of the Jewish-Christian dialogue on which I consider myself qualified to speak. A fundamental goal of the dialogue, of course, is the overcoming of mutual fears. My topic, at first glance, might seem to simply compound those fears. And yet, ironically, it is only this most primordial of all fears—the fear of *YHWH,* our mutual Lord and Master—that can ultimately overshadow and obliterate all our petty, anthropocentric phobias. Let me elaborate.

First, some preliminary remarks are in order on the overcoming of mutual fears. Whatever bond of unity can be discovered between two groups deserves to be exploited for its potential to create or increase harmony. I maintain that the *Tanakh*—the Hebrew Scriptures or Old Testament constitutes such a bond and has the potential for establishing some harmony, despite a history during which it has also been a bone of contention. Even though my remarks are necessarily conditioned by my Christian point of view, I learn much from my Jewish colleagues and I try earnestly to understand and explain the Bible on its own terms. In 1965 I participated in a symposium of Jewish and Catholic theologians, the proceedings of which were eventually published as the book, *Torah and Gospel.*[1] Samuel Sandmel and I were to address the topic,

---

1. P. Scharper, ed., *Torah and Gospel* (New York, 1966).

"Biblical Scholarship: Bond or Barrier?" The late Professor
Sandmel addressed himself positively to "Jewish and Catholic
Biblical Scholarship" and pointed out the distinction between
the "pristine" (or literal-historical) sense and a "developed"
sense of the Bible. He also indicated the analogous roles played
by the Oral Torah and by Church Tradition among Jews and
Catholics. My topic was "Current Biblical Scholarship as a bond
of Understanding." I, too, evaluated our common approach to
the Bible positively, as a bond of understanding. At that point
in time, American Catholic biblical scholarship had made great
strides and was totally open to learning from both Protestant
and Jewish quarters. And yet, as I observed at the time, there
was still at least one missing link in the bonds of our scholarly
dialogue, namely, "the fact that there exists no *Theology of the
Old Testament* written by a Jewish scholar in the genre of those
by Christian scholars."[2] Today, however, there is a new wave
abroad, set in motion by the formidable Israeli scholar, Moshe
Goshen-Gottstein, who is urging a "Tanakh theology."[3] This
point must not be misunderstood. Goshen-Gottstein admits that
there is an inevitable bias in the selection and development of
the biblical data. For example, one can contrast the amount of
attention given to the topics of sacrifice, sabbath, and *miṣwôth* in
a Christian biblical theology with the amount that will properly
be given to it in a Tanakh theology, and the contrast is not merely
quantitative. There is no perfect agreement in this area (just as
there is no perfect agreement among Christian theologians on
less sensitive topics). But the achievement of modern scholarship
is such that Christians and Jews have learned to interpret the
Hebrew Bible on its own terms. Here there is much common

---

2. *Ibid.*, p. 92.
3. M. Goshen-Gottstein, "Tanakh Theology: The Religion of the Old Testament and
the Place of Jewish Biblical Theology," in P.D. Miller, et al, eds., *Ancient Israelite Religion:
Essays in Honor of Frank Moore Cross* (Philadelphia, 1987) pp. 617–44. See also his challenge
to the scholarly community, "Christianity, Judaism and Modern Bible Study," *Congress
Volume Edinburgh 1984 V Test Sup* 28 (1985) 69–88. For a different perspective, see J.
Levenson, "Why Jews Are Not Interested in Biblical Theology," in J. Neusner, ed., *Judaic
Perspectives on Ancient Israel* (Philadelphia, 1987) pp. 281–307. However, in my judgment,
Levenson is doing "Tanakh theology" in his *Sinai and Zion* (Minneapolis, 1985).

ground where scholars must learn from one another and where Christians and Jews can stand together.[4]

The Biblical Emphasis

I would open my discussion of "fear of the Lord" against the background of a quotation from Dietrich Bonhoeffer. In his *Letters and Papers from Prison* he wrote: "My thoughts and feelings seem to be getting more and more like the Old Testament, and no wonder, I have been reading it much more than the New for the last few months. It is only when one knows the ineffability of the Name of God that one can utter the name of Jesus Christ."[5] Understandably, there is a Christian outlook or orientation in his appropriation of the biblical data. But unmistakably he recognizes the profound biblical reverence for God, as manifested in the practice of not pronouncing the tetragrammaton, the sacred name of the Holy One. Without this sense of God that is communicated in the ineffability of the divine Name, one's Christian understanding of God is itself undermined. Bonhoeffer often attacked the "cheap grace" so often marketed in Christianity. He is thinking along those lines here, at least implicitly. On Christian terms, the Incarnation can be properly understood only against the background of the Jewish and biblical reverence for

---

4. The common ground to which I refer is the interpretation of the Hebrew Bible according to historico-critical methodology. I readily grant that this methodology only approximates its goal of establishing the historical meaning, and also that it does not exhaust the meaning of the text. With all its limitations, however, it does succeed in establishing a shared understanding that is ecumenically important.

If someone were to reply that I necessarily interpret the *Tanakh*/Old Testament in a Christian manner, I suppose I would have to admit that I cannot escape a certain bias. But I would maintain that there is a difference between Christian interpretation and christological interpretation. The latter is carried out knowingly in the light of the New Testament and the position of the Christian faith. But a Christian understanding is an exploration of the God of the (Hebrew) Bible, YHWH, the Holy One. It is a second hermeneutical step to proceed to identify the Holy One as the God and Father of Jesus Christ, but this does not vitiate interpreting the Bible in the first instance on its own terms. I think this reasoning is similar to that of my Jewish colleague who also goes on to interpret the Tanakh in the light of the Oral Torah and rabbinic tradition. The common task is to define, according to biblical categories, the God who is revealed in the Bible. One may allow that the more complex the definition becomes, the more room there is for a construction that might go beyond sheer biblical data and thus constitute a more pronounced Christian or Jewish understanding.

5. D. Bonhoeffer, *Letters and Papers from Prison*, rev. ed., E. Bethge, ed. (New York, 1967) pp. 103–04.

the ineffable God. This "reverence" leads into my topic of biblical "fear of the Lord."

I do not think it is pertinent for our purposes to distinguish between fear of God and fear of the Lord, or to distinguish between the nominal phrase, "the fear of God/the Lord," and the verbal expression, "(to) fear the Lord." I will explore the basic meaning of these expressions as well as the appropriation of the idea by Israel's sages in the Wisdom literature.

The Numinous Aspect of the Fear of the Lord

Although Rudolph Otto did not set out to investigate exclusively the *biblical* experience of the numinous, his study of The Holy does provide us with concepts that help to explicate the biblical fear of the Lord.[6] He spoke of divinity as being Wholly Other, of the *mysterium tremendum et fascinosum*, and of the feeling of the numinous. These ideas can be legitimately associated with the fear of God that is described in several texts of the Bible.[7]

The numinous experience of the Israelites is vividly described in Exodus 20:18–20, in the account of the Sinai theophany, the purpose of which is explicitly stated: "that the fear of the Lord may ever be with you." Similarly, in Genesis 28:17, Jacob's reaction to his dream-vision of *YHWH* is described thus: "and he feared, and he said, 'how fearsome *nôrā>)* is this place!' " In the "call" narratives of several prophets there is a clear reference to the feeling of the numinous, even if the word "fear" is not used (cf. Isaiah 6:5; Ezekiel 1:28). Particularly important is the biblical belief that the vision of God brings death. This belief is evident in the stories of Jacob at Peniel (Genesis 32:30); the people at Sinai (Exodus 19:21; cf. Moses in Exodus 3:6 and 33:18ff.); Gideon and "the angel of the Lord" (Judges 6:22–23); the parents of Samson (Judges 13:22); Elijah in the cave at Horeb (1 Kings 19:13); and the prophet Isaiah's call (Isaiah 6:5). Interestingly enough, we know of this attitude because the characters involved lived to tell the tale! Although the word "fear" *(YR>)* is

---

6. R. Otto, *The Idea of the Holy* (New York, 1958).
7. In what follows I am guided mainly by J. Becker, *Gottesfurcht im Alten Testament* (AB 25; Rome, 1965).

mentioned explicitly in these texts only once (Judges 6:23), there is a clear understanding that the presence of God is threatening and thus fearful.

Similarly, the divine "deeds" are described as fear-inspiring, especially the deeds surrounding the Exodus (nôrā>ôth: Deuteronomy 10:21; Isaiah 64:2, etc.; cf., môrā>îm in Deuteronomy 4:34). The adjective nôrā>, "fearful," is used to characterize the deeds of the Lord in Exodus 34:10 and Psalm 66:3. He is nôrā> tĕhîllôth ("fearsome in splendor," Exodus 15:11 [NJV]) and nôrā> <ălîlāh ("fearsome in deed," Psalm 66:5).

In Israel the mysterium could be fascinosum as well as tremendum, drawing human beings to it and releasing a mood of celebration. Although the note of fear generally predominates, both fear and joy are expressed in several texts. Fearing and trusting are united in Psalm 40:4. Fear gives way to praise of God for his intervention in the cause of justice in Psalm 64:10. In Psalm 96:9, the whole earth is summoned to "tremble" (ḥîlû) in the presence of the Lord, while heavens and earth rejoice and exult. In Psalm 119:120, the psalmist says; "My flesh shudders from fear of you; I fear your ordinances." But in the same psalm the Law is repeatedly an object of delight (vv. 14, 16, 24, etc.).

From this basic notion of fear before the numen derives the later meanings frequently found in the Bible, namely cultic and moral, and from the latter what may be called nomistic (devotion to the Law). In the deuteronomic writings, it designates "worship of the Lord under the particular aspect of loyalty to him as the God of the covenant."[8] Thus, proper worship of Yahweh and observance of his covenant laws are connected, as in Deuteronomy 6:13, 24. In fact, even "love" of God is synonymous with fearing him and observing the covenantal statutes (Deuteronomy 5:10; 6:5, etc.). In Joshua 24:14, "fear" is parallel with "serve" (<BD). In the Psalms the worshippers are described as those who "fear" the Lord (Psalms 22:24, 26; 66:16, etc.).

The moral connotation of fear of the Lord may derive from fear of his actions, especially those of judgment. The fear of sanctions tended to support a given moral conduct. The moral nuance is found in Genesis 20:11, where Abraham can find no "fear of God" in Abimelech's kingdom. Joseph describes himself

---

8. Ibid., p. 84.

as a God-fearing man (Genesis 42:18) and hence ready to deal gently with his brothers. It is this moral aspect of fear of the Lord that one finds in the book of Proverbs.

Fear of the Lord in the Wisdom Literature

Proverbs 1:7 is set off from the long introductory period in vv. 1–6 as a kind of motto: "The fear of the Lord is the beginning of knowledge" (rēʾshîth dāʿăth). The epigrammatic character of this saying is indicated by its many variants (Proverbs 9:10; Job 28:28; Psalm 111:10: Proverbs 15:33). Fear of the Lord is the "beginning" (rēʾshîth; Psalm 111:10) or "unleashing" (tĕḥillāh; Proverbs 9:10) of wisdom in the sense that it eventually leads into wisdom; it is also the "discipline" (mûsar; Proverbs 15:33) that leads to wisdom. The "knowledge" (dāʿăth) referred to by the Hebrew sages (and prophets) is no merely theoretical matter, but rather the practical conduct of life under divine guidance, without which life quickly deteriorates (Hosea 4:1). Thus, "knowledge" often is used in parallelism with "wisdom" (ḥokhmāh; Proverbs 1:7; 30:3). Fear of the Lord is also associated with knowledge (Proverbs 1:7; 2:5; 2:29; 9:10); the two terms are practically interchangeable.

A strong moral connotation comes from the association of fear of the Lord with "turn(ing) from evil" (Proverbs 3:7; cf., 8:13). In the Book of Job this association is conspicuous, for it characterizes Job's virtue (1:1, 8; 2:3) and even becomes the only "wisdom" available to human beings who cannot fathom that wisdom which is hidden with God (28:28). In the collections of sayings (Proverbs 10ff.), fear of the Lord guarantees life (10:27; 14:27; 19:23) and also issues in wealth and honor (22:4). Those who fear God have a future (23:17–18; cf., 24:14), which is, however, left undefined. Thus fear of the Lord also serves to promote the optimistic doctrine of retribution that is characteristic of the Book of Proverbs.

Qoheleth, who in so many ways jousts with traditional wisdom, has his own views about fearing God.[9] They are not those of the writer of the epilogue in Qoheleth 12:13, where fear of

---

9. Cf. E. Pfeiffer, "Die Gottesfurcht im Buche Kohelet," in H.G. Reventlow, ed., *Gottes Wort und Gottes Land* (Göttingen, 1965) pp. 133–58.

God is joined with keeping the commandments *(miṣwôth)*. Such an understanding, however, goes beyond Qoheleth's own thought and reflects a thematizing given to the book by a later writer who is thinking along the lines of Sirach (a nomistic interpretation of fear of the Lord).[10] Rather, Qoheleth returns to the numinous aspect of fear. He does not use the abstract phrase, "fear of God"; he prefers the verbal expression, "(to) fear God," as in 3:14 and 5:6. The context of 3:14 gives us to understand that this is far from the consoling fear of God that is so common in the wisdom tradition. Qoheleth gives a purpose to God's utterly mysterious action in the world: that human beings may fear God. This attitude is also reflected in his curt command, "fear God!"—a command that derives its businesslike tone from the reminder that "God is in heaven and you are on earth; therefore let your words be few" (5:1). Qoheleth clearly espouses the fear of God, but in his treatment the concept entails nothing of the security and certainty that it traditionally does in the wisdom literature. Since God is very much a mystery and his actions cannot be understood, a numinous fear is in order.

Since Sirach identifies Lady Wisdom with "the Law that Moses commanded us" (24:23), it is not surprising that wisdom displays a nomistic aspect in his book. But nomism is far from legalism. There is certainly a clear emphasis on the Law, but this is in the style of the author of Psalm 119, who finds his joy in the Law. Interestingly, Sirach does not deal with the Law directly, but in what might be called a sapiential manner. As G. von Rad has remarked, "we see Sirach endeavouring to legitimatize and to interpret Torah from the realm of understanding characteristic of wisdom."[11] One learns more about his attitude towards the Law from what he says about fear of the Lord than from any direct statements he makes about the Law. Thus, fear and love often alternate:

> Those who fear the Lord disobey not his words;
>   those who love him keep his ways.
> Those who fear the Lord seek to please him,
>   those who love him are filled with his law.

---

10. So G.T. Sheppard, *Wisdom as a Hermeneutical Construct* (BZAW 151; Berlin, 1980) pp. 121–29.
11. G. von Rad, *Wisdom in Israel* (Nashville, 1972) p. 245.

> Those who fear the Lord prepare their hearts
> and humble themselves before him. (2:15–17)

In three passages there is a clear parallelism between fearing God and loving him (Sirach 2:15–16; 7:29–30; 34:15–16). Fear of the Lord is very much interiorized in this book and is virtually identified with wisdom:

> He who fears the Lord will do this;
> He who is practiced in the law will come
> to wisdom.
> (15:1)

> All wisdom is fear of the Lord;
> perfect wisdom is the fulfillment of
> the law.
> (19:17)

> He who keeps the law controls his impulses;
> he who is perfect in fear of the Lord
> has wisdom.
> (21:11)

Josef Haspecker has argued that fear of God is the key to the literary structure of the book: it figures prominently in 1:1–2:18 and is resumed at midpoint (25:7–11); a final counterpoint to the opening chapters occurs in 40:18–27.[12] One may not agree that fear of the Lord is central to the *structure* of the book, but it is certainly a favorite theme. The first two chapters are an extraordinary mixture of wisdom and fear of the Lord. Sirach opens with a theme already celebrated in Job 28, "all wisdom comes from the Lord" (Sirach 1:1) and he alone knows her. After creating her (vv. 4, 9; cf., Job 28:27), God lavished her upon all of his works, upon all humankind, upon all who love him (vv. 9–10). How does one receive this gift? Through fear of the Lord (cf. Job 28:28), which is described as "the beginning" (v. 14), the "crown" (v. 18), and the "root" of wisdom (v. 20). It is not surprising that in the colophon of 50:27–29, where Sirach gives his name and his purpose, wisdom and the fear of the Lord are again joined (read, with the Hebrew text, "fear" instead of "light"). The theme of fear of the Lord keeps echoing throughout his work,

---

12. J. Haspecker, *Gottesfurcht bei Jesus Sirach*, AB 30 (Rome, 1967).

e.g., 9:16; 10:19-23; 15:1 (which unites 14:20–15:10); 19:20–24 ("all wisdom is fear of the Lord"); 21:11; 25:10; 34:13–15; and 40:26–27. In this extensive treatment, Sirach is able to develop both the moral and the nomistic aspects of "fear of the Lord"—the inner and outer dimensions of his theme.

Conclusions

In the light of the foregoing treatment of the fear of the Lord, I view the entire Tanakh/Old Testament as a bond of union between Jews and Christians, provided that it is interpreted on its own terms. Thus it can serve as a means of lessening tensions and fears. When we look to common elements in our traditions, there is hope for some agreement and respect. Specifically, fear of the Lord, taken in all its aspects, is a necessary and positive ingredient in the spiritual life of Jews and Christians.[13]

---

13. Since writing these lines I find that my essay, "Old Testament/*Tanakh*—Canon and Interpretation," is pertinent to the theme of mutual understanding; see R. Brooks and J.J. Collins, eds., *Hebrew Bible or Old Testament? Studying the Bible in Judaism and Christianity* (Notre Dame, Ind., 1990) pp. 11–29.

CHAPTER FIFTEEN

Unmasking Fear and Suffering: An Encounter with Russian Anti-Semitism

Christopher M. Leighton

The largest seminary in the Soviet Union is garrisoned in the ancient monastery of Zagorsk, on an isolated hilltop forty-four miles northeast of Moscow. Our small procession of American academics was marched through a maze of courtyards, towers, and tombs into the depths of the monastic enclosure surrounded by impregnable walls. There, behind closed doors, we were greeted with the formality of ancient custom. At the head of the conference table sat Archbishop Alexander, rector of the theological academy—a large, commanding presence wrapped in a cassock of battleship grey. Dark, penetrating eyes, stern and unblinking, with two bushy tangles above and a massive prickly beard below, gave me the feeling of being watched from the depths of an impassable thicket.

We were ten seminary and university educators selected from around the United States to particpate in the 1990 Emerging Leaders Summit, an event coordinated by the American Center for International Leadership and the Soviet Committee of Youth Organizations. Our assignment was to meet our religious counterparts, explore the theological landscape of our respective countries, and determine the fault lines of religious

This article is a revised version of an earlier paper entitled "Suffering the Difference: Reflections on Russian Anti-Semitism," published in *Occasional Papers on Religion in Eastern Europe* 11, no. 1 (February, 1991): 25–31.

upheaval. Though our commission arrived with poorly marked maps of an unknown land, it was the question about Soviet Jewry that got us lost—a question shaped at home and impossible to leave behind. The question moved us in unexpected directions and finally pushed us over the border into unstable territory. From all that we Americans had seen and heard about the disillusionment of Communist ideology, the hopes of many people appeared to be shifting toward the Russian Orthodox Church. "With the prospects of greater recognition, openness, and freedom," I asked, "what will church leaders say on behalf of those who are still vulnerable, those who live outside the sanctuary of the official ecclesia? Does the church have an obligation to stand up on behalf of those who remain marginalized? In particular, will Russian Orthodox Christians accept responsibility for the survival of the Jews?"

On the outskirts of Moscow, the climate is thick with fear and suspicion. In such an atmosphere, questions must be stripped and searched; they often harbor clandestine problems and destabilizing uncertainties. Unless disarmed, a question can explode, exposing crucial vulnerabilities. So the scent of a hidden accusation provoked a flurry of gestures from the rector. In retaliation for probing regarded as intrusive, the Archbishop shot back:

> Do you think that we have not also suffered? Twenty-seven million lost in the Great Patriotic War. As many as forty million murdered in Stalin's purges. Why single out the Jews for special treatment, as though their suffering counts for more? There are other ethnic groups that continue to endure horrendous oppression. The danger is that we will cling to our separate ways and fail to overcome our differences. We must journey beyond our particularities, transcend divisive national affiliations, and find unity in our spiritual journey to God.

Over the course of two weeks, "the Jewish question" surfaced repeatedly, pushing our group to the edges of civility with several prominent leaders in the Russian Orthodox Church. Invariably the glare of anger displaced the flush of embarrassment. Repeatedly awkward silence would blister and break, an uproar of incriminations filling the void, as when one of the Americans clamored:

> In our country massive efforts to evacuate Jews from the Soviet

Union are underway. A resurgence of anti-Semitism coupled with rumors of new pogroms mandate the condemnation of prejudice. Moral passivity will once again prove damning.

Without diplomatic tuning, the cautions arrived as dissonance, noise in a pitch which tripped alarms. The Americans drummed their responses on an ideal of theological inquiry that champions diversity. Trained in institutions where interreligious dialogue animates the lunchroom and frequently spills into the classroom, these Americans noted the creative tensions which can emerge when the distinctiveness of our respective communities is recognized and explored. For most of the American participants, the Christian-Jewish encounter has been central to this process, teaching us to relinquish theological certainty and encouraging us instead to distinguish the command to repair the world from the impulse to wiggle out of it. The Jewish-Christian conversation has challenged the practice of pouring religious truth into static doctrinal formulations which promise life everlasting to the credulous consumer. However disruptive, the confrontation has enlarged our memory, compelling a more generous recollection and a more modest hope in the things to come.

The officials from the Russian Orthodox Church were agitated by the zeal of these proclamations and the apparent self-righteousness of our assessments. The promises of pluralism seemed empty, even false; incompatible with pressing organizational challenges; a move which would further fragment the church and compromise its mission in the Soviet Union. With a desperate shortage of priests, a platoon of novices who have yet to master the liturgy much less biblical exegesis, a theological faculty straining to harness its students to the traditions of the Church Fathers and struggling to provide a working knowledge of homiletics and Orthodox spirituality, Jewish-Christian dialogue registers as an extracurricular pastime, a bourgeois indulgence, a vacuous distraction. When a people stumble out of the wilderness after seventy years of privation, they do not need loading up with hot apple pie, but a simple diet that will settle the stomach and fortify the spirit. Before turning to the outsider for cooperative nourishment, the church has the duty to reestablish itself, the imperative to reclaim its own historic calling, and the obligation to reconcile those divergent factors which are ripping the social fabric. Is not the church entitled to ensure its own survival by leaving aside disruptive ethnic divisions and resuscitating that ancient vision of the peaceable Kingdom?

With staggering consistency, we Americans were informed that anti-Semitism was not a problem within the Russian Orthodox Church. The obstacle was portrayed as a problem of misplaced allegiances, a peculiar ethnic alignment. After all, if Jews can leave aside their Zionist idiosyncrasies, they are welcome to pitch their tents in the church's camp. Resolution can always be earned the old-fashioned way, through conversion and cultural assimilation. This rationale failed to prick any religious scruples, because Jewishness was reduced to a sociological category. Ignorant of the cultural content of the Jewish tradition, as well as the ethical and spiritual vitality of its people, the Russian Orthodox imagination simply did not leave room for a Jewish identity shaped by an autonomous faith. The spokesmen for the official church insisted that the withholding of the saving truth of the Gospel on the basis of ethnicity would signal the worst kind of Jew hatred. Aren't Jews good enough to receive what we believe to be the very best?

This evangelical "outreach" was intensified by a romantic longing to transcend our ethnic differences, bury our peculiarities, and forget our tribal resentments. In an era of glasnost and perestroika, this call for oneness was tantamount to unity with a Russian accent. Having been boiled in one melting pot, the feast which our Russian Orthodox hosts were preparing set the Americans' teeth on edge. The corporate ideal of the Church Universal overshadowed ethnic and religious distinctions. I noticed something omnivorous in the way these officials deployed that all-inclusive pronoun "we." In one conversation after another, this pronoun rumbled like an empty stomach. The "we" who are seizing the country's future seemed content to swallow "them," the outsiders, the resident aliens, the others. "They" were seldom mentioned; apparently they lived in exile or were kept under lock and key, safe in amnesia's dungeon.

So it was the expansive ambitions and the unqualified enthusiasm in the church's age-old answers that stood out. The ardor and the confidence of our Russian hosts might have suggested an inspired response to destiny's demands. Yet, inspiration, being fragile and fleeting, was maintained by means of a highly selective memory, the gift of historical revisionism. The hope and the glory of religious restoration which dazzled these official strategists was built on a foundation of quicksand. Out of extravagant promises the builders have chiselled "forgetful monuments" to an ascendent church.

As the American commission issued its concerns, the Russian hierarchs were stunned by an audacity that cast shadows upon their own authenticity. How seriously should one regard visitors who sputter down the postmodern strip, intoxicated with their diversity, crashing into conventions and calling it "necessity," swerving into dangerous pitfalls, blithely ignoring oncoming traffic? What can "we" learn from individualists who have canonized personal preference; iconoclasts who know how to multiply choices, not how to make them; mavericks who ironically touch everything, but grab hold of nothing? When a people coddled in modernity's lap, sheltered from persecution, young and untested, start hurling accusations, need "we" listen?

At the end of two weeks, my colleagues and I limped onto the plane and headed for home. After skidding into the walls of mutual suspicion, I was bruised in the discovery that ancient hostilities can take on many hard-hitting guises. There are commitments that reach for the skies, and between their allegiances and ours stretches a chasm difficult—perhaps impossible—to traverse. How does one cross over? How does one reckon with the militaristic impulses within their ranks and ours? How does one disarm distrust? Slowly. Laboring under a common weight. Feeling a common strain. Lifting up the buried memories around which suspicions have hardened.

This is no simple task, for it draws the inquirer into the murky depths of the other's pain. Yet this much was clear: there is an anguish among the Russian Orthodox that lies beneath the glittering hopes of the church triumphant. This ache gets into the bones, and the throbbing does not stop. Every time I now try to get a fix on this distress, I am drawn to the memory of another encounter on the outskirts of Moscow the night before returning home.

In the cramped quarters of an eviscerated apartment complex, we sat huddled around a coffee table: four Americans and three representatives of the "catacomb" church. These three expressed

tremendous confidence in Russian Orthodoxy, but maintained
that the "True Orthodox" reside outside the walls of the officially
recognized ecclesial establishment. When Metropolitan Sergii issued the 1927 Declaration of Loyalty, a movement was launched
which has refused to associate administratively or sacramentally
with the Moscow Patriarchate. According to the witness of our
three hosts, this underground movement has preserved the faith
from extinction.

Branded as disruptive renegades by the state and largely ignored by the official ecclesiastical powers, the dissidents who
make up the "catacomb" movement have long claimed that an
aphasic church can only regain its voice after it has identified
the administrative compromises that have corrupted both
church and state. They insisted that only when the ideological
deformities and bureaucratic malignancies are cleaned up can
the church provide moral and spiritual direction. To recover from
its subservience to the Soviet regime, the church must fill in
memory's gaps and then repent in word and deed.

This idea crystallized around two o'clock in the morning,
when the nagging questions reemerged:

> Why is there no word in Russian for the Holocaust, the *Shoah*?
> Why has the particularity of the Jewish plight been uniformly
> denied? Why the refusal to acknowledge anti-Semitic attitudes
> within the church or even the society at large?

A long pause followed before Father Alexei, a leading intellectual and spiritual force within the "catacomb" community, who
earns his daily bread as an electrician in a local hospital, finally
spoke:

> Our inability to confront the legacy of anti-Judaism reflects a fail-
> ure to work through the agony in which the church as been
> caught. We have not yet found adequate ways to bring our own
> suffering to consciousness. We are still emerging from the cata-
> clysm of the last war and the trauma of the purges. But you must
> understand that more was lost than lives. Our sense of values
> died. Our tradition broke down. We found ourselves living among
> former Christians, folks who had become barbarians. When we
> looked in the mirror, we were terrified by the beasts that stared
> back. How does one come to terms with such a monumental col-
> lapse? A living faith was reduced to a religious artifice. We drifted
> into an ideology with a set of self-serving allegiances. In the proc-

ess, our church found itself in a passionate rivalry with Armenians, Protestants, Roman Catholics, Muslims, and of course Jews. We live in an unacknowledged fear. Were we to acknowledge the suffering of others we would diminish the claims of our own community.

The way in which a community derives meaning from suffering, the way a people encounters, interprets, and responds to affliction at home and abroad reveals its ethical and theological core. The inability which Father Alexei was attempting to name reflects a theological impairment which extends beyond the boundaries of the Soviet Union and the Russian Orthodox Church.

The prevailing wisdom is that the corporate heart has its limits, for it can pump only so much pity into the bloodstream before giving out. The supply of human kindness is drawn from a shallow reserve, easily exhausted. So whichever group can establish itself as the most oppressed can convert pain into political clout. Suffering becomes the ticket that wins the victim a seat in an exclusive club, and membership has its privileges. If this fraternity extends an invitation to every group that has paid its pound of flesh, the value of victimization declines and thereby prevents a decent rate of exchange. Since scarcity determines worth, each group has a stake in minimizing the other's suffering, or denying it altogether. So suffering is wedged within an ideological framework. Pain is politicized, society polarized.

This zero-sum logic is compounded by an ancient theological tradition which extracts meaning from suffering by transmuting victims into martyrs. Affliction must be rescued from the abyss, because the only terror greater than physical torment is the horrible possibility of its senselessness. The concept of vicarious suffering fits atrocity into a serviceable religious equation. The one suffers on behalf of the other. The one is slain that the other might live.

At home and abroad, this notion of atonement is buckling under the weight of mass destruction. If God can only balance the cosmic scales by feeding Jewish children to the flames of the crematorium, by crushing Cambodian innocents under the heel of Pol Pot, and by deporting Russian civilians to Stalinist Gulags, then we are left with an explanatory calculus that derives a moral monster from an inscrutable diety. Not only does the idea of

martyrdom mask the reality of death behind a facade of enno-
bling results, but the victims increasingly refuse to allow advan-
tages from their persecution to be expropriated by others who
remain at a secure distance. No longer are Jews, Armenians,
Kurds, Native Americans, Afro-Americans, or women willing
to permit their degradation to maintain the status quo. Increasingly the victims of oppression resent a national body that as-
similates their particular anguish. They insist that death is
misrepresented when made to appear as sacrifice—that one person's agony cannot be used for another's advantage.

If suffering can no longer assume national, much less cosmic
signficance, if a theological model which one brought order out
of atrocity no longer works, what checks do we have on the
Balkanization of oppression and the political exploitation of suffering? Current theological formulations that highlight "God's
preferential option for the poor" guarantee that the world gets
split into factions. The rich versus the poor. The powerful versus
the downtrodden. A group that can demonstrate the severity of
its oppression not only can trade on public assistance, but can
also derive comfort in the knowledge that God is on its side.
The open wound becomes the distinctive badge of authenticity.

Obviously there are many victims in the U.S.S.R. and the
U.S.A. who are unable or unwilling to profit from their suffering. There are victims who need and deserve redress, and these
reflections are not intended to devalue their affliction. The point
is that suffering is frequently filtered through the lens of politics
and economics, producing a dark image of competitiveness
which promotes callous indifference in the face of deadly rivalries. This mind-set reinforces a disposition that blinds the Russian Orthodox to the beleaguered minorities in their midst, and
there are few theological correctives on the horizon. Closer to
home, this outlook highlights one of the difficulties in putting
together a rainbow coalition. No wonder a segment of Christian
feminism simply reframes the legacy of anti-Judaic polemics,
portraying Jesus as the one who saves the marginalized from
the yoke of Jewish patriarchy. No surprise many Jews agonize
within their own ranks about the plight of the Palestinians, but
consistently minimize the struggle in public. When suffering is
measured by the rules of the marketplace, the reason that many
Afro-Americans do not want to hear about anti-Semitism and

the Holocaust becomes more comprehensible: Why pour millions of dollars into a museum when widespread unemployment, teenage pregnancy, drugs, crime, and a failing educational system are leaving inner cities devastated? When the anguish of the oppressed is translated into the language of public relations, minorities are apt to wrap themselves tightly in their own misfortune and elbow each other in the scramble to ensure their own survival.

Many of us at home and abroad have settled for flattened renditions of our generative stories. Our accounts of struggle lack theological gravity and ethical direction. Unless affliction is transformed into a metaphor, a memory which extends the boundaries of the imagination, the Other remains invisible, an anonymous outsider, an outcast, an untouchable. As Cynthia Ozick notes:

> By turning the concrete memory of slavery into a universalizing metaphor of reciprocity, the ex-slaves discover a way to convert imagination into a serious moral instrument. . . . "And a stranger you shall not oppress," says Exodus 23, verse 8, "for you know the heart of the stranger, seeing you were strangers in the land of Egypt." Without the metaphor of memory and history, we cannot imagine the life of the Other.[1]

Memory is shaped by a vision of the future. The Russian ideologues who constitute *Pamyat* (memory) also want to stake their claims on the past. So the pressing questions return to haunt the Russians no less than us. Will our religious communities retrieve ancient memories which open doors? Can Jews remember the oppression of Egyptian slavery so that they can remove the yoke from the outsider? Can Christians recollect the crucifixion in ways that leave no one hanging? Can they reclaim the redemptive power of their focal metaphors? Can they restore those founding stories so that they are pushed beyond the familiar into the company of the Other?

Lines are being drawn, sides chosen, even though the enemy remains elusive and largely unknown. Already battles are underway at home and abroad. Whose rendition of good and evil will prevail? This much is certain: the metaphors deployed and

---

1. C.Ozick, *Metaphor and Memory* (New York, 1989) p. 278f.

the memories enlisted will determine the terms of engagement. From my encounters with various religious leaders in the U.S.S.R., it appears that a protracted struggle is in the making. The long march is still ahead. In this sense, Americans and Soviets labor under a common strain. The future will depend upon how the story gets told, the depth of metaphor, the reach of memory, the fear of meaninglessness, the grip of hope. Where are the sages, prophets, and poets who can help us to overcome our fears? Can we build a society that works through suffering by making room for the stranger? Until religious communities learn to articulate their stories in ways that stretch the imagination and redefine the boundaries of duty, the walls of indifference and hostility will remain intact; and we will gird ourselves for a warfare where no prisoners are taken.

Index of Names

Index of Ancient Sources